Arnold Swanberg
October 14, 1985

The American Flying Boat

The American Flying Boat

AN ILLUSTRATED HISTORY

BY CAPTAIN RICHARD C. KNOTT USN

NAVAL INSTITUTE PRESS
Annapolis, Maryland

Library of Congress Catalog Card No. 79-84247
ISBN 0-87021-070-X

Printed in the United States of America

TO MY FATHER

Foreword

THE FLYING BOAT has played a prominent role in American aeronautical progress, and this is especially true in the case of naval aviation. Designed to operate in the marine environment, this aircraft was ideally suited to the Navy's mission. Unfortunately, in those early days the idea that airplane and warship might compliment each other's capabilities did not find immediate acceptance. It was the flying boat which first demonstrated the feasibility of the concept, and made naval aviation a working reality. Moreover, it was the flying boat that tested the theories of naval aviation proponents during World War I and established the value of the long-range seaplane, particularly with regard to antisubmarine warfare. Commercial aviation can also trace its roots to these aircraft. When World War I ended, Navy surplus flying boats became available to the public, and many were employed as air mail and passenger carriers. Naval aviators who chose to return to civilian life became part of the fledgling air transportation industry, and ultimately found their way into many of the cockpits of the early Pan American Clippers. During the 1920s and 1930s the Navy continued to develop improved versions of the flying boats and when World War II erupted, these aircraft functioned in a variety of combat and support missions around the globe.

Much of my early flying experience was in the PBY Catalinas. These were slow, unwieldy aircraft, very vulnerable to fighter attack. But because they could operate from a tender or a hastily prepared Pacific island base, they were highly mobile, enabling the U.S. Navy to range over wide ocean areas at a time when available naval forces were extremely limited and thinly spread. Of necessity, these planes were often pitted against unfavorable odds, and performed incredible feats never intended by their designers.

The many contributions of the flying boat have been overlooked by historians to a great extent. This book redresses the oversight, and brings more than half a century of flying boat aviation into sharp focus. Captain Knott relates the story in colorful detail, from Glenn Curtiss' wooden F-Boat, to Convair's supersonic Sea Dart and Martin's four-engine jet Seamaster. *The American Flying Boat* is an absorbing slice of aviation history.

T. H. Moorer
Admiral, U.S. Navy (Ret.)

Acknowledgements

CREDIT FOR THE FIVE COLOR PLATES which appear in this book belongs to artist John Ficklen of Atlanta, Georgia, whose reputation for high quality airbrush renderings of aircraft is clearly well deserved. I am also indebted to Mr. Walter Hinton, pilot of the *NC-4* on the epic first flight across the Atlantic, for relating his flying boat experiences, and for providing a direct insight into the formative years of American aviation history. Mr. Merrill A. Stickler, Curator of the Glenn H. Curtiss Museum at Hammondsport, New York, generously contributed his extensive knowledge of the life and times of the inventor of the flying boat, and provided helpful suggestions and advice on that portion of the book. Mr. Dominic Pisano of the National Air and Space Museum was of considerable assistance in locating obscure documents and hard to find information.

Much of the material used in this endeavor came from Navy sources. I would particularly like to thank naval aviation historians Mr. Clarke Van Vleet and Mr. Wes Pryce of the Office of the Deputy Chief of Naval Operations (Air Warfare), Dr. William J. Armstrong, Naval Air Systems Command Historian, Ms. Barbara Gilmore of the Naval Historical Center, and Mr. Robert A. Carlisle of the Navy Office of Information, for making available a wealth of research material, both documentary and photographic. Special thanks go to Mr. W. F. Waddington of Forest Industries Flying Tankers Limited, for furnishing little-known information on the last two remaining Mars aircraft, and to Mr. George Bunker and Mr. Roy Calvin of the Martin Marietta Corporation, for opening the old Martin Company photographic archives for my research. Mr. George Rodney, also of Martin Marietta and Mr. George Trimble, President of the Bunker-Ramo Corporation, provided specialized knowledge and commentary on the Martin Seamaster project.

The following organizations also provided information and illustrative material, and their assistance is gratefully acknowledged:

American Aviation Historical Society
Douglas Aircraft Company–McDonnell Douglas Corporation
Grumman Aerospace Corporation
Hughes Aircraft Corporation
Lockheed Aircraft Corporation
National Aeronautic Association of the USA
National Air and Space Museum
Naval Aviation Museum
Naval Aviation News
Newport Historical Society
Pan American World Airways, Incorporated
Sikorsky Aircraft Division of United Technologies
Sperry Division of Sperry Rand Corporation
U.S. Coast Guard Headquarters
U.S. National Archives
U.S. Naval War College Archives
Western Airlines

Finally and most important is my appreciation for the patience and support of my wife and children during the three years it took to complete this project.

Chapter-Opening Photographs

Page 1: Glenn H. Curtiss, Hammondsport, New York. (Curtiss Museum)

Page 21: The *America*, grande dame of the flying boats, and some of its admirers, at its launching ceremony, 1914. (Curtiss Museum)

Page 39: The *NC-4* lands triumphantly at Lisbon, thereby completing the first airborne transatlantic crossing. (U. S. Navy)

Page 59: Aeromarine cruisers flew passengers on their "Highball Express" between New York City and Havana, Cuba, and Nassau in the Bahamas during the Prohibition years. (Smithsonian Institution)

Page 73: The Boeing PB-1 after being refitted with Pratt and Whitney GR-1690 Hornet engines. (U. S. Navy)

Page 91: The Douglas XP3D-1. It first flew on 6 February 1935. (McDonnell Douglas Corp.)

Page 115: A Sikorsky S-42 Clipper making a takeoff run at Dinner Key, Florida, 1934. (Pan American World Airways)

Page 141: PBM-1s and PBM-3s in formation. Note retracted floats on the PBM-1s. (U. S. Navy)

Page 157: A painting of an Army Air Corps Catalina. (Robert Lansing)

Page 181: Like a huge giant hovering over its offspring, the Martin JRM-1 *Hawaii Mars* dwarfs a Grumman Widgeon amphibian. (U. S. Navy)

Page 201: A Sikorsky S-41 monoplane amphibian basks in the sun alongside a river. (Sikorsky Aircraft Corp.)

Page 231: VP-40's P5M-2 Twelve-Boat comes home for servicing by the seaplane tender *Currituck* at Cam Ranh Bay, South Vietnam, in 1967. (U. S. Navy)

Contents

Introduction

THE FIRST HALF-CENTURY of powered flight from 1903 to 1953 was a period truly reflective of the spirit of human innovation. It was a time in which anyone with sufficient imagination, courage, and tenacity could literally soar to great heights, or fall to an untimely death. No one compelled the early aviation pioneers to wager life and fortune against undependable machines in an unpredictable environment. They were drawn to it like steel to a magnet, driven by deep personal obsessions to achieve—to fly higher, faster, farther—and to be first! It was a time of breathless change, with continual new challenges to meet, new obstacles to hurdle, and old ideas to disprove. Yet it was much more than an age of engineering breakthroughs. It was the opening chapter of man's success story in his age-old struggle to defy the force of gravity, and revel in the thrill of flight.

The first fifty years of powered flight in the United States marked the heyday of an aircraft which, like the Wright Brothers' biplane, typified the American knack for innovation—the flying boat. Born of the inspired dream of Glenn Curtiss, then shaped by major improvements to his initial concept, the first great American ocean-going flying boat was built in 1914. It was named the *America*, and was one of the most advanced flying machines of the day. With a wingspan of 72 feet, it was designed as a twin-engine aircraft, but was also operated for a short time in a trimotor configuration. Although the *America* never flew the Atlantic, it nevertheless became the grande dame of future generations of American flying boats.

In the early days there was a romantic aura about the giant seaplanes. Maybe it was their colorful exploits, or perhaps their impressive size, which made them seem more like airborne ships than flimsy flying machines. Perhaps it was the similarity they bore to the mysterious ocean birds, whose casual grace has fascinated men since the beginning of time. Whatever the case, the flying boat was a hybrid which, more than any other aircraft of its time, fostered an appreciation of manned flight and its many possible practical applications.

It is a little-known fact that a flying boat inaugurated the world's first scheduled airline service in the United States in 1914. Five short years later, a descendant of *America* thrilled the world with the first flight across the Atlantic. By this time, the versatile flying boats had become a mainstay of naval aviation. They were a most effective countermeasure against the other great weapon developed in World War I, the fleet submarine. They also proved themselves as long-range scouts, with their own bombing capability and a lethal sting. Later, their large cargo capacity and ability to carry heavy loads made them a logistician's dream for moving quantities of men and material across the oceans. Because of their ability to cover large areas in a timely manner, and to make open-sea landings when necessary, they became the preferred platform in maritime search and rescue operations, and remained so until the advent of the helicopter.

Perhaps the most valued attribute of the flying boats, and the one which probably had the most effect in assuring their longevity, was their ability to operate independently of expensive fixed installations. Thus, they provided world-wide mobility and striking power at modest cost. It was this economic feature, coupled with the belief that flying boats were inherently safe for overwater travel, that enabled Pan American Airways to blaze the world's transoceanic air routes during the glamorous era of the great Clippers, long before airports with concrete runways and adjoining facilities proliferated throughout the world.

The zenith of the American flying boat occurred during World War II, when literally thousands of them were built. Operating from places inaccessible to other aircraft, they became the sentries of the sea-lanes, protecting vital allied shipping from the depredations of the undersea U-boat menace. They were angels of mercy to downed pilots and sailors adrift from ships torpedoed in shark-infested seas. They were cavernous transports, and in the early days of the Pacific conflict after Pearl Harbor, they constituted an important part of the few assets left with which the United States could prosecute the war. In this regard, no mission was inconceivable. Consider, for example, the spectacle of the docile Catalina flying boat hurtling out of a night sky to rain death on Japanese fleet units, or diving through an Aleutian overcast to bomb an entrenched enemy ground force.

Although World War II was perhaps the finest hour of the American flying boat, it was also the beginning of the end for them. The increasing availability of hard-surfaced airfields brought about by the war, and the advantages of operating and maintaining aircraft from such facilities, signaled the demise of its golden age.

This is a narrative of the American love affair with these mighty leviathans of the sky, and of those who conceived, constructed, and flew them through the pages of early U.S. aviation history. The great flying boats are gone now, but *America*, the *NC-4*, *China Clipper*, the Black Cats, and a host of others have indelibly written their colorful sagas in the annals of flight. Each type was unique, each had its legends, and each made its contributions. All were imbued with the composite soul of those who designed and built and flew them. The exploits of the flying boats and the men who built them are an everlasting tribute to the searching, soaring spirit of man.

The American Flying Boat

CHAPTER ONE

The Hero of Hammondsport

FROM THAT DAY FORWARD, the world would never be the same. The continents would be drawn closer together, the great oceans would be shrunk in size, and even the unalterable element of time would henceforth seem less formidable. Yet, the great event that occurred on 17 December 1903 at Kitty Hawk, North Carolina, went almost unnoticed, heralded only by the boom of the Hatteras surf, and applauded by the raucous voices of a few kindred feathered spirits circling overhead. Man's first successful flight in a mechanically-powered aircraft had been accomplished.

Perhaps it is significant that aviation came to life in a young land with an unusual attachment to the work ethic, and a philosophy which held that any man could aspire to greatness, sustained by belief in his dream, and limited only by the strength of his personal commitment. This was the essence of the age and the wellspring of American vitality. Cynics who now question the validity of that philosophy might do well to take a penetrating look at the dour, comical-looking Orville and Wilbur Wright, bicycle mechanics by trade, peering out from under their derby hats in every child's history book. These unassuming brothers were the first to achieve powered flight, a fact that many of their contemporaries found difficult to believe. They had achieved the impossible, because they believed they could.

But this was only the beginning. Other men and even more innovative ideas were needed to transform this shaky start into something more substantial, and considerably more dependable. There were many who were anxious to try. Some of these became folk heroes of their day, and later, barnstorming legends of a "death-defying era." A very few became masters of the guild, undisputed giants of the new profession.

Such a man was Glenn H. Curtiss, a bona fide small town American hero. Born to a family of modest means in the little town of Hammondsport, New York, at the southern end of Lake Keuka, he was left fatherless at the age of seven. By the time he reached fifteen, he had decided that education was a callous luxury for a capable boy with a widowed mother and a deaf sister. He abandoned any thought of further schooling, and went to work for the Eastman Company in Rochester, New York, for $3.50 a week. Times were hard in the middle 1890s, and often thereafter he found himself without work. Eventually he returned to Hammondsport, and by the age of twenty had opened his own business selling harnesses and bicycles. His capital consisted mostly of boundless energy and confidence in his ability to succeed, but this was enough to enable the shoe-string operation to blossom into a small chain of bicycle shops. Soon, Curtiss was designing and producing bicycles under his own brand name. Encouraged by his modest success and driven by a fascination for things mechanical, he began experimenting with gasoline engines which he painstakingly adapted to his cycles. At the turn of the century, while still only twenty-three, Curtiss was operating his own motorcycle factory, albeit one of unpretentious proportions.

To publicize the superiority of his machines in the face of stiff competition, he began racing them, and quickly made a name for himself as an aggressive contender and frequent winner. A few years later, in January 1907, he would startle spectators at the Florida Speed Carnival by covering a measured mile on one of his motorcycles at the unprecedented speed of 136.3 miles per hour. No machine operated by a human being had ever traveled so fast. No motorcycle would do so again for more than two decades. This record-setting feat brought him national acclaim as "the fastest man on earth."

In conjunction with his successful motorcycle developments, in 1903 Curtiss decided to expand his business to include a new and exciting field of interest. Captain Thomas Scott Baldwin, a well-known balloonist and aerial exhibitionist, had contracted with him to build a light air-cooled engine for his dirigible the *California Arrow*. So successful was that engine and airframe combination, that Curtiss found himself becoming a popular supplier of light-weight airship engines. The success of this endeavor was indicated by the fact that several devotees of lighter-than-air craft, led by Baldwin, decided to make Hammondsport their center of operations, to be close to their source of engines.

While he welcomed and encouraged the airship trade, Curtiss had not taken much personal interest in aviation up to this point. He thought of himself as a businessman, with the manufacture of motorcycles and engines being his business. In June 1907, he tried his hand at flying one of Baldwin's machines, and discovered that he had a natural feel for aerodynamics. Still, even at that late date, he was not particularly impressed with flying as a useful pursuit.

Three months later, however, he became involved with a group which called itself the Aerial Experiment Association. Guided by the famous Dr. Alexander Graham Bell, the five members set out, ". . . In pursuance of their common aim 'to get into the air,' by the construction of a practical aerodrome [sic] driven by its own motive power and carrying a man."* From that time forward, the name Curtiss would be eminently associated with aviation, and the man himself would become one of the world's most prolific contributors to the science of manned flight.

The Wrights, of course, had already flown their machine in 1903, but in those early years their penchant for secrecy led some people to question the authenticity of their claims. Many Americans voiced skepticism that they had flown at all. Ignoring public cynicism, the brothers quietly applied for patents, and set to work improving their original machine. They continued to avoid public exposure, and by 1905 they felt confident enough to offer an improved model of their original airplane to the United States government. Incredible as it may seem, the government was not interested. Shaken but undaunted, they turned to Great Britain. The response was substantially the same. After having been rejected by their chosen beneficiaries, and somewhat piqued by their countrymen's refusal to recognize their achievements, the brothers lapsed into a period of relative inactivity. During this time competitors were developing their own designs, and soon thereafter, the Wrights' clear lead was lost.

Meanwhile, the Aerial Experiment Association had proceeded at a fast pace. Experimenting first with a man-carrying tetrahedral kite, the association progressed rapidly through the glider stage, and in less than a year they had constructed and successfully flown two powered aircraft over short distances. Then in the spring of 1908, the association produced a Curtiss-designed aircraft known as the *June Bug*. Its performance was so encouraging that the members decided to hazard a try for the coveted *Scientific American* trophy, which had been offered for the first public flight of one kilometer or more. On the Fourth of July 1908, Glenn Curtiss flew his *June Bug* a distance of about 5,000 feet, well beyond the kilometer required to capture the prize.

*The agreement creating the Aerial Experiment Association was signed at Halifax, Nova Scotia on 30 September 1907. The five signatories were Alexander Graham Bell, G. H. Curtiss, F. W. Baldwin, J. A. D. McCurdy, and T. Selfridge.

On the Fourth of July 1908 Curtiss flew his *June Bug* a distance of more than 5,000 feet to win the *Scientific American* award. (Curtiss Museum)

It is difficult in the present day to comprehend the excitement caused by a flight of only 5,000 feet. But in 1908, with a significant segment of the American population still expressing serious doubt that man could really fly, the news was electrifying. This time there was no question about it. A crowd including newsmen, scientists, and officials representing the *Scientific American* and the Aero Club of America, had witnessed the feat.

In December of that same year Curtiss made his first serious attempt to take off in an aircraft from water. To accomplish this, he reconfigured the *June Bug* with lightweight, fabric-covered, canoe-like floats, and renamed it the *Loon*. It rode well enough on the pontoons, and when Curtiss opened full throttle, it sped across the waters of Lake Keuka with perfect form, but refused to fly. The added weight of the floats, and the suction created by the calm lake surface, was too much to overcome. Undismayed, Curtiss fitted the *Loon* with a more powerful engine and tried again. Still there was no lift-off. Unfortunately, one of the floats was damaged during the attempt to become airborne, and the *Loon* sank, after which the project was shelved for the rest of the winter.

Having accomplished its mission of documented powered flight, the Aerial Experiment Association disbanded on the last day of March 1909. Earlier in March, Curtiss and Augustus Herring had formed the Herring-Curtiss Company to manufacture aircraft, motorcycles, and other engine-driven conveyances. This proved to be an ill-fated venture, with the company ending in receivership. A partnership with Herring had been particularly attractive to Curtiss, because Herring had assured him that he possessed patents from his

The *Loon* was used by Curtiss for his first serious experiments with waterborne aircraft. (Curtiss Museum)

early experiments sufficient to ward off legal attacks initiated by the Wright brothers in an attempt to control the aviation industry and inhibit competition. The gist of the Wright claim was that Curtiss had infringed on the patented Wright system of aircraft control. In point of fact Curtiss' aircraft employed ailerons perfected by the Aerial Experiment Association, while the Wrights' aircraft used a less effective wing-warping technique later discarded by the aircraft industry as inefficient and impractical. Nevertheless, early court decisions liberally interpreted the Wright patents and found the similarity sufficient to constitute infringement. It was not until World War I that the internecine patent battle came to an end, as a result of a cross-licensing agreement among aircraft manufacturers. Unfortunately, the damage wrought by litigation within the American aircraft industry prior to World War I had the effect of retarding the growth of aviation in the United States during that period. Only Curtiss and a few other brave souls had been willing to take the serious risks involved in defying the Wright suits.

The first Herring-Curtiss airplane was built under contract for the Aeronautical Society of New York. It was called the *Golden Flyer,* later mistakenly referred to by some as the *Gold Bug.* On 17 July 1909 Curtiss flew this machine to capture once again the *Scientific American* trophy. This time the award had been offered to the first man to fly 25 kilometers. The following month he entered another of his aircraft, the *Rheims Flyer,* in the first international air meet, La Grande Fenaine d'Aviation de la Champaigne, held at Rheims, France. There, before an estimated crowd of more than two hundred thousand people, he bested the finest aviators of Europe to capture perhaps the most prestigious award of the meet, the Gordon Bennett International Aviation Trophy. For this achievement, the French subsequently awarded him that nation's Pilot's License Number 2. In aviation circles, it was now clear that this shy, almost reticent American from Hammondsport, New York, was someone to be reckoned with.

Meanwhile, a French marine engineer named Henri Fabre had begun to experiment with the idea of flight from the surface of the water. His first seaplane, powered by three Anzani engines driving one propeller, failed to fly. On his second machine, which he called the *Hydravion*, however, he used a more powerful new Gnome rotary engine, which he mounted at the rear of the aircraft to power a pusher propeller. The wings were also positioned in the extreme rear. The whole contraption somewhat resembled a sawhorse with a man astride; set on three long legs with each ending in a hollow wooden float, it was a weird and unlikely-looking aircraft, but on 28 March 1910 it lifted off the water and flew. Fabre duplicated the feat several times, until on 18 May 1910 he made a bad landing, which wrecked the *Hydravion* and threw him into the water. Although he apparently gave up piloting aircraft at this point, Fabre rebuilt and improved his machine, only to have it wrecked by another pilot during a demonstration at Monaco the following year. Unable to continue his work any further because of a lack of financing, he contented himself with the manufacture of floats for other early aircraft pioneers.

Back in Hammondsport, Glenn Curtiss had been preparing a machine to compete for a $10,000 prize offered for the first flight from Albany, New York, to New York City. Since the trip would be flown over the course of the Hudson River, he wanted to be able to land his *Albany Flier* on the water if it became necessary. Therefore, he attached two metal tanks as pontoons, plus a long tubular flotation device made of fabric and filled with cork. He then tested the system by landing in Lake Keuka. It was a complete success. On 29 May 1910 Curtiss took off from Van Rensselaer Island in the Hudson River at Albany, New York, and landed just under five hours later on Governor's Island in New York City Harbor. He made the trip with two fuel stops along the way, in an actual flight time for the 143 miles of 2 hours and 51 minutes. He had won the $10,000 prize as well as the *Scientific American* trophy for the third time, retiring it in his name. Although the use of the makeshift flotation gear had proven unnecessary, another small step had been taken toward development of a practical seaplane. In the course of all this activity, the man from Hammondsport had become the most popular figure in American aviation, lauded in story and song.

About this same period of time, the military value of the airplane began to be recognized. In September 1908, the Wright brothers had demonstrated their improved aircraft to the Army at Fort Myer, Virginia, and about ten months later the machine was officially accepted as *Army Aeroplane Number One*. Two U.S. naval officers who attended the September demonstration expressed interest in constructing an aircraft on floats for the U.S. Navy. The Navy Department was not yet ready to accept the new concept at this stage, though, and the idea was quietly allowed to die. By late 1910, however, the Navy's curiosity had been aroused to the point that one of Curtiss' airplanes was permitted to attempt a takeoff from a wooden deck mounted on the bow of the USS *Birmingham*. Eugene B. Ely, a member of the Curtiss Exhibition Team, made the noteworthy flight on 14 November 1910. Two months later, on 18 January 1911, Ely established another first, when he landed his Curtiss aircraft without incident on a platform erected over the stern of the USS *Pennsylvania*. After refueling, he took off again and landed ashore.

Proponents of the new idea called naval aviation felt certain that the Secretary of the Navy could not ignore the implications of such sensational demonstrations. They were wrong. The Secretary, Truman H. Newberry, apparently felt that the concept of an aircraft which could take off from the deck of a warship and return later to land aboard had little practical application. He made it clear that before the Navy Department would show an official interest in aviation, it would have to be demonstrated that an aircraft could be lowered over the side by a ship's crane, take off from the water to pursue its mission, and return to land alongside the ship and be hoisted aboard.

Lesser men might have given up in exasperation. Curtiss, who had already done much developmental work on the concept, doubled his efforts to find the key to water operations.

By this time the Herring Curtiss Aircraft Company had gone into receivership, and Curtiss had moved his winter flying operation to North Island at San Diego, California, where the weather was nearly optimum for his purposes. North Island was flat, mostly barren, uninhabited, and could be reached only by boat or via a sandspit usually covered by water at high tide. Here amid the sandy beaches, Curtiss planned to pursue his work on waterborne aircraft to a successful conclusion, free from interruption by curious sightseers. Concurrently, he planned to accumulate badly needed working capital and spur interest in aviation by conducting a flying school. In a letter to the Secretary of the Navy he had already offered to instruct a naval officer free of charge, "in the operation and construction of the Curtiss aeroplane." The Navy accepted his offer, and sent him Lieutenant T. G. "Spuds" Ellyson, a submariner who would later become Naval Aviator Number 1.

Curtiss and Ellyson worked well together and became good friends. Curtiss' approach to a problem tended to be based on instinct, tempered by a vast store of practical knowledge gained from trial and error experiences. Ellyson, on the other hand, was trained as an engineer, and was proficient in the methodology of theoretical problem-solving. He quickly developed an intense interest in Curtiss' "hydroaeroplane," as it was called, and he spent much of his time not otherwise engaged in flying lessons in assisting Curtiss in solving the perplexing problems associated with getting airborne from the water. They determined that the answers had something to do with not only the size and weight of the floats, but also their shape, and they experimented with numerous configurations. Finally on 26 January 1911, after one of the more promising float configurations had been installed, the aircraft left the water, flew a short distance, and landed. An increased water-plane surface and an upturned lip on the main float were credited with the success; doubtlessly, a slight chop on the bay that day had also helped to break suction and bounce the aircraft into the air. Afterwards, all that remained was to incorporate the desirable characteristics of the experimental arrangement into a stable, permanent float design.

Work began almost immediately, and Curtiss was soon operating his aircraft on a single, shallow, box-like planing float 12 feet long by 2 feet wide. On one occasion, while seeking ways to improve takeoff characteristics, Ellyson rode on the float while Curtiss flew the airplane. After takeoff, while the aircraft cruised about a hundred feet over the water, Ellyson was surprised by his ability to discern fish and other submerged objects from his precarious perch on the float. Having been a submariner, he was struck by the implications of this experience as it related to antisubmarine warfare. This may have been the first realization of the potential of the airplane as a effective weapon to combat the submarine.

By the middle of February 1911, Curtiss had perfected his hydroaeroplane to the point where he was ready to give a demonstration. The USS *Pennsylvania*, which had been used by Ely for his innovative landing and takeoff the previous month, was anchored in San Diego Bay, California. On 17 February Curtiss contacted the Commanding Officer of the *Pennsylvania*, Captain Charles F. Pond, and asked if he might fly out to the ship to make a call. The captain, who was at that time one of a very few senior naval officers sympathetic to naval aviation, readily agreed. After sending Ellyson ahead by boat to assist

Ellyson (left) and Curtiss aboard the latter's hydroaeroplane. (Curtiss Museum)

him when he arrived, Curtiss took off from his base at North Island, and within minutes landed alongside the ship. The machine he used on this flight was a tractor-type, the only one of its kind, as Curtiss preferred pusher-types. The ship's boat crane was swung over the side and the hook was lowered to engage a sling which Curtiss had rigged on the aircraft beforehand. Standing on the upper wing with one leg slung casually over the hook, Curtiss rode the aircraft up and onto the deck of the *Pennsylvania*, where he then climbed down to pay his respects to Captain Pond. Following a brief visit, Curtiss and his hydroaeroplane were lowered into the water, and he took off and flew back to North Island. Curtiss had met all the requirements imposed by the Secretary of the Navy. There could be no more equivocation. Naval aviation was an idea whose time had come.

Curtiss had one more refinement to his machine in mind. He fitted the aircraft float with retractable wheels arranged in tricycle-fashion, to provide the option of operating from land or water. Then he proceeded to demonstrate the practicality of this feature by taking off from the water at North Island and flying to Coronado Beach, California, where he extended his wheels and landed. After a leisurely lunch at the local Coronado Hotel, he reversed the procedure and returned to his base at North Island. This first American seaplane-turned-amphibian was named *Triad*, because of its ability to function on land, water, or in the air.

In May of 1911, the Navy formally ordered its first two Curtiss airplanes. This occurred at an opportune time for Curtiss, because he had just regained

Curtiss returning to his base at North Island aboard the *Triad,* following a luncheon
at Coronado, 1911. (Title Insurance and Trust Co., San Diego, Cal.)

control of his factory at Hammondsport, and he had split his original company
into two new organizations, The Curtiss Aeroplane Company and The Curtiss
Motor Company. The Navy's first Curtiss airplane, designated *A-1,* was accepted on 6 July 1911. Captain Washington Irving Chambers, Officer-in-Charge
of Naval Aviation, and its most vociferous champion within the bureaucratic
structure at that time, was on hand for the occasion. Chambers watched Ellyson qualify in the *A-1* for his Aero Club of America license on 2 July, and
afterwards experienced his first airplane ride aboard the *A-1* with Curtiss at
the controls. The *A-2* was accepted later that month.

In addition to the purchase of its first two aircraft, the Navy also acquired
another pilot, Lieutenant Junior Grade John H. Towers, from Rome, Georgia.
Ellyson became his instructor, under the watchful eye of Curtiss. Towers was
an enthusiastic student, and, despite a broken ankle and some minor scrapes
sustained on his first encounter with an airplane, he qualified for his Aero
Club license in September of 1911. Later, when the Navy began formalizing
such things, he would be designated Naval Aviator Number 3. Eventually he
was to become Chief of the Bureau of Aeronautics. Hammondsport itself soon
evolved into a sort of miniature naval air facility, complete with tent hangar
and a small contingent of Navy personnel who had been ordered there to
learn about aviation from Curtiss, one of the men most prominent in the new
field.

Having advanced this far with his hydroaeroplane, Curtiss now pushed
on with the next logical evolutionary step in the development of waterborne
aircraft—a flying boat. He designed and had constructed a larger flat-bottom
hull to which the lower wing was directly attached, but with the tail assembly
supported by an outrigger framework extending aft as in the hydroaeroplane.
A 60-horsepower engine was mounted in the hull in front of the pilot, and it
drove two tractor-type propellors by means of a chain-drive. The craft was
built in Hammondsport and shipped to the winter flying base at North Island.
There the old suction problem was reencountered. While the engine developed
what should have been sufficient power to get the machine airborne, the aircraft
obstinately refused to lift off. Eventually, on 10 January 1912, it broke the
surface and flew, but refused to do so again. Although Curtiss knew he was
close to success, he was unable to solve the problem that winter.

Upon returning to Hammondsport from California in the spring of 1912, Curtiss made some radical changes to his flying boat, and tried again to take off. (Curtiss Museum)

Upon returning to Hammondsport in the spring, Curtiss made some major changes. He moved the engine to a position up between the wings, and eliminated the chain-drive, so that the engine drove a single pusher-type propeller directly, as in the *A-1*. This accomplished, he again tried repeatedly to coax his flying boat into the air, but again without success. Some elusive but essential element was missing. One day he decided to observe the aircraft at full power from the vantage point of a motor-boat running alongside, to try to discover the answer to this frustrating problem. With Naval Constructor Holden Richardson, later to become Naval Aviator Number 13, Curtiss intently watched the attitude of the hull and the flow of the water around it at various speeds. Finally, he came ashore, made a rough drawing, and instructed one of his workmen to fashion two wedge-shaped blocks of wood in accordance with his sketch. These he fastened to the hull to form a break in the flat bottom. This simple device proved to be the solution which had eluded him for so long. When power was added, the world's first flying boat rose on its crude step and took to the air. From that moment onward, every flying boat constructed would employ the step principle conceived by Glenn Curtiss that day, and patented by him in 1915.

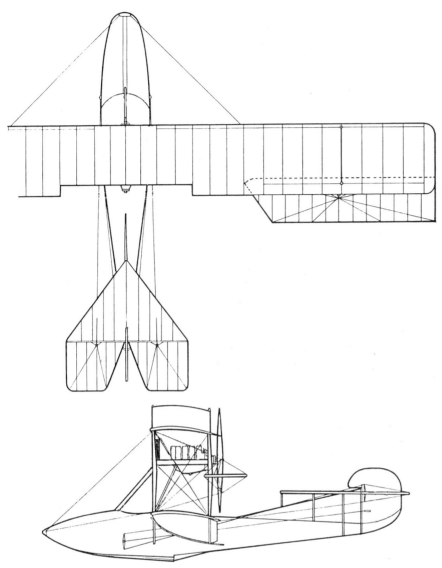

The Curtiss F-Boat.

The first few production boats had hulls somewhat redesigned with integral tail assemblies, but with the flat bottom characteristic of the prototype. By late 1913, however, the hull shape of the F-Boat, as the model came to be called, had undergone important modifications, including the addition of a streamlined bow and a V-shaped bottom. This latter feature, along with the step principle, completely eliminated the problem with suction. The reshaped bottom also served to keep spray away from the propeller and the pilots during the takeoff run. As new engines became available, horsepower was increased from the original 60 horsepower to 75, 90, and eventually 100 horsepower, with the advent of the Curtiss OXX engine.

Finding buyers for the fledgling flying boat was another problem. While fully recognizing the importance of keeping his military customers happy, Curtiss felt that the American sportsman might become interested in it as well if the right approach were taken. Once the fad caught on, he reasoned, this segment of the market could be further developed to produce substantial profit. The sportsman had to be wealthy, though, because these early flying boats were priced upward from about $6,000, a large sum of money in the early 1900s. The machine was marketed as the Aeroyacht, and men such as Harold

F. McCormick of International Harvester, George L. Peck of the Pennsylvania Railroad, and William B. Scripps the publisher were among Curtiss' first customers.

Logan A. "Jack" Vilas, son of a wealthy industrialist, was also one of Curtiss' early customers. Upon ordering one of the new 100-horsepower Curtiss F-Boats, he enrolled in the Curtiss Flying School at Hammondsport. The course, which took about four weeks to complete, was probably the first commercial flight training program in the United States. Upon completing it, Vilas was awarded the Aero Club of America License Number 6 for hydro-aeroplanes.

Vilas quickly became a proficient pilot, and decided to attempt a significant aviation first—a flight across Lake Michigan. The feat had been attempted on at least two previous occasions, without success.

At about 3:00 P.M. on 1 July 1913, with a local resident named William Baster aboard for company, Vilas set out from Saint Joseph, Michigan, and flew west toward Chicago, Illinois. He had no compass, but by pointing his aircraft in the direction he thought that city ought to be, and by keeping the sun in the same relative position to maintain heading, he landed at his intended destination and taxied into the Chicago Yacht Club sometime around 4:30 P.M.*

By 1913 other aircraft manufacturers had decided to take advantage of Curtiss' invention, and they began producing their own versions of this new type of aircraft. W. Starling Burgess, a well-known boat-builder from Marblehead, Massachusetts, built three models that year, one of which was purchased by the Navy. The Burgess Model K was accepted for service on 13 May, and designated the D-1. It was a two-place, single-engine pusher aircraft, powered by a 70-horsepower Renault V-8. Burgess produced other aircraft for the U.S. Navy, but in 1916 the Burgess organization was destined to become a division of the Curtiss Aeroplane and Motor Company.

Even the Wright brothers, who had been engaged in a costly patent battle with Curtiss, had to concede the advantages of the new type of aircraft. Toward the end of 1913, they too produced a flying boat, a twin-propeller airplane known as the Model G Aeroboat, powered by a 60-horsepower Wright engine mounted in the hull. The Navy considered purchasing this aircraft in 1914, but ultimately decided its performance was not as good as that of other available designs.

On the west coast of the United States, the Christofferson brothers had begun building their Model D flying boat, which featured a 110-horsepower V-8 engine, and boasted a speed of up to 75 miles per hour. These aircraft were used for nonscheduled passenger service primarily between San Francisco and Oakland, California. Two Christofferson flying boats were built to the order of Roald Amundsen for his Arctic explorations, but the intervention of World War I prevented their use on this adventure.

The Benoist Company of St. Louis, Missouri, had also begun building these new and increasingly popular aircraft. On New Years Day 1914, a Benoist Type XIV flying boat belonging to the newly-formed St. Petersburg and Tampa Airboat Line and flown by Tony Jannus, made the world's first airline flight.† The capacity of the Type XIV was limited to a pilot and one passenger, and the flight distance between the two cities was about eighteen miles. The fare for the twenty-three minute flight was five dollars. This brave venture did not prove to be profitable, however, and folded only a few months after the inaugural flight, when the contract expired on 31 March 1914. During its short ex-

*Vilas is also believed to have instituted the first aerial forest patrol on 22 June 1915, when he took Wisconsin Forest Service Officer E. M. Griffith aloft in his Curtiss F–Boat to look for forest fires.

†Jannus was killed in Russia on 12 October 1916, while demonstrating a Curtiss flying boat.

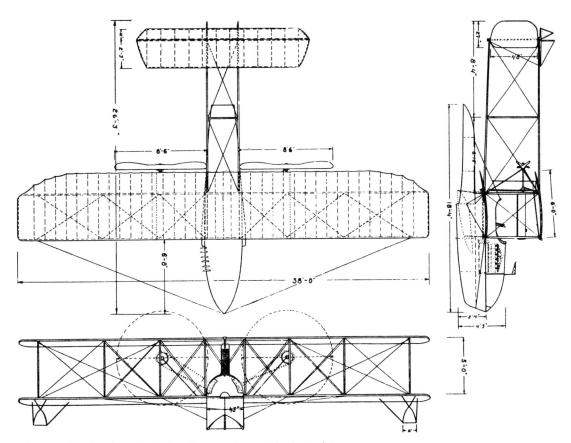

The Wright Aeroboat. It had twin propellers with chain drives.

istence, however, the St. Petersburg and Tampa Airboat Line carried over 1,200 passengers, and the experience proved that an airplane could operate point-to-point on a regularly scheduled basis with remarkable reliability. The idea had been premature, but only a few years were to pass before the concept would be validated.

During these same years, flying boats produced by Thomas, Patterson-Francis, and others also began to make their appearance. During the summer of 1913, a well-publicized race for waterborne flying machines was organized over a course extending from Chicago along the eastern edge of Lake Michigan, through the Straits of Mackinac, and down the western shore of Lake Huron to Detroit, Michigan. The "Aero and Hydro Great Lakes Reliability Cruise," as it was called, attracted six flying boats of various makes, and one hydroaeroplane designed and flown by Glenn L. Martin. The race would be a veritable proving ground, testing not only the dependability of each aircraft, but also its ability to survive adverse weather. On the afternoon of 8 July 1913, one week after Vilas had crossed Lake Michigan, the race began, with only five of the seven original entries starting. The five starting aircraft and their pilots were:*

Curtiss F-Boat—Beckwith Havens/J.B.R. Verplanck
Benoist Flying Boat—Antony Jannus/Paul McCullough
Thomas Flying Boat—Walter Johnson/Earl Beers
Martin Hydroaeroplane—Glenn L. Martin/Day
Patterson-Francis Flying Boat—Roy Francis/Irving

It has since been agreed that the event took place during some of the most mischievous weather ever encountered on the Great Lakes.

*The entries who did not start were Weldon B. Cooke in his Cooke flying boat, and L. A. "Jack" Vilas in his Curtiss F-Boat.

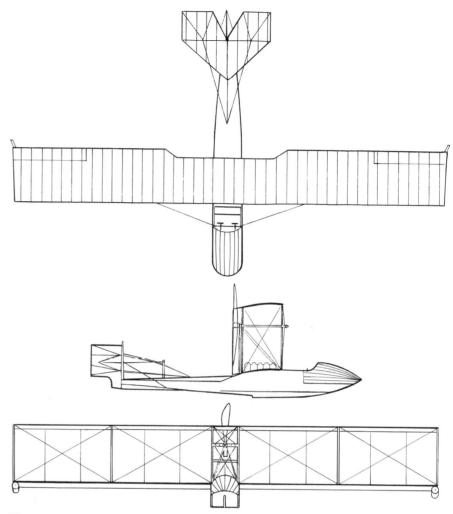

The Benoist Type XIV, used by the first scheduled air carrier, the St. Petersburg and Tampa Airboat Line. (Charles Cooney)

Three of the aircraft left on the eighth, just ahead of an approaching storm. The Benoist boat flown by Tony Jannus became the first casualty when it made an emergency landing near Gary, Indiana, shortly after departure. It was towed to shore, but was later destroyed by the storm. Walter Johnson, in his Thomas aircraft, had flown an even shorter distance, when mechanical difficulties forced him down at Robertsdale, Illinois, for repairs. Later, as he was making his take-off to continue the race, his aircraft hit some floating debris, causing serious damage to the hull and ending his chances of finishing.

Roy Francis in his Patterson-Francis aircraft started late and reached Pentwater, Michigan, but the grueling pace, compounded by the miserable weather, caused him to quit the race at that point and go home. Martin, the other late starter, also made Pentwater on the fourteenth, but was ruled out of the race there because he did not continue within the time allowed.

Beckwith "Becky" Havens and J. B. R. Verplanck in the latter's Curtiss F-Boat had been the second contestants to leave Chicago on the eighth. They proceeded along the coast ahead of the storm to Michigan City, Indiana. From there they flew to Soutl· Haven, Michigan, and on to Pentwater. They lost a whole day at South Haven and two days at Pentwater due to high winds and rough water conditions, but on the fifteenth they took off again to cover some 260 miles to Point Lookout on Lake Huron. The following day they flew to Bay City, Michigan, and on the next made Port Sanilac, Michigan, after battling

The Navy C-2 Flying Boat, one of five purchased from Curtiss on the first F-Boat order. (Curtiss Museum)

severe storms and on one occasion running out of fuel. The eighteenth was the day of triumph, when the exhausted pilots and their Curtiss F-Boat landed at Detroit, Michigan, at 3:30 P.M. They were the only ones who completed the race. The flight of approximately 800 miles had taken them ten days; the total flight time was not quite fifteen hours. The victory was largely due to the skill and perseverance of Havens and Verplanck, but it was also a testimonial to the ruggedness of the Curtiss F-Boat.

In the meantime the U.S. Navy had placed an order for five of the early F-Boats, and as they were delivered, designated them C for Curtiss, one through five. Later, in March 1914, the five Curtiss boats were redesignated AB-1 through AB-5. The letter A became the designation for Curtiss, the first manufacturer of aircraft for the Navy. B signified flying boat, and the number indicated the sequence of Navy acquisition. During the Mexican hostilities of 1914, the F-Boats went to war aboard USS *Birmingham* and *Mississippi*. In April, the AB-3 made a reconnaissance flight over Veracruz, Mexico, searching for enemy troops ashore and mines in the harbor. This was the first American operational flight against belligerent forces, and while it was uneventful, it served as a beginning for expanding the military use of aircraft.

Ellyson and Richardson had both participated in the development of the first flying boat, and knew that this type of aircraft had characteristics which made it particularly suitable for naval use. One of these was its rugged construction, which made it capable of enduring the stress of launching by catapult. As early as September 1911, Ellyson, in the *A-1* hydroaeroplane, had demonstrated a simple wire launching device which he and Curtiss had devised, and which both hoped could be developed into an acceptable shipboard launching system. It soon became apparent, however, that while the device worked well on land, it would not be adaptable for launching an aircraft from a rolling, pitching warship at sea. Naval Constructor Richardson was next to fabricate a compressed-air catapult, which he built from discarded ordnance parts. The first attempt at launching an aircraft with this contraption wrecked the *A-1* and threw Ellyson unharmed into the Severn River. Using the information derived from this experience, Richardson made some basic changes in his launching device, and in November he succeeded in catapulting the *A-3* into the air from

The Navy AB-3 is launched by catapult from the USS *North Carolina*. (U.S. Navy)

a barge in the Anacostia River. This feat was later repeated using the C-1 flying boat, but it was not until November 1915 that an improved Richardson-built catapult launched the AB-2 from the deck of the USS *North Carolina*. A Curtiss aircraft had chalked up another first.

Several hundred F-Boats were built, but they were not altogether uniform in design. Each aircraft tended to be a slightly improved version of the previous

Artist's conception of Lawrence Sperry's dramatic demonstration of gyro-stabilized flight over Paris in June 1914, using a Curtiss F-Boat. (Sperry Div. of Sperry Rand Corp.)

one. Certainly the C-1, the first of the F-Boats accepted by the Navy, was considerably different from the later models, and some, like the triplane F-Boat, were obvious departures from the norm. A successful monoplane version was constructed, and was particularly noteworthy because monoplanes were not characteristic of the Curtiss line. It was made especially for R. V. Morris to compete in the Schneider Trophy Race. Four-place F-Boats were also built, but the one unalterable rule which was applied to all the variations was Curtiss' total insistence upon structural strength and superior workmanship. In its day, the F-Boat was clearly an advanced flying machine. It was probably for this reason, as well as its inherent stability, that Dr. Elmer A. Sperry and his son Lawrence chose an F-Boat for their work with the forerunner of the modern autopilot. Lawrence, nicknamed "Gyro" by his fellow student aviators, was a graduate of the Curtiss Flying School, and qualified in the F-Boat in the summer of 1913. The following year, for a 50,000-franc French prize, he demonstrated to the French War Department by means of a dramatic stunt that the Sperry Gyro-Stabilizer had been developed to such a point that it was capable

The Curtiss F-Boat was used to train early naval aviators at Pensacola, Florida. (U.S. Navy)

of keeping an aircraft in straight and level flight by itself, while the pilot climbed out onto one wing and the gyro compensated for the weight shift. During the years from 1915 to 1917, the Sperrys also conducted the first American guided missile experiments, employing a Curtiss F-Boat fitted with a preset automatic guidance system.

Curtiss found a good market for his F-Boat in Europe and even in Japan. European countries were beginning to feel the diplomatic rumblings foreshadowing World War I and were making hurried preparations. Russia bought eighty F-Boats, and when war finally broke out, Curtiss was swamped with orders for them both at home and abroad. The U.S. Navy bought a large number of F-Boats, and used them extensively at Pensacola, Florida, to train early naval aviators.* In 1916 the F-Boat gave way to the model MF or Military Flying Boat, a larger, improved aircraft which incorporated all the knowledge gleaned from other Curtiss seaplanes. After World War I, the U.S. Navy would build about eighty of these improved models in its own Naval Aircraft Factory. The basic design type culminated in the Curtiss Seagull, a four-place flying boat built after the war for the civilian market.

By 1913, the name Curtiss was already closely linked with aviation in America. The factory at Hammondsport was producing several different types of float planes and flying boats, and Curtiss had established himself as the largest aircraft manufacturer in the United States. Among his many achievements in the development of aviation in five short years were:

*The Navy's first formal flying school under Lieutenant John H. Towers was established at Pensacola, Florida, in January 1914. Towers made the first flight in a Curtiss F-Boat. The U.S. Army also acquired a total of seven F-Boats between 1912 and 1918, for training purposes.

—The first officially-observed flight in the United States, for which he was awarded Pilot's License Number 1 and the Aero Club of America Gold Medal

—The capture of the Gordon Bennett trophy at the first international air meet

—The capture of the *Scientific American* Trophy three times in succession for record-setting flights

—The award of the Collier Trophy for his hydroaeroplane and flying boat

—The award of the Langley Gold Medal by the Smithsonian Institution for his spectacular achievements in marine aviation

Notwithstanding his many successes, however, Curtiss considered the flying boat his crowning achievement. He had foreseen the coming of commercial aviation, and knew that hulled aircraft, because of their unique qualities, would establish the international ocean routes. He looked ahead with the confidence of a visionary to the day an aircraft would cross the Atlantic, and had already begun working to ensure that the aircraft would be a Curtiss flying boat.

Most authorities would agree that Glenn H. Curtiss ranks high among the early aviation pioneers. He was also somewhat of a controversial figure, who even today evokes different reactions, depending on one's point of view. To most aviation enthusiasts of his time, he was an American hero of the first order; to his rivals the Wright brothers and their supporters, he was an unabashed patent infringer. To still others, he was a socially inept person who shunned parlor conversation, and who frequently made early disappearances from parties and other social functions including even his own. The evidence suggests that he was in a fact a modest man incapable of small talk, whose restless mind constantly spirited him away from superficial activity to the pursuit of solutions to some vexing problem.

Curtis is widely credited as the first American to achieve flight from the water's surface. Because of this some have claimed for him the title, "Father of Naval Aviation." If any one person can rightly lay claim to this title, Glenn Curtiss would have to be a leading contender. The evidence is persuasive. For it was Curtiss who made the early beginnings of naval aviation possible by satisfying the difficult requirements set by the Secretary of the Navy for a practical seaplane. It was he who built the first aircraft to land on and take off from a ship, and it was a Curtiss-trained pilot who accomplished the feat. It was he who built the U.S. Navy's first operational aircraft and many hundreds more, and it was he who taught the Navy's first pilot to fly. The Navy's first aviation mechanics learned the idiosyncrasies of aircraft and their engines under his tutelage, and the Navy frequently called upon him for his services as the world's foremost authority on hydroaeroplanes and flying boats. It was the Curtiss Transatlantic Flyer that became the prototype for U.S. as well as British maritime patrol aircraft of World War I, and Curtiss flying boats were the only American-built combat aircraft to be used in that war. It was a Curtiss flying boat design that would enable the Navy to be the first to conquer the Atlantic by air.

Glenn Curtiss was a prodigious achiever, a man who rose from a modest background to attain fortune and fame in his lifetime, a living testimonial to the validity of the American dream. Yet, despite his success, he continued to retain much of his small-town identity. To the people of Hammondsport, he was their most illustrious son, and for a brief moment in time they basked with him in the limelight of world acclaim. In his later years he moved his residence to sunnier climates, but he always seemed to remain in character, if not in fact, G. H. Curtiss, Hammondsport.

Glenn Curtiss died on 23 July 1930 at the age of 52. He is buried in Hammondsport near the spot where he first made aviation history in July 1908.

CHAPTER TWO

The Americas

MAN IS INHERENTLY an audacious creature who cannot be permanently intimidated by the unknown or the untried. His curious mind is always at work devising means to overcome any impediments to his progress, and he cannot resist the temptation to see how far he can stretch his knowledge, and his luck. He is an impatient being, and when he has achieved beyond his greatest expectations, he cannot rest but rather must continue onward, to improve upon his accomplishments, and to seek even greater challenges.

On the first day of April 1913, the Englishman Lord Northcliffe, publisher of *The London Daily Mail* in London, England, made a startling announcement. The sum of 10,000 pounds sterling ($50,000) was proffered to the first person or persons who could successfully fly over the Atlantic Ocean, "From any point in the United States, Canada or Newfoundland, to any point in Great Britain or Ireland, in seventy-two consecutive hours." The offer was greeted with skepticism by many who thought the feat impossible to accomplish. But there were others who considered it an entirely realistic challenge. An attempt had already been made in an airship three years earlier, and, although it had failed, the fact that the participants had gone some distance before going down was encouraging.

On 15 October 1910, Walter Wellman, newspaperman turned adventurer, had ascended in his airship *America* from Atlantic City, New Jersey, and headed eastward. The *America* was a "flying boat" in a literal if not a conventional sense, for beneath a 228-foot-long gas-bag hung a large lifeboat, which served as galley, lounge, and sleeping quarters, and which in the event of an emergency, would revert to its original function. After three days of punishment by foul weather and high winds, *America* was forced down into the sea about 400 miles east of Cape Hatteras, North Carolina. Wellman and his crew in the lifeboat were picked up by a passing ship, thus ending in defeat man's first serious attempt to fly across the Atlantic. But intriguing questions remained. What if weather conditions had been more favorable? Suppose there had been a tailwind? Would more powerful engines or improved design characteristics have made a difference? No one could say with certainty. In any case, Northcliffe's rules specified an aeroplane [sic], and serious competitors made their plans accordingly.

In Hammondsport, New York, Glenn Curtiss, who only five years earlier had been satisfied when his *June Bug* flew a distance of some 5,000 feet, had already given the idea of a transatlantic flight much serious thought. By the time Northcliffe made his announcement in the spring of 1913, there was little question in Curtiss' mind that he could build a flying boat capable of crossing the Atlantic.

In the fall of 1913, Curtiss sailed to England on a business trip to promote his products. His English agents, White and Thompson Company Limited, had in their employ a pilot named John Cyril Porte, a tall congenial fellow whose appearance and manner gave no indication of a serious health problem. He had been a promising young submarine officer in the Royal Navy until he developed tuberculosis, which had led to an early retirement in 1911. Shortly

Towers, Curtiss, and Porte in front of the *America*, 1914. (U.S. Navy)

thereafter, he had become involved with the new science of flight at the Deperdussin Flying School in France, and subsequently made Curtiss' acquaintance during the latter's visit in 1913. Porte was impressed with the American's flying boat demonstrations, and quickly became a dedicated enthusiast. He was soon caught up in Curtiss' transatlantic obsession, an involvement which would ultimately lead him to achieve a permanent place in aviation history, for his contributions to the development of the flying boat for naval use.

In December 1913, Rodman Wanamaker, a wealthy department-store magnate, secretly agreed with Curtiss to finance the design and construction of a flying boat capable of crossing the Atlantic. His decision to underwrite this expensive project had been made after lengthy feasibility discussions with Curtiss and others knowledgeable in the field. Wanamaker was an idealist who was prompted by a desire to join the United States and Great Britain by air, in commemoration of one hundred years of peace and friendship between them. He saw the airplane not as a war machine, but rather as an instrument of peace, which he thought would render armed conflict obsolete by bringing prosperity and understanding to all men and nations. It was his belief that a transatlantic flight would dramatize this theme, while helping to alleviate the prewar tension then building in Europe.

The Transatlantic Flyer, as the model came to be called, was to be flown by two pilots, one an Englishman and the other an American. The two men chosen for the honor were Lieutenant John Cyril Porte, Royal Navy (Ret.) and Lieutenant John Towers, U.S. Navy. Porte accepted the offer immediately, but Towers was on active duty as Officer-in-Charge of the Navy Flying School at Pensacola, Florida, and was obliged to defer to the Navy Department for approval.

The U.S. Navy was very interested in the Curtiss-Wanamaker venture. If successful, the flight would not only signal a significant advance in the field of aviation, but also an aircraft capable of crossing the Atlantic would have immediate application in the Navy. On the other hand, much skepticism was voiced concerning the ability of Curtiss, or anyone else for that matter, to produce such a machine. In 1912, Towers had set an endurance record in the *A-2* of 6 hours, 10 minutes and 35 seconds, which, translated into distance at a speed of 60 miles per hour, would amount to only about 370 miles, far short of the endurance required to cross the Atlantic. Finally it was decided to send Towers to Hammondsport in the capacity of observer and advisor, with the final decision on his participation to be withheld pending results of flight tests.

Originally, the Transatlantic Flyer was envisioned as a 200-horsepower single-engine tractor-type aircraft, with a cruising speed of about 60 miles per hour. The flight was planned to be made from St. Johns, Newfoundland, direct to the southwestern tip of Ireland, with great reliance placed on expected tailwinds of as much as 50 miles per hour. This would give the aircraft an actual speed over the ocean of 110 miles per hour, enabling it to transit the 1,870 miles of the planned route in 17 or 18 hours. Also under initial consideration had been a track about 2,100 miles long from Labrador to England via Greenland and Iceland, but that plan had been quickly discarded as infeasible.

On 14 February 1914 Wanamaker officially announced his entry, sending a letter of intent via the Aero Club of America to the Royal Aero Club in England, which was acting in Northcliffe's behalf. The value of the prize had since been increased to $55,000, by the addition of a trophy worth $5,000 offered by Mrs. Victoria Woodhull Martin on behalf of the Womens Aerial League of Great Britain.

The acceptance of the challenge was well-received on both sides of the Atlantic, with only the old Curtiss-Wright patent dispute surfacing to mar the occasion. A recent decision by the U.S. Court of Appeals had gone against Curtiss, and the Wright Company took the opportunity to express its position that Curtiss should neither be permitted to build his aircraft in the United States, nor begin the trip there, in defiance of the latest patent ruling. Although Curtiss considered moving the operation to Canada, where the Wright claims were not recognized, he ultimately decided to go on with the work in Hammondsport in spite of the court ruling. As it happened, the Wright Company did not pursue its threat vigorously, probably because public sentiment had begun to build against them.

Following the official announcement of the entry, work proceeded with all deliberate speed, and the plans for the new aircraft quickly began to take shape. Curtiss obtained considerable assistance from a British engineer, B. D. Thomas, who had returned with him from England. Thomas arrived in the United States with excellent credentials and practical engineering experience gained from earlier work with T. O. M. Sopwith.

Even in the planning stages, it was obvious that the Curtiss-Wanamaker Transatlantic Flyer would be an impressive machine. The original concept of a relatively small single-engine tractor aircraft had been scrapped early in the

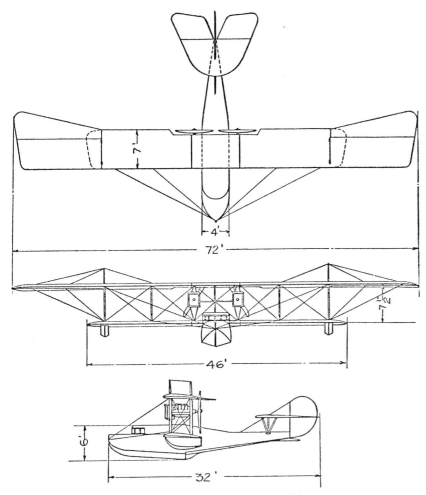

The *America*, 1914. The dimensions shown are those of the final configuration. The dimensions were changed at least twice previously, in an effort to obtain the optimum configuration by trial-and-error. (Smithsonian Institution)

game, primarily because the engine earmarked for the project failed on the test-stand. It was decided to utilize instead two pusher-type 90-horsepower Curtiss OX-5 engines mounted between the wings. This change necessitated a larger aircraft to support both the extra weight of the second engine and the additional fuel required for its operation.

In its final configuration, the Transatlantic Flyer was one of the largest airplanes built up to that time, and by the standards of 1914, it represented a very advanced design. The upper wing had a span of 72 feet, and the lower, 46. Each wing had a 7-foot chord. The aircraft was 32 feet in length, and the hull measured 4 feet across at its widest point. The pilot's compartment was completely enclosed, and featured clear celluloid windows affording reasonably good pilot visibility. A close friend of Curtiss, Dr. Alfred F. Zahm from the Smithsonian Institution, spent much of his time at Hammondsport during the construction and trials of the transatlantic flying boat, and he wrote several articles on its progress for the *Scientific American* and *Popular Mechanics*. He described the foreward part of the hull as "shaped like a slipper," while the after part resembled "the rear of a whale." The idea, he advised his readers, was for the aircraft to first skate across the water on the sole of the slipper, and then rise on the heel preparatory to takeoff.*

*Albert F. Zahm, *Aeronautical Papers of Albert F. Zahm Ph.D.* (Notre Dame, Indiana: The University of Notre Dame, 1950, p. 354.

The hull was constructed of quarter-inch thick planking attached to a light wooden frame; its V-bottom had a double layer of planking, to take the pounding which occurred during takeoff and landing. The entire hull was covered and made completely watertight by two layers of fabric generously saturated with marine glue.

The wing structure was formed of spruce and covered with Japanese silk, on which several coats of varnish were applied. The wing roots were strengthened so they could sustain the weight of one of the pilots, if the engines required adjustment or repair in flight.

In the cockpit the pilots were seated side-by-side. Behind them in the hull was a narrow one-man sleeping area, and still further aft were located three gas tanks with a total capacity of about 300 gallons. The rearmost section of the hull had four watertight compartments to provide for flotation should the hull be damaged.

And so the work continued into the spring of 1914. On 18 April Towers was summoned to Pensacola, Florida, under urgent orders from the Navy Department to report aboard the USS *Birmingham*, which shortly thereafter got underway to take part in the Veracruz operation in Mexico. By the time he was able to return to Hammondsport in June 1914, the Transatlantic Flyer had been nearly completed, and he had been replaced as copilot.

While Towers had been in Mexico, Porte had been in England. He had been giving much thought to the direct route which had been planned between Newfoundland and Ireland. He pondered whether the critical fuel situation might not make an alternative route more suitable. As a result of discussions with Captain F. Creagh Osborne, a noted navigation expert of the Royal Navy, a new route was developed, and on Porte's return to Hammondsport, it was quickly accepted by Curtiss and Wanamaker. Consequently, on 17 June the change was announced. The crossing would now be made from St. Johns, Newfoundland, to the Azores Islands and thence to Vigo, Spain, and then finally to Plymouth, England. This track greatly improved the chances for success, because the first and longest leg of the trip was shortened to about 1,200 miles. The time-distance-fuel load calculations were now more realistic, since the speed of the aircraft was computed assuming no-wind conditions, rather than on the hope of a tail-wind. It was thus estimated that it would take about twenty hours at sixty miles per hour to reach the Azores. Equally important was the fact that the new route would cut across numerous shipping lanes, greatly improving the chances of survival should the Flyer be forced to go down at sea.

Instrumentation aboard the aircraft was extremely primitive by today's standards. In fact, anyone familiar with present-day air navigation techniques and instruments would think it astounding that two sane men would even attempt an Atlantic crossing under the conditions existing in 1914. The risk inherent in the adventure was compounded by the fact that fairly precise navigation was required on the first 1,200-mile leg of the journey, to avoid a complete miss of the Azores.

According to Dr. Zahm in an article written for the *Scientific American*, navigation was to be accomplished by the use of a sextant, a magnetic compass, watches, an anemometer, and a crude drift instrument. In addition, a simple inclinometer, which was no more than fluid in a sealed glass, would provide the pilot with information concerning the "dip and tilt of the aeroplane." An instrument to measure height above the water was also to be included, probably an aneroid barometer. The accuracy of this latter instrument would be a problem, however, because of the need to reset it constantly to allow for changing atmospheric pressure, as the aircraft moved across the Atlantic. An accurate indication of the state of instrumentation at that time can be obtained from a discussion by Dr. Zahm in the same article, concerning the possible use of a "plumb line" for measurements at low altitude.

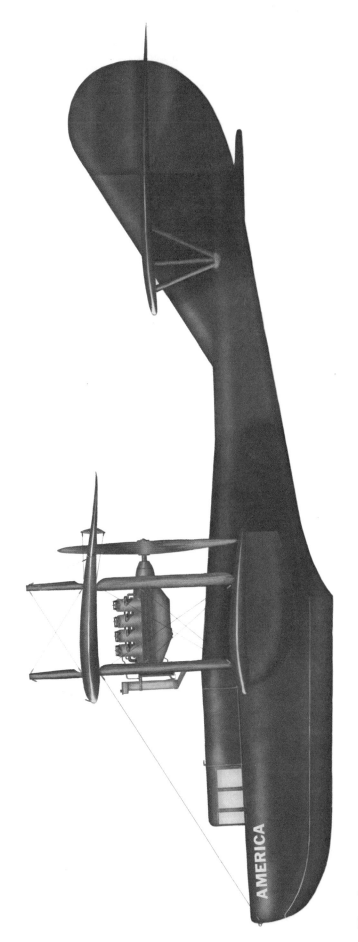

The *America*, painted bright red with the name lettered boldly on each side of the bow, was a fitting symbol of the dynamic society after which it was named. (John Ficklen)

There was to be no radio carried on board. Instead, ships would be expected to provide information by signal flags, with carrier pigeons used to communicate from the aircraft if necessary.

At some point during the advance preparations in early 1914, Towers was replaced as prospective copilot. The precise timing and reason for his withdrawal is not clear, but it appears that Curtiss and Wanamaker began looking for a substitute when Towers was abruptly called away to report to Pensacola on 18 April. Although he did ultimately return to Hammondsport in June, there was no way in April to predict that he would return in time to make the summer flight date. One reason frequently stated in various sources for his withdrawal is that the Secretary of the Navy did not want him to participate in a subordinate capacity to the British aviator, but this explanation has been denied by other sources. It is probable that the real reason for the Navy's reluctant attitude pivoted around serious questions concerning the capabilities of the aircraft. In any event, Towers was replaced as copilot by a very able Curtiss employee named George Hallett in May or early June.

Hallett had first become associated with Curtiss at North Island, California, in 1910. Because of his work with homemade airplanes, Hallett was loaned to Curtiss by the owner of a machine shop where Hallett worked as a foreman. Hallett's timing was fortunate, because he arrived on the scene in time to become one of the small number of men to be involved in the development of the world's first practical seaplane. He proved to be a gifted mechanic, and soon after his arrival, he was hired by a Curtiss exhibition pilot, Charles C. Witmer, for twenty-five dollars a week. It was not long before his skill with engines came to the personal attention of Curtiss, who soon thereafter gave him increased responsibility. Hallett and Witmer were sent abroad as a team to deliver Curtiss aircraft to European nations, who were by then rapidly building up their war arsenals. The aircraft were delivered complete with flight instruction by Witmer, and a short course in maintenance by Hallett. Their best customers in continental Europe were France, Germany, Austria, and Russia.

In the spring of 1914, Hallett, now back in Hammondsport, was given the responsibility for the testing and preparation of the engines for the Transatlantic Flyer. It was at about that time that Curtiss decided to offer him the copilot position for the flight across the Atlantic. Not only would his prowess with engines be a valuable asset, but he was also a capable pilot who could relieve Porte while the latter attended to navigation or rested. Hallett enthusiastically accepted the offer, thus resolving the question of who the second pilot would be.

On 21 June 1914 the Curtiss-Wanamaker Transatlantic Flyer was made ready for takeoff on the first test flight. It had been painted a bright red for maximum visibility in case it became disabled at sea, and was dazzling to the eye. They named it *America,* which was lettered boldly on each side of the bow. No other name would have been as appropriate, for indeed the aircraft was the product of the dynamic society for which it was named, and a fitting symbol of a free and vigorous people.

By late the following afternoon, a crowd of several hundred people had gathered at the test site at Lake Keuka, New York, to witness the official christening ceremony. History was being made that day, and they wanted to be present. In response to public interest across the country and in Europe, the press was well represented.

America rested on a launching cradle at water's edge, with a national ensign flying from the supports between the wings. Katherine Masson, sixteen-year-old daughter of a local vintner, christened the aircraft. She was dressed in a long white gown, and read a poem by Doctor Zahm which proclaimed *America* to be the "Peace herald of the century."* Following the reading, she

*C. R. Roseberry, *Glenn Curtiss: Pioneer of Flight* (Doubleday & Company, Inc., Garden City, New York, 1972), p. 374.

Porte, Hallett, Curtiss, and Katherine Masson prepare to christen *America*. (Curtiss Museum)

slammed a bottle of local champagne against the bow of the aircraft. The bottle did not break, and after trying again without success, she was assisted by Lieutenant Porte. After he too had failed to crack either the bottle or fortunately the aircraft in two tries, the dilemma was satisfactorily resolved by securing the bottle to the bow and smashing it with a hammer. The champagne, having been tossed about so rudely, exploded like a bomb. As the laughing onlookers applauded, Curtiss' workmen slid the Transatlantic Flyer into the waters of the lake.

America's first flight test was made the following day. Before takeoff, Curtiss taxied the big aircraft for about fifteen minutes to be certain that everything was operating satisfactorily. *America* had been provided with a unique control system which, it was hoped, would lessen pilot fatigue during the long flight. The ailerons were controlled by foot-bars, while a turn of the wheel attached to the control column operated the rudder. This was a departure from the traditional Curtiss shoulder-yoke control, and would prove to be the exact opposite of today's standard aircraft control system arrangement.

The first flight was made at about 3,500 pounds gross weight, considerably less than the estimated 5,000 pounds *America* would have to lift if it were to have enough fuel on board to reach the Azores. The airplane performed handsomely. Subsequent flights were made with Porte and Hallett at the controls. They were pleased with the flight characteristics, and Hallett, on one flight, even demonstrated the machine's ability to fly with only one engine operating.

But as they increased the loaded weight, trouble began. *America* would without doubt fly at 5,000 pounds gross weight, but would neither plane nor

America on her maiden flight over Lake Kueka, New York, 1914. (Capt. F. Creagh Osborne, R.N. Collection)

America, in three-engine configuration, on a takeoff run. (Curtiss Museum)

leave the water at that weight. There followed a period of experimentation with various kinds of fins and lifting devices to help raise the aircraft to a planing position. Some progress was made toward solving the problem, but none of several novel ideas, including a sea-sled bottom, worked well enough to enable the pilots to coax *America* into the air at the desired weight.

The flight had by this time been postponed until August. Well-wishers who had planned to sail to Newfoundland, Canada, to give *America* a proper sendoff, postponed or canceled their steamship reservations.

Another bothersome problem involved spark plugs, which in 1914 were highly unreliable. Frequently they required replacement after only an hour or two of operation, and several were almost certain to fail on a flight of twenty hours' duration. In order to cope with this problem, Hallett had deep pockets sewn into his overalls. While *America* was in flight, he would crawl out of the cockpit onto the lower wing root. There, using a specially designed tool, he would jam open a valve on the bad cylinder to relieve compression, and remove the offending spark plug with a socket wrench. While hanging on to the wing-bracing with one hand, he would place the socket wrench and plug into one of his pockets with the other hand, where he replaced the old plug in the socket with a new one. Withdrawing the tool with the new plug nested in the socket, he would complete the procedure by inserting the plug into the cylinder with the wrench and removing the decompression device. Using this technique, he could change as many plugs as was necessary to obtain maximum performance from the engines at all times.

Finally, after all the hull-design experiments alluded to above proved fruitless, Curtiss decided to install a third tractor-type engine on the upper wing along the centerline. On 23 July *America* lifted off with ease at a gross weight of 5,500 pounds. Later that same day, this was increased to 6,100 pounds with similar success. The plan now called for the third engine to be shut down soon after takeoff to save fuel. Unfortunately, the drag of the windmilling prop resulted in an unacceptable fuel consumption rate, and it was estimated that in this configuration *America* would barely remain airborne until reaching the Azores, with no reserve left over for headwinds or navigation error.

Again the flight was postponed, and Curtiss began to work on reducing structural weight. He also postulated that if he idled the third engine instead of shutting it down completely, drag would be reduced, thereby avoiding excessive fuel consumption. Unfortunately, before he was able to prove his theory, Europe was plunged into World War I.

The dream of a transatlantic flight appeared to have ended, at least temporarily. Wanamaker, however, refused to give up on the idea, and in 1916 he formed the America Trans-Oceanic Company, to try again. The entry of the United States into the war in 1917 prevented him from making his second try, but he continued to keep the company going in hopes that it would one day become the first transatlantic airline.

Porte returned to England when the war began for duty with the Royal Naval Air Service. He was sorely needed, for the Royal Navy possessed very little aviation expertise at the commencement of hostilities. In August 1914 two Curtiss F-Boat aircraft, previously imported into England by White and Thompson for civilian use, were pressed into military service. Meanwhile, Porte was using his influence to persuade the British Admiralty to purchase *America* and its sister ship. Apparently his idea was well received, because a price was quickly agreed upon, and the two Americas, as the type came to be called, were delivered via steamship in November 1914.

Sixty-two more of these aircraft were ordered from Curtiss' factory at Hammondsport, and eight were assembled by manufacturers in England. The original Curtiss engines supplied with the aircraft were not considered by the British to be satisfactory for operational use, and were therefore replaced as the aircraft arrived with more powerful Anzani, Beardmore, Clerget, or Sunbeam engines. The aircraft were designated H-4s, and later nicknamed "Small Americas." They were used to a limited extent for patrol duties, and in that capacity, they carried twelve twenty-pound bombs or two one hundred-pounders. Even with more powerful engines, however, the small Americas were still considered underpowered for the military application. In flight, they were nose-heavy with power on, and tail-heavy with power off in a glide. On takeoff, there was a marked tendency for the nose to submerge into the water. In addition, the endurance of the hulls fell short of expectations when the aircraft were subjected to the continual grind of wartime operations, and the abuse of repeated landings and takeoffs in rough, unprotected waters. To remedy these defects, John Porte at the Royal Navy Air Station, Felixstowe, England, began to experiment with improved hull designs.

A Curtiss H-12 Large America rides open water at rest. (U.S. Navy)

Most of the H-4s were employed as training planes. Toward the end of the war, one of the few which survived was put aside for preservation because of its historic significance. Unfortunately, it was later disposed of, apparently by shortsighted persons who thought that the storage space it occupied could be put to better use.

An avalanche of orders descended upon the relatively small Curtiss organization. By March 1915, the British were taking the total output of his factory, and by 1916, that country had awarded him contracts totaling eleven million dollars. Immediate expansion was essential to meet this demand, but Curtiss at that time did not possess the necessary capital to finance such an undertaking. He therefore cabled a request to the British Admiralty for an advance of "seventy-five thousand"; being a frugal businessman, he left out the word "dollars" to save the cost of the extra word, and assumed the British would understand his meaning. They did not, and instead sent him a draft for 75,000 English pounds, several times the amount he had asked for when converted to U.S. dollars. This windfall catapulted the Curtiss Aeroplane and Motor Company into operations on a grand scale.

By July 1916, Curtiss had developed a new flying boat, which he designated the H-8. It was considerably larger than the H-4, and its hull design had been improved as the result of Porte's feedback regarding weaknesses in the H-4. The H-8 had two Curtiss 160-horsepower engines, but it was still considered underpowered for use in combat operations.

From this prototype, however, developed the best known American flying boat of World War I—the Curtiss H-12. These aircraft, referred to as "Large Americas," had a wingspan of 92 feet 8 inches, and were 46 feet in length. They carried a crew of four which included two gunners, one of whom was situated forward in the bow with two 30-caliber Lewis guns, and the other aft, with one Lewis gun. The H-12s built for the Royal Navy were powered by two 275-horsepower Rolls-Royce Eagle engines. They could carry two 230-pound bombs or four 100-pounders, and proved to be an effective combat aircraft. It was an H-12 on 14 May 1917 which destroyed the German zeppelin *L-22,* thereby accounting for the first enemy flying machine ever to be shot down by an American-built aircraft. On 20 May another British H-12 was credited with the sinking of the German submarine *UC-36.* The aircraft reportedly caught the U-boat on the surface, and scored fatal direct hits with two bombs. An H-12 also took part in a remarkable dogfight on 4 June 1918 while in company with four Felixstowe F-2A flying boats. The flight was attacked by a dozen or more German fighter float-planes. Two enemy planes were shot down and others were damaged. The H-12 and one of the F-2As landed in the open sea off the Dutch coast, and the crews were captured and interned for the duration of the war.

H-12s were also credited with destroying or damaging other enemy submarines, particularly in the so-called "Spider Web" patrol area positioned in the

North Sea between England and the Netherlands, where there was considerable U-boat activity. This famous search pattern was octagonal in shape, 6 nautical miles in diameter, and covered approximately 4,000 square miles of ocean. In the area covered by the patrol, flying boats saved many an allied ship from destruction, and the hunters became the hunted.

In all, fifty H-12s were built for the Royal Navy, and they established an enviable record of service. Twenty-one improved model H-12Bs were also delivered to the British in 1918. These required hull modification and strengthening before they were serviceable, and they came to be called "Large America Converts."

In 1916, the U.S. Navy, perhaps anticipating that the United States would soon be drawn into the world conflict, ordered its first H-12, and soon thereafter, another nineteen of them. These were originally fitted with Curtiss VXX 200-horsepower engines, but later some were refitted with 330-horsepower Liberties.

Before the second order of nineteen H-12s could be delivered, Curtiss was at work on a larger version designated the H-16, also known as a "Large America." The hull, though similar to that of the H-12, incorporated several new improvements suggested by the continuing work of John Porte at Felixstowe. The wingspan of 95 feet ¾ inches was about 2 feet greater than that of the H-12, while the length of 46 feet was the same. It had a maximum speed of 95 miles per hour, and a range of 378 miles. Perhaps one of its most important features was its greater armament, consisting of six 30-caliber Lewis machine-guns and four 230-pound bombs. Seventy-five of these aircraft were delivered to the British in early 1918, but only twenty-five were fully assembled with their 375-horsepower Rolls Royce Eagle engines, and of these, only fifteen saw action before the end of hostilities.

Meanwhile, in the United States, Curtiss had begun to produce another excellent model of combat aircraft, known as the HS-series. The prototype of this single-engine pusher-type aircraft, designated HS-1, was equipped with a 200-horsepower Curtiss VXX engine and was first flown early in 1917. Later that year in October, it became the first aircraft to use the new 375-horsepower twelve-cylinder Liberty engine, whereupon its designation was modified to HS-1L. In its original production version, the engine was upgraded to 400-horsepower, and later to 420-horsepower in subsequent production versions.

On 6 April 1917 the United States, though militarily unprepared, declared war on Germany. For all practical purposes, the naval air forces were initially incapable of performing combat duty. Altogether there were only thirty-eight qualified naval aviators, one naval air station, and a total of fifty-four aircraft of all types. Only one of these aircraft, an H-12, was suitable for operational use.

While foresight may have been lacking, this deficiency was compensated by enthusiasm and quick and effective response to some difficult problems. By the first of May 1917 expansion of aviation training programs was well underway, and Lieutenant John Towers was assigned as Supervisor of the Naval Reserve Flying Corps. The U.S. Navy contracted with the Curtiss Flying School which had been established at Newport News, Virginia, to turn out naval aviators to supplement those being trained at Pensacola, Florida. On 23 May, the First Aeronautic Detachment, consisting of seven officers and 122 enlisted men, sailed for France. The first group of these men arrived at Pauillac, France, on 5 June, and the remainder at St. Nazaire, France, a few days later. They were the first organized American aviation unit in Europe.

The First Aeronautic Detachment was commanded by Lieutenant Kenneth Whiting, Naval Aviator Number 16. The group arrived ready to go to war, but they were seriously hampered by the fact that they had no aircraft and only four members who were qualified pilots. Whiting on his own initiative enrolled some of his men in the French flying school, Ecole d'Aviation Militaire, at Tours, France, and he sent others there to train as mechanics. Then, without

A Curtiss H-16 at Killingholme, England, 1918. (Naval Aviation Museum)

authorization or further instructions, he began a series of talks with the French government concerning the establishment of U.S. Naval Air Stations (NAS) on French soil. Whiting obtained an agreement that as a beginning the U.S. Navy should establish a seaplane training station at Moutchic and three operational stations at Dunquerque, Le Croisic, and St. Trojan. By mid-August the first American students had completed the flying course at Tours, and on 27 September the first flight was made at NAS Moutchic in a French flying boat. By the end of the following month NAS Moutchic had begun training American pilots and mechanics.

In the meantime Whiting had reported his unsponsored negotiations with the French government to Admiral Sims, then commander of U.S. Naval forces in Europe. Sims was somewhat surprised by the bold activities of the audacious young lieutenant, but apparently he felt that his was the kind of initiative needed to get naval aviation effectively involved in the war effort as soon as possible. On 8 August 1917 the Secretary of the Navy approved Whiting's proposal for one training and three operational naval air stations in France. By the end of the war, naval aircraft would be operating from twenty-seven U.S. naval air bases in England, France, Ireland, and Italy.

One of these overseas bases was the U.S. Naval Air Station, Killingholme, England. It was acquired from the British on 20 July 1918 to serve as the base for an unusual mission. The adventurous plan called for a group of flying boats to be loaded aboard lighters which would be towed out into the North Sea to a position within striking distance of certain German naval facilities. The flying boats would then be hoisted over the side onto the water, take off for bombing raids against the German bases, and return alongside the lighters to be hoisted back aboard upon completion of the mission. For a number of reasons, this imaginative plan was never carried out, but nevertheless the Killingholme station proved to be a useful base for the U.S. Navy.

One particularly awkward aspect of early U.S. naval aviation activities in Europe was that the Americans were obliged to fly French, British, and Italian flying boats, since no U.S. combat aircraft were available. Back in the United States, however, American industry had begun responding to this unsatisfactory situation. Top-level planners had already contracted for 134 H-16s and 1236 HS-type aircraft for service in naval aviation. Later, in December 1917, the number of H-16s to be purchased for the Navy was increased to 864. Curtiss ultimately built 124 H-16 and 675 HS aircraft for the U.S. Navy. In addition, several other manufacturers were awarded contracts to produce the HS type; among them were Boeing, Loughead (later Lockheed), Lowe, Willard and Fowler (LWF), and Standard.

One of the more significant accomplishments of the U.S. Navy during World War I was the establishment of the Naval Aircraft Factory. Following

A Navy H-16 on patrol. (U.S. Navy)

U.S. entry into the war in 1917, it became immediately apparent that the production capacity of the contemporary private aircraft-manufacturing industry was insufficient to meet the urgent requirements of the U.S. Army and Navy and of the European allies as well. Moreover, the large amounts of money being disbursed to civilian contractors made it difficult to insure that the maximum value was being obtained from each wartime tax dollar spent. Another problem was the lack of a secure facility which could produce experimental aircraft under close Navy supervision.

On 17 July 1917 the Secretary of the Navy approved construction of a Naval Aircraft Factory to be located at the League Island Navy Yard, Philadelphia, Pennsylvania. Ground was broken on 10 August 1917, and on 27 March 1918, only 228 days later, the facility's first aircraft, an H-16, was successfully test-flown. A few days later this aircraft and a second H-16 were shipped to England. In total, the Naval Aircraft Factory built 150 H-16s during the years 1918 and 1919.

On 16 March 1918 the first HS-type flying boat was accepted for Navy service at the naval air station at Miami, Florida. Soon thereafter HS-type aircraft were being produced in large numbers. The twelve-cylinder Liberty engines were incorporated in the model in 1918 as they became available, and the wingspan was extended to 74 feet by the addition of a 6-foot section to both the upper and lower wings. The resulting extra wing area enabled the HS-2L, as the version was designated, to carry two 230-pound bombs vice the two smaller 180-pounders carried by the HS-1L.

The HS-1 models were the first American-made aircraft to be delivered to the U.S. naval aviation forces in France. On 25 May 1918 the first 6 of an eventual total of 182 HS-type American-built flying boats shipped to U.S. naval aviation units in France arrived at NAS Pauillac, France, aboard the USS *Houston*. These HS aircraft eventually replaced almost all of the French flying boats used by Americans operating in France out of the bases located at Brest,

A Navy HS-2L on patrol over European waters. (U.S. Navy)

Dunquerque, Fromentine, Ile Tudy, L'Aber Vrach, Le Croisic, St. Trojan, Treguier, and the training station at Moutchic. Approximately 20 of these were of the improved HS-2L type. A few HSs also operated from NAS Lough Foyle in Ireland, and some were sent to Italy to replace the Macchi M-5 Flying Boats then being flown by American pilots at Porto Corsini. The U.S. Marine Corps also used this aircraft to good purpose. During 1918, the Marine First Aeronautic Company flew HS-1Ls and HS-2Ls on antisubmarine patrols out of Ponta Delgada in the Azores Islands.

Whiting in the meantime had been back in the United States organizing assets for the Killingholme station. He returned to England on 1 June 1918 aboard the USS *Jason*, bringing with him a second detachment of aviation personnel and twenty-three new H-16s. By the time the station was placed under American control on 20 July, several of these aircraft had been assembled and were already in operation. Between 20 July 1918 and the signing of the Armistice on 11 November of that year, the Americans at Killingholme flew 233 operational flights, each averaging better than four hours, and they escorted some 6,243 ships through submarine-infested waters.

One other model of American flying boat emerged in 1918—the F-5L. Although it was placed in service too late for wartime use, it represented the culmination of U.S. and British efforts to produce a superior naval flying boat. John Porte in England had developed the famous Felixstowe Flying Boats (F-1, -2, -3, and -5) from the Curtiss America-series. The Felixstowe F-1, or Porte-1 as it was sometimes called, was in fact a modified H-4 Small America with Hispano-Suiza engines and a completely redesigned hull. The F-2, -3, and -5 were inspired by the H-12 Large America. The wings and tail-assemblies of the Felixstowes were almost identical to those of the Curtiss boats, but the hulls had been greatly strengthened by Porte to withstand the beatings they had to endure during North Sea operations. So successful had the British been with the F-5 that in late 1917 the U.S. Navy decided to produce an American version featuring the new Liberty engine. It came to be known as the F-5L. The Navy ordered 480 of these machines from the Naval Aircraft Factory, 60 from Curtiss, and 50 from Canadian Aeroplanes Limited. The first of these aircraft entered service at NAS Hampton Roads, Virginia, on 3 September 1918. Two months later the Armistice was signed, and the number of F-5Ls originally ordered was reduced. Ultimately, Canadian Aeroplanes Limited produced 30, Curtiss 60 as originally planned, and the Naval Aircraft Factory 138.

Table 2-1. Flying boats built by the Naval Aircraft Factory

Model	No. Produced	Date Completed
H-16	150	1919
F-5L	138	1919
F-6L	2	1919
NC-5, -6, -7, -8	4	1920
HS-3	2	1920
MF	80	1920
NC-9, -10	2	1921
GB-1	1 partially completed	1922 (discontinued)
TF	4	1923
PN-7	2	1924
PN-8	1	1924
PN-9	1	1925
PN-10	2	1926
XPN-11	1	1926
PN-11	1	1929
PN-12	2	1928
XP4N-1	1	1931
XP4N-2	2	1932
PBN-1*	156	1944

*NAF production version of the Consolidated PBY

During the war years, important changes took place in naval aviation, and great strides were made in the development of waterborne aircraft. At the conclusion of the war on 11 November 1918, there were twenty-seven naval aviation bases overseas and twelve in the United States, almost all of which were commissioned to support the flying boat. In just over nineteen months, the air arm of the U.S. Navy had recruited and trained 6,716 officers, 30,693 enlisted men, and had acquired 2,017 aircraft. Of these aircraft 1,865 were seaplanes, mostly flying boats. These machines adapted extremely well to the Navy mission and proved themselves to be worthy opponents of the fleet submarine, the other new weapon which made its debut in World War I.

While no enemy submarines were known to have been sunk as a result of direct action by U.S. Navy aircraft, at least twenty-seven recorded attacks were made on U-boats, and several of the attacked submarines were damaged. An unknown but significant number were crippled or destroyed by surface vessels directed to the scene or otherwise assisted by naval aircraft. Many enemy submarines undoubtedly missed opportunities to destroy allied shipping, or were forced to break off attacks, at the sudden appearance of these ever-present sentinels.

American flying boats patrolled thousands of square miles of ocean, and it is very significant that during 1918, only three allied ships were sunk in areas assigned to aircraft of the U.S. Navy. Over 4,000 patrols were flown, more than 450 convoys were escorted, and 100 tons of explosives were dropped on the enemy.

It seems ironic that in a few short years *America,* the dove of peace, had been completely transformed into a bird of prey. Perhaps Wanamaker took some satisfaction from the bonds of friendship descendents of his aircraft helped to strengthen between England and the United States. In any case, the flying boat had proven itself to be an effective war weapon, and it would be an indispensable asset to the U.S. Navy for many years to come.

CHAPTER THREE

The Nancy Boats

WARS HAVE ALWAYS BEEN heavily influenced by logistics, the ability to produce the material essentials and to deliver them to combatant forces in the field. World War I was no exception. For the United States with its gigantic industrial capacity, wartime production was fundamentally a question of organization and priority. Delivery, however, was a more complicated matter. After the Kaiser had made the decision to engage in unrestricted submarine warfare and the United States had responded with a declaration of war, the Germans moved quickly to exploit their U-boat advantage. Their goal was to cut the American supply line and strangle their adversaries into submission. This strategy was sound, and the effort was rewarding. Indeed, a few months after the entrance of America into the war, the allies were losing almost a million tons of vital shipping every month. Ships were being destroyed faster than they could be built.

The only weapon which seemed to offer relief from the depredations of the U-boat was the airplane. Existing patrol aircraft had given a good accounting of themselves against the submarine, but their range was insufficient to provide adequate coverage, and there never seemed to be enough of them where they were needed. The situation was ironic, inasmuch as while flying boats were desperately needed to decrease shipping losses, they were being stacked in their crates on American piers because there was no space available for them aboard the remaining ships.

No one was more concerned over this dilemma than Rear Admiral David W. Taylor, who headed the Navy's Bureau of Construction and Repair. After mulling over the problem for some time, he reasoned that it could be solved by a more advanced flying boat, having the range to seek out and attack submarines far out to sea, and the reliability and fuel-carrying capacity to deliver itself across the Atlantic. He assigned the formidable task of producing such an aircraft to two able officers with impressive credentials.

Lieutenant Commander Jerome C. Hunsaker headed the Bureau's Aircraft Division. He had graduated from the U.S. Naval Academy in 1908 as the top man in his class. Prior to his Bureau assignment, he had served on loan from the Navy as an instructor at the Massachusetts Institute of Technology (MIT), which had established this country's first graduate program in aeronautical engineering. There, he taught the new science to such future leaders of the aviation industry as Donald Douglas and LeRoy Grumman. Hunsaker was joined in the flying boat project by another Lieutenant Commander then serving in the Bureau, George C. Westervelt. In 1915, Westervelt had teamed with William E. Boeing to develop a single-engine float plane which would be the first of a long and distinguished line of Boeing aircraft. Shortly before reporting to the Bureau of Construction and Repair, Westervelt had toured allied aircraft factories in Europe, and had thus acquired detailed knowledge of the latest European aircraft manufacturing techniques.

In spite of, or perhaps because of, their wealth of theoretical and practical experience in aircraft design, Hunsaker and Westervelt were both skeptical as to whether the specified airplane could be produced by the technology in

The Curtiss BT-1 Flying Lifeboat was designed to land in the open sea beyond the surf, rescue those in distress, shed its wings and tail structure, and motor to shore as a boat. (Curtiss Museum)

existence at that time. There was, however, one gentleman who might be able to do it if anyone could. Both officers were personally acquainted with G. H. Curtiss and his achievements. Hunsaker had established a lasting friendship with him a few years earlier, and Westervelt had served for a time as a naval aircraft-inspector at the Curtiss plant in Buffalo. They quickly dispatched a telegram to the quiet man from Hammondsport.

Curtiss responded immediately to the call for assistance. The two naval officers filled him in on the details, and Hunsaker asked pointedly if an aircraft capable of crossing over the Atlantic could really be built. Without hesitation, Curtiss assured them that it could. He was perhaps slightly annoyed by the question, because he had already built and flown an aircraft intended for that purpose, although it had never had the opportunity to prove itself in a contest with the great ocean. In any case, he was back in Washington three days later with plans to support his contention.

Curtiss was at that time working on a small single-engine flying boat, a project he had taken on at the request of the U.S. Coast Guard. It was known as the BT-1 Flying Lifeboat, and was designed for the rigors of open-sea rescue operations. It is probable that he used this plan as a point of departure in developing the two designs he presented to the Navy in September 1917. They were unusual in that they provided for an abbreviated compartmented hull, from which protruded a boom-like structure supporting a high tail assembly. The novel idea had several advantages. The high tail would be above all but the highest waves which might be encountered if it became necessary to land on the open ocean. At the same time it would provide an unobstructed sector through which an aft-mounted machine gun or recoilless rifle might be fired without hazarding the aircraft. The abbreviated hull would weigh less, enabling the aircraft to carry an increased fuel load, and its compactness would afford better chances of survival in the open sea. The two aircraft which Curtiss proposed were similar in concept, but differed in size and power. One was a huge five-engine monster, while the other, also with rather large dimensions, was smaller and boasted only three engines.

Admiral Taylor, doubtlessly translating size into range, originally favored the larger aircraft. In the final analysis, however, the engineering problems inherent in constructing such a giant aircraft caused the planners to focus their efforts on the smaller of the two. The planning went forward in earnest, and by December, the Secretary of the Navy formalized the Navy-Curtiss partnership with a contract for Curtiss to build four of these aircraft. They were to be called Navy Curtiss, abbreviated *NC, -1, -2, -3* and *-4.* At some point apparently as a result of careless journalism, the NCs came to be called "Nancies." Navy officials were not pleased with the nickname and tried to discourage its use, but the public seemed to like it, and, much to the Navy's consternation, the name stuck.

In the meantime Admiral Taylor had called in one more key officer, Lieutenant Commander Holden C. "Dick" Richardson, a recognized authority on flying boat hulls. Richardson, like Hunsaker, had done his graduate work at MIT and possessed that rare combination of extensive theoretical knowledge and the ability to put it to practical use. Making him even more of an asset was the fact that he was a designated naval aviator, having acquired his wings in 1916 at the unusually advanced age of thirty-eight. He had been on hand at the birth of the flying boat in 1912, and he had developed the first successful shipboard aircraft-catapult, which launched a Curtiss F-Boat from the deck of the USS *North Carolina* in 1915. And, like other Curtiss-trained naval aviators, he had become an admirer and friend of the famous pilot, inventor, and aircraft manufacturer.

From the beginning, it had been agreed by all concerned that the new flying boat would be powered by the Liberty engine which had recently been developed. When the United States entered World War I in April 1917, military planners were faced with the disconcerting fact that this country produced no aircraft engines which were suitable for the severe demands of combat. An Aircraft Production Board was hastily formed, and a commission was sent to Europe to study the aircraft and engine designs of the allies, while the latter sent experts to the United States to advise and assist in any way they could. The Americans soon discovered that the Europeans had some serious difficulties of their own. They had developed so many different engines that the problems of efficient production, maintenance, and parts supply were staggering.

In the midst of the confusion two American engineers, J. G. Vincent of the Packard Company and E. J. Hall of Hall–Scott, met at the Willard Hotel in Washington, D.C., to write a report for the Aircraft Production Board describing the nature and extent of the aircraft engine problem in the United States. The meeting began just before noon on 29 May 1917; by the afternoon of the thirty-first, they had produced not only the report, but also the first drawings and specifications for the Liberty engine.

With American manufacturers cooperating to provide components that each was best suited to produce, the first eight-cylinder Liberty engine was completed in a month. The twelve-cylinder model was installed on a Curtiss HS-1 flying boat and successfully flight-tested on 21 October 1917. The Liberty engine was so designed that it could be manufactured from standardized components in four-, six-, eight-, or twelve-cylinder versions. This concept of using identical parts for four different engines, any one of which could be rapidly mass-produced to meet power requirements of specific aircraft, represented a revolutionary engineering breakthrough. In all, more than twenty thousand Liberty engines were built, and until about 1926, they were used in more American aircraft than any other engine.

Another consequence of American entry into the war affected the Curtiss operation directly. Congress began allocating millions of dollars for the products of the American aviation industry, and the resulting surge in demand for military aircraft exceeded the capacity of American manufacturers. The Curtiss

The Liberty engine revolutionized American aviation. It could be produced in four-, six-, eight-, or twelve-cylinder versions. (U.S. Navy)

Aeroplane and Motor Company was no exception, and to meet the challenge it elected to join forces with the Willys-Overland automobile interests. In the reorganization which accompanied this development, John Willys, an expert on mass production techniques, replaced Curtiss as president of the expanded company, with Curtiss becoming chairman of the board. A huge new Curtiss plant sprang up in Buffalo, New York, almost overnight. The original little harness and bicycle shop of Hammondsport had grown into the largest aircraft manufacturing organization in the world.

Curtiss was not altogether comfortable with the new arrangement. He had become a very wealthy man preeminent in the aviation industry, but he found that as a result he had less time to devote to aeronautical experimentation. Moreover, the new management seemed preoccupied with the problems of production efficiency and securing the largest possible segment of the aircraft manufacturing market. A potential conflict of interests and personalities was averted by the establishment of the Curtiss Engineering Company at Garden City, Long Island, New York, directed by Curtiss himself. It was set up to function as a research and development facility for the parent company. In December 1917, Curtiss and some of his closest associates, many of whom had been with him since the company's humble beginnings, moved to the new location, and set to work. It was here that the Navy's new flying boats were first assembled.

Prior to the move to Garden City, the preliminary design and production work on the new aircraft had been accomplished at the Buffalo plant. Components for the big aircraft were subcontracted to expedite the project. Thus, while Curtiss built the hull for the first flying boat in Buffalo, two New England boat-builders were awarded contracts to construct the hulls for the second, third and fourth. The wings and tail-assemblies were produced in New York City, while the Liberty engines were assembled in Detroit. All the components were brought together for initial assembly at the Garden City plant, then taken apart and transported to the Naval Air Station at Rockaway Beach, New York, some twenty miles from Garden City. Here final assembly took place in a large hangar specially constructed to house the big flying boats.

The hull of the *NC-1* arrived at Garden City from the Curtiss plant in Buffalo in the spring of 1918. Its unusual lines were the work of Richardson, the authority on hydrodynamics. Ten feet wide and almost forty-five feet long, it weighed 2,583 pounds, and was formed from two layers of thin wooden planking glued together with a sheet of fabric sandwiched between, attached to a light wooden framework. The decking was made of white cedar with a canvas covering. The hull had six compartments divided by wooden bulkheads and watertight doors. The forward compartment was assigned to the aircraft commander who also served as navigator. A hatch was provided from which he could take celestial sights and calculate wind direction and velocity from observations of the surface of the water. The cockpit in the original design was located in the center engine nacelle between the wings, but in the final version, it was moved to the second compartment in the hull. The third and fourth sections carried the main fuel tanks, while the fifth compartment housed the radio operator, two mechanics, and an additional 200 gallons of fuel. The sixth and last section contained radio-direction-finding equipment.

During the summer of 1918, the other components arrived at Garden City, and *Nancy One* as it was called began to take shape in initial assembly. The upper wing of the aerial giant measured 126 feet in length with a 12-foot cord, while the tail assembly spanned 37 feet 11 inches. It stood over 24 feet in height and was 68 feet in length overall. Never before had an airplane approaching such size been built in the United States.

In September 1918, the *NC-1* was declared complete, disassembled, and transported piece by piece by horse-drawn wagons to Rockaway Beach for final assembly. On 4 October with propellers turning, it was eased into the waters of Jamaica Bay off Rockaway Beach for the first test flight. The test pilot and aircraft commander was Lieutenant Commander "Dick" Richardson, whose hull design gave him a personal stake in the day's events. The copilot, Lieutenant David McCulloch, like Richardson and so many other Navy pilots of that period, was a Curtiss-trained aviator. A Navy mechanic and two Curtiss engineers made up the remainder of the crew for the maiden flight.

Richardson began the test with some high-speed taxiing. Then, satisfied by its performance, he opened the throttles for the takeoff run. The big Liberties responded with a surge of power. *Nancy One* rose on the step and became airborne.

Further testing and minor adjustments continued through October, but by the following month the *NC-1* was ready for an extended trip. On 7 November it took off for Washington, D.C. on the first leg of a cross-country proving-flight. A precautionary landing was made in the ocean off Barnegat, New Jersey, to repair a radiator leak, following which the big flying boat took off with little difficulty through ten-foot swells, and arrived at the Naval Air Station, Anacostia, Washington, D.C., in the late afternoon. On the eighth, *Nancy One* proceeded further south to Hampton Roads, Virginia, and returned to Rockaway Beach the following day without further incident.

Two days later, on 11 November 1918, the war ended.

Curtiss' dream of a transatlantic flight, which had been interrupted in 1914 by the beginning of World War I, was now threatened by the termination of that conflict. The successful conclusion of the "war to end all wars" had rendered the Nancies' antisubmarine potential and transatlantic delivery capability irrelevant. Work on *Nancy Two* slowed to a snail's pace and stopped altogether on *Nancy Three* and *Four*.

Meanwhile, an English Handley-Page bomber set a new world record by carrying forty-one people on a short flight over London. The *NC-1*, with its considerable weight-lifting capability, was at least equal to that challenge. On 27 November the Navy flying boat, at a gross weight of over 22,000 pounds, shattered the British record by lifting aloft fifty designated passengers and crewmembers, plus one over-enthusiastic stowaway who was discovered only after the flight. His presence brought the actual record number of people on board to fifty-one.

Commander John Towers proposed the NC flight across the Atlantic, and was assigned responsibility for bringing the project to fruition. (U.S. Navy)

No doubt the record flight buoyed the spirits of all those who had worked on the NCs, but the road ahead looked very uncertain. According to popular belief, the world had been made "safe for democracy," and there was little interest in new machines of war. Fortunately, an old champion of naval aviation managed to join the project at just the right moment. John Towers, then a Commander in the Office of the Chief of Naval Operations (Aviation), proposed, in a memorandum written only eleven days before the armistice, that the U.S. Navy take advantage of the unique capabilities of the NCs and attempt a flight across the Atlantic. He felt that it was important for the United States to sustain and strengthen its image as a great power by dramatically establishing its aeronautical prowess in the arena of international competition. He had been watching apprehensively as other would-be contenders, anticipating the war's end, began to make their own preparations for the record flight. A board of officers including Towers was assigned to study his proposal. Their favorable report recommended that preparations be undertaken at once. Three days after its submission, the Secretary of the Navy gave the approval for which everyone had hoped, and John Towers subsequently was assigned the welcome responsibility for bringing his proposal to fruition.

At first the Navy tried to keep the project secret, but it was soon discovered and triumphantly exposed by the ever-probing Washington press corps. In the meantime, several would-be competitors, spurred by Lord Northcliff's renewal of the 10,000-pound *Daily Mail* prize offer, had announced their intentions of making the transatlantic flight as soon as their aircraft could be made ready. The U.S. Navy, of course, was not participating in the competition for the money. It was made clear from the beginning that crew members who were to participate would be forbidden to accept any prize money even if it were pressed upon them; they would have to be satisfied with the honor of being first. For the men who were finally chosen to make the flight, this was enough.

The course to be flown was similar to that plotted for Curtiss's *America* in 1914—Newfoundland, Canada, to the Azores, then to Lisbon, Portugal, and finally to Plymouth, England. Still, despite the many improvements which had been made in engines and aircraft in the intervening years, success was hardly a certainty. Weather forecasting techniques in the North Atlantic Ocean were still extremely primitive, and reliable predictions of conditions aloft were non-existent. Nor were there any proven instruments for long-range overwater-navigation. These had to be improvised by an intelligent young Lieutenant named Richard E. Byrd. One of his innovations, the bubble sextant, became an indispensable tool for future aerial navigators. Radios were often undependable, and radio-direction-finding devices aboard the Nancies had a maximum range of only about fifteen miles. In fact radio equipment was almost left off the aircraft entirely, because of its questionable value and heavy weight.

If these and other problems created apprehension, Towers and his associates showed none of it. On the contrary, their outlook was optimistic, and they were eager to prove the validity of their judgement.

Progress on the assembly of the other Nancy flying boats continued but was not without problems. The *NC-2* was originally put together as a tri-motor model, but, unlike the *NC-1*, its center engine was mounted as a pusher in order to allow the pilots seated in the nacelle ahead of the propeller better visibility. The arrangement did not prove to be as satisfactory as had been anticipated, however, and a new four-engine configuration was effected by the placement of two big 400-horsepower Liberty engines on each side of the center-line in tandem fashion, with the two forward-facing engines pulling, and the two aft-facing ones pushing. This arrangement provided considerably more power and a greater weight-lifting capability, but was still not considered the best possible configuration. The pilots continued to occupy the center nacelle, which was now engineless.

Nancies *Three* and *Four* were also completed as four-engine machines, but with engine arrangements which were different from either of the two previous models. Two of the engines were mounted back-to-back along the centerline, while the remaining two were positioned on either side as tractor-types. This configuration necessitated moving the cockpit to the number-two compartment in the hull, where it probably should have been located from the beginning.

In March, while the *NC-3* was still undergoing final assembly, *Nancy One* was badly damaged when it dragged anchor and went aground on the shore. The action of wind and wave battered the lower port wing beyond repair. Unfortunately, there were no new wings available, and it seemed that *Nancy One* would have to be eliminated from the plan. In the end, however, it was decided that *Nancy Two,* with the unsatisfactory engine configuration, would be sacrificed to render *NC-1* flyable. Along with the wing repair, a fourth engine was added to give *Nancy One* the same configuration as *Nancy Three* and *Four.*

During April, the tension began to mount. Two British aircraft and their crews had already arrived in Newfoundland, and were ready to make their transatlantic attempts as soon as the weather was deemed suitable. And these were not the only contenders. Other teams had completed preparations, and were on their way to Newfoundland to join in the contest. It was a free-for-all scramble, and the Nancies would not be ready until May.

During the second half of April, a sense of urgency sparked by the threat of competition permeated the atmosphere at Rockaway, and Navy and Curtiss people alike worked late into the night, seven days a week, to get the Nancies

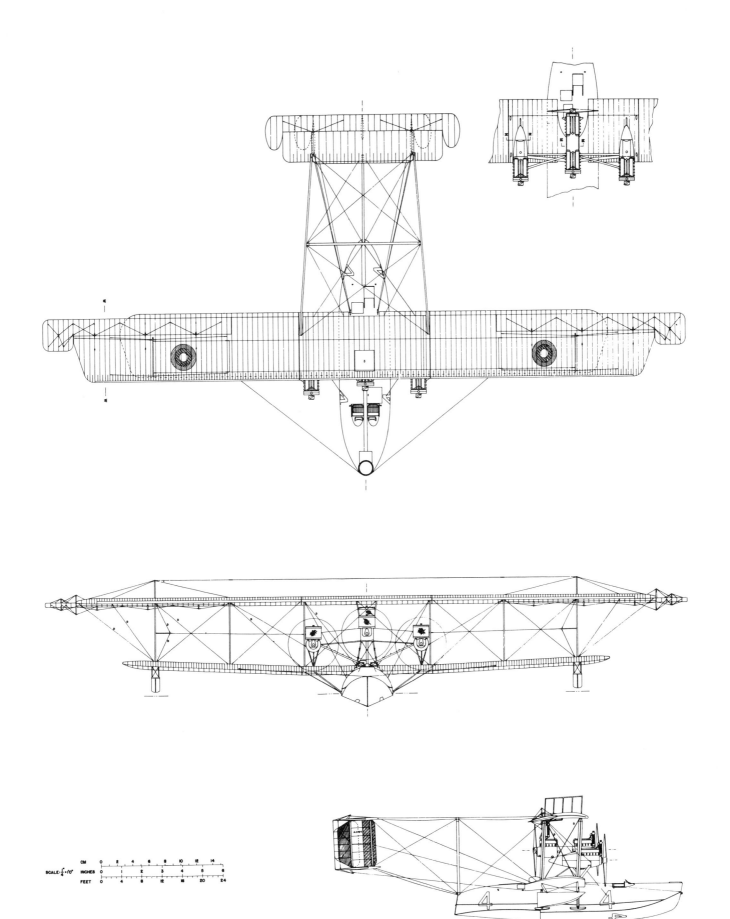

SCALE·$\frac{1}{8}$·1'0"

CM
INCHES
FEET

The *NC-4.* (Smithsonian Institution)

Commissioning of Seaplane Division One. Cdr. John Towers, commanding officer, reads their orders to the NC crews. (U.S. Navy)

ready. *NC-3* made its first flight on the twenty-third, whereupon the new center-line tandem engine configuration was adjudged a success. *NC-1* was rendered airworthy again after being fitted with its fourth engine and the port wings of the luckless *NC-2*. Work continued around the clock on the *NC-4*. Meanwhile, commanding officers of the ships to be stationed along the route received final briefings.

The Navy had planned well for this epic event in aviation. Every possible precaution had been taken to give the Nancy crews the best chance of survival, should they be forced down in the cold waters of the merciless North Atlantic. Ships were assigned to take positions at fifty-mile intervals along the route. As the aircraft passed over each station, the next ship in line was to be notified by radio to begin firing star shells to the northwest until the planes had passed. When they were almost overhead, a searchlight beam was to be rotated to indicate surface-wind direction. Each ship had laid out a numeral outlined in lights on deck, to advise the aircraft which station they were passing. Toward the end of April these ships put to sea.

On the first of May, *Nancy Four* was towed out of the hangar for the first flight. It performed well in the air, but the hull leaked badly and required some repair work. Nevertheless, all three aircraft which were to make the trip had been flown at least once, and the press began to sense that preparations were in their final stages. On 3 May John Towers formally took command of NC Seaplane Division One.

As the pieces of the enterprise came together, the influence of Glenn Curtiss could be discerned in every essential element. He had originated the design for these machines from which so much would soon be demanded. From the very beginning he had provided an unwavering confidence so necessary to the success of such an undertaking. The assembly of all four Nancies had taken place under his careful scrutiny, and several of the key figures who would now put his confidence to the test bore the Curtiss stamp of approval: Towers, the mission commander, Richardson, the pilot of *Nancy Three,* and Bellinger, who commanded *Nancy One,* were all Curtiss-trained aviators. This was Curtiss' last great aviation endeavor. No one had done more to make the dream of transatlantic flight a possibility.

In the early morning hours of 5 May the task of fueling the big aircraft began. It was a time-consuming chore, because the tanks of each held more than 1,800 gallons of gasoline. As the work progressed, one of the electric fuel pumps suddenly caught on fire, and in a matter of seconds the blaze spread across the hangar, enveloping the starboard wings of the *NC-1* and the lower tail surfaces of the *NC-4* in flame. The fire was extinguished expeditiously, but not before it had done major damage. Undaunted, the Navy-Curtiss team set to work to repair the affected sections. Eighteen hours later, the two aircraft had again been made ready, *NC-4* having been outfitted with a refurbished tail assembly, and *NC-1* with new starboard wings from the now completely-stripped *NC-2.*

Next it was the weather that postponed the departure, and while the crews waited, two grim occurrences added to the somber atmosphere, and served as a stern reminder that theirs was a profession which was cruelly unforgiving of human error. A Curtiss HS-1 flying boat on a local flight stalled as it made a turn over the air station. Unable to recover at low altitude, it struck a fuel storage tank, killing its two-man crew. On the seventh, Machinist's Mate Chief Edward H. Howard, a crewman on the *NC-4,* inadvertently thrust his left hand into the arc of a spinning propeller, which instantly severed the hand at the wrist. So deeply involved had Howard become in the transatlantic attempt, that his primary concern was that the loss of his hand would prevent him from participating in the flight.

The weather outlook continued to be discouraging for several more days, but on the morning of the eighth it was promising enough for Towers to make the decision to start. The three Nancies were launched into Jamaica Bay, and by 10:10 A.M., all were airborne, bound for Newfoundland via Halifax, Nova Scotia. The first leg of the great transatlantic adventure had begun.

Nancy One and *Three* arrived in Halifax that evening following uneventful flights. *Nancy Four,* which had flown only once before, was not so fortunate. Off Cape Cod, Massachusetts, oil pressure was lost on the centerline pusher, and it had to be shut down. Later at about 2:30 P.M. local time, the centerline tractor threw a rod, leaving only the two outboard engines operating. There was no alternative but to land in the open ocean.

Nancy Four spent the rest of the afternoon and all that night taxiing in a calm sea. No contact was made with destroyers which were searching for the downed aircraft, and by morning it had arrived off the Chatham Air Station on Cape Cod under its own power. At Chatham a new tractor engine was installed, and the pusher was overhauled. On the morning of the fourteenth *Nancy Four* was off again for Halifax.

Nancy One and *Three* had arrived at Trepassey Bay, Newfoundland, on the tenth. The crews were quartered aboard the base ship USS *Aroostook,* and the planes were moored nearby. The press had also arrived on the scene, and were accommodated in a dining car acquired from Newfoundland Railways. It was parked on a spur overlooking Trepassey Bay, and sported a large sign on its side proclaiming it to be "NANCY-5."

The competition had been waiting for the weather to improve since mid-April at St. Johns, Newfoundland, about sixty-five miles north of Trepassey Bay. The Englishmen Harry G. Hawker and Lieutenant Commander K. Mackenzie Grieve, with their Sopwith *Atlantic,* vied with their countrymen Frederick F. Raynham and Captain William F. Morgan, and their Martinsyde *Raymor,* for the £10,000 prize and glory of Great Britain. On the tenth, the same day that *Nancies One* and *Three* arrived at Trepassey, the British contenders were joined at St. Johns by still more of their compatriots who were eager to get into the race. Admiral Mark Kerr and his crew arrived by ship with a dismantled four-engine Handley-Page V/1500 bomber. Undismayed by the fact that the departure of the other teams seemed imminent, Kerr and his men went to work readying their entry. To them it was still an open race.

Meanwhile, all contestants were being held on the ground by weather, and all were eager to depart. At Trepassey Bay the Nancy crews worked on their aircraft, while Towers anxiously pored over the weather reports. Skies overhead were clear on the tenth and the eleventh, but the weather over the treacherous North Atlantic was prohibitive. On the thirteenth a thick fog rolled in and lingered until the afternoon of the fourteenth, when patches of blue sky began to appear. On the fifteenth the weather all along the route looked as good as it would probably get, and Towers decided reluctantly that he must depart without waiting for *Nancy Four* to arrive. And so at about 1:00 P.M. the two remaining aircraft from Seaplane Division One taxied out toward the head of the sea-lane for takeoff.

Trepassey Harbor is a narrow, elongated body of water running northeast and southwest, affording only two choices of direction for a long takeoff run. Unfortunately, the prevailing wind with only occasional variation blows from the northwest and this day was no exception to the norm. Towers felt that the heavily-loaded Nancies needed all the takeoff room they could get, and thus decided to run the length of the harbor toward the southwest, rather than traverse the narrow width of the harbor into the northwest wind.

Upon reaching the northernmost end of the harbor, the two aircraft turned toward the southwest, and with throttles open, went careening down the sea-lane in the direction of the open sea. The pilots of both aircraft, inundated with spray that poured over them in great sheets and struggling to maintain control in the thirty-knot, ninety-degree crosswind, were forced to abort the takeoff as the entrance to the harbor rushed to meet them.

About this time *Nancy Four* was observed making its approach to Trepassey Bay. Frustrated by his inability to get airborne, but delighted by the arrival of *Nancy Four*, Towers decided to delay the flight another day, so that all three aircraft might try again as a team. *Nancy Four* was back in the game.

While these events were taking place, another drama was unfolding nearby. Having a considerable investment in the transatlantic venture and with an eye toward the public indignation that would result should the enterprise fail, the Navy had decided to hedge its bet. At 10:00 A.M. on the morning of the 15th, the Navy airship *C-5* arrived at Pleasantville near St. Johns and was moored not far from the British airplane *Raymor*. Its crew, who had been flying for almost twenty-six hours, retired to the USS *Chicago* anchored at St. Johns. While they rested, weather at the mooring site took a sudden turn for the worse. The wind rose, gusting up to sixty knots, and the mooring lines began to part. A caretaker crew barely had time to abandon the airship before it broke loose and headed out to sea. Thus it was that as the *NC-4* approached St. Johns, its occupants observed what appeared to be the *C-5* making its transatlantic departure ahead of them. *Nancy Four* turned south, and a short time later, arrived at Trepassey Bay. Here they were greeted by another demoralizing sight: the other two Nancy flying boats on their takeoff run. They thought that it had all been for nothing, that they had arrived too late.

They were soon to learn of the bizarre events that had preceded their arrival and to discover that their fears of being left behind were unfounded.

The morning of 16 May dawned bright and sunny for a reunited Seaplane Division One, and reports of good weather were coming in from the ships at sea. Throughout the night mechanics had successfully labored to install a new centerline tractor-engine in the *NC-4*, as the one received at Chatham

Mechanics at work completing the installation of a new centerline engine on *NC4* at Trepassey on 16 May 1919. (U.S. Navy)

had been a low-compression type not suitable for the trip ahead. That evening, the NCs cast off from their buoys and positioned themselves for takeoff, with *Nancy Three* in the lead. Again *Nancy Three* drove down the entire length of the harbor as it had done the previous day, and again it failed to become airborne. The plane commander of the *NC-4,* however, had decided that with the full-capacity fuel load, a takeoff into the wind was essential for lift-off. Consequently, he conned the *NC-4* to the extreme southeast corner of the harbor, taxiing so close to the shore that the tail passed very near to the rocks as the aircraft swung around into the wind. The pilot opened the throttles wide, and about three-quarters of the way across, eased the overloaded boat into the air, with very little landing room left for an emergency. It was not an ideal situation, but it was the only way to get airborne.

In the meantime *Nancy Three* continued to have trouble getting airborne. The pilot made three attempts to coax the aircraft into the air running cross-wind, but to no avail. Finally, everything was offloaded which could reasonably be called excess—extra oil, water, the emergency radio, and finally the Chief Engineer, Lieutenant j.g. Braxton Rhodes. While this was going on, *Nancy Four* had landed again to conserve fuel, and both it and *Nancy One* taxied about waiting for the problem on *Three* to be resolved.

At six o'clock *Nancy Three* tried again. This time, however, the takeoff run was made across the bay into the wind, as *NC-4* had done previously, and this time the effort was successful. *Nancies Four* and *One* followed, and by 6:10 P.M. all three were airborne and heading east into the gathering darkness toward the Azores, a pinpoint in the North Atlantic.

As the planes departed, the word that the great adventure had begun was radioed to the waiting station ships. The three aircraft flew at low altitude in a very loose formation, attempting only to stay within sight of one another. Aboard the Nancies, the radio operators established contact and began to transmit among themselves. *Nancy Four,* the fastest of the group, experienced some difficulty keeping position behind the lead aircraft, *Nancy Three.* This situation was made potentially hazardous by the fact that *Nancy Three's* running lights were not functioning. As the first station-ship passed beneath them, all seemed to be going smoothly, when suddenly *Nancy Four* narrowly averted a midair collision with the tail of *Nancy Three.* From then on *NC-4* continued independently.

Of the three, *Nancy One* was the slowest and straggled along in the rear. This was actually a composite of two aircraft, and, because there had been insufficient time for adjustments before the trip, it had a tendency to fly with one wing down. As it proceeded on course, its commander's concern that it might not be able to keep up was forgotten at the sudden appearance of the unlighted *Nancy Three* a few yards ahead. *Nancy One* veered away sharply, and put some lateral distance between the two aircraft. From this point on, the epic tale divides into three separate experiences.

Lieutenant Commander Patrick N. L. Bellinger, Naval Aviator Number 8, was the aircraft commander and navigator aboard *Nancy One.* His pilot, Lieutenant Commander Marc A. Mitscher, was a competent officer who would have had his own command if *Nancy Two* had been flyable. Both men were destined to become luminaries in naval aviation history.

Bellinger, peering from the navigator's station in the nose, checked-off one station after another with satisfaction. Two and a half hours out of Trepassey, they were favored by a full moon which made the darkness less forboding. The four big Liberty engines droned steadily through the night as *Nancy One* made its way over the water expanse. Morning, however, brought a deteriorating weather situation, and *Nancy One* was unable to locate USS *Craven* on station eighteen. The pilots now were experiencing difficulty maintaining straight and level flight using the primitive instruments, and Bellinger elected to climb above the weather. Here the flying was easier, but the thick carpet of fog below made it impossible to see the station vessels as they were over-flown. Bellinger obtained a sun line of position with Dick Byrd's bubble sextant, but judged it to be unreliable. The radio-direction-finder, or RDF, was extremely limited in range due to engine interference, and gave no indication as to the whereabouts of the next station-ship in line.

Finally, Bellinger decided that they must descend if there was to be any hope of establishing their position. After feeling the way down through the clouds, *Nancy One* leveled off just above the surface of the ocean. There was nothing in sight. As they flew along through rain and patches of fog not knowing where they were, with the realization that they could easily miss sighting the Azores in that weather, Bellinger concluded that the only prudent thing to do was to set the aircraft down on the water, shut down the engines, and try for an RDF bearing.

From the air, the surface of the ocean can be deceiving. Even under ideal conditions, an open-sea landing is not something to be taken lightly. Primary and secondary swell systems often run at right angles to one another, and a wind with no tendency to conform to either is often a third and dangerous factor. Moreover, it is sometimes difficult to accurately assess both the direction and intensity of these forces, all of which can tear the most rugged aircraft to pieces under unfavorable conditions.

Nancy One came down in twenty-foot swells with a strong crosswind blowing parallel to the crests. Miraculously, no damage was suffered on landing, but it was clear that the aircraft could not possibly take off again under the existing sea conditions. The outcome was only a matter of time. Despite

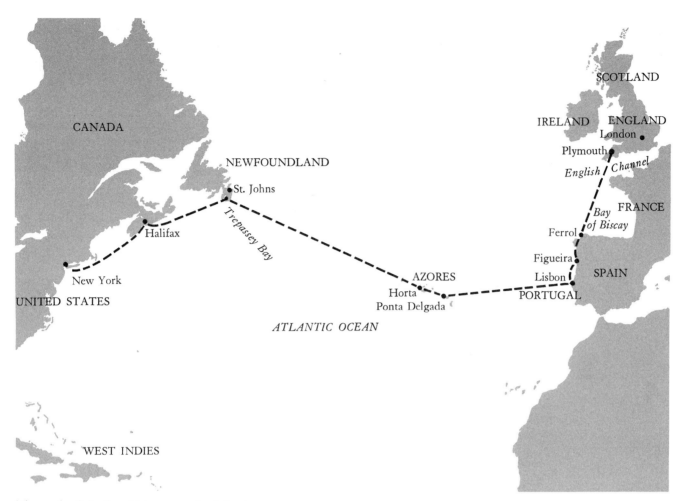

The track of the first flight across the Atlantic.

valiant efforts by the crew, wind and waves soon took their toll, and before long the *NC-1* had been permanently disabled.

Seven hours elapsed before the Greek freighter *Ionia* appeared on the scene, quite by chance, and took the crew of *Nancy One* aboard. With the battered flying boat in tow, she headed for Horta in the Azores. Unfortunately, the towline did not hold, and *Ionia* was obliged to stand by the stricken aircraft until relieved a short time later by the destroyer USS *Gridley*. As *Ionia* steamed toward port, the bedraggled *Nancy One* wallowed in the sea. Two days later, in spite of several attempts to save the damaged aircraft, it was claimed by the North Atlantic.

Nancy Three's fate was similar to that of *Nancy One*. Its undoing came when Towers mistook a passing ship for USS *Maddox* on station fifteen. Using the ship's position as a fix, he adjusted his course for the Azores. Unfortunately, the ship was not the *Maddox,* and after flying for some time with no further sightings, Towers realized that he was off course. As they continued on their last best heading, Towers was able to get a sun line during a brief break in the clouds. The line ran northeast through one of the Azores Islands, and he elected to fly along this line of position until he made a landfall. The sun line might have been in error, a possibility of which he was keenly aware, but it was the only positive indication of position he had.

The fuel situation was another constraint to consider. Towers certainly did not want to fly a random pattern over the ocean in a fruitless search for the proverbial needle-in-a-haystack, while the big Liberty engines used the last remaining fuel. Finally, after careful consideration, he arrived at the same conclusion that Bellinger had reached only a short time before. They would land on the sea, and attempt to determine an RDF bearing.

Upon contacting the water, *Nancy Three* skipped twice like a flat stone on the wave crests, and then ploughed headlong into one of the big swells. The sudden stop bent the struts supporting the forward centerline engine, causing it to wrench downward and hang askew. The flight was over for *Nancy Three*. Buffeted by the elements, it drifted tail-first toward the Azores. Two days later, with the fabric torn from the lower surfaces, both wing-tip floats missing, and balanced precariously by crewmen on the wings, *Nancy Three*'s engines were started, and the aircraft was taxied into the harbor at Ponta Delgada in the Azores under its own power.

After separating from the other two aircraft, *Nancy Four* had soon out-distanced them. Like the others, this aircraft had an easy time of it during the night, with the station-ships appearing when expected along the route. Aboard *Nancy Four,* Lieutenant Commander Albert C. "Putty" Read, the aircraft commander, looked forward to the remainder of the flight with quiet confidence. He was a navigator of no mean ability, who had taken up flying in 1915 and quickly became a competent pilot. In the copilot's seat was Lieutenant Elmer Stone, the U.S. Coast Guard's first aviator. In the pilot's seat, the steady hands of Lieutenant junior grade Walter Hinton held *Nancy Four* steadily on course; a former quartermaster, he had an uncanny ability to maintain heading with extreme accuracy. Although junior to Stone in rank, he was an accomplished aviator with a wealth of experience in flying boats. Read and Stone had apparently agreed between themselves that Hinton should fly in the pilot's seat for the entire trip. In the cramped radio operator's compartment, Ensign Herbert Rodd kept continuous guard over the radio circuits. Lieutenant James Breese, a designated naval aviator, served as chief engineer, while Machinists Mate Chief Eugene "Smokey" Rhoads filled in as the second mechanic for the unfortunate Chief Howard, who had lost his hand at Rockaway. Rhoads was an extremely competent mechanic and a welcome addition to an outstanding crew.

As the night merged with the dawn, it became increasingly apparent that the weather ahead would be less than ideal. As *Nancy Four* approached station seventeen, the gray haze thickened, and the air became turbulent. It became a problem just to maintain straight-and-level flight, using the primitive instruments. Walter Hinton recalled this part of the trip in an interview with the author in July 1976.*

Q: Where did you start encountering bad weather?
A: I'd say it was about three-quarters of the way.
Q: Was anybody ever concerned that you might not be able to find the Azores? It's really just a pinpoint.
A: Yes, and we had some very rough weather before that. We ran into a very turbulent situation. Read thought we were in a spin. The bottom just dropped out. Even the bilge-water was coming up. No control. With a slow plane in rough air you just fight it out with the controls. It's prolonged at seventy-seven knots average speed. We just wallowed in it. Read crawled back and pulled my leg. He thought I'd fallen asleep or something had happened to me. But I just had no control. We got out of that and straightened. But that seemed like a close one. [*NC-4* climbed on top of the overcast after this incident].
Q: When you climbed on top of the overcast, did you see the station-ships anymore? Were you able to use your radio compass?
A: No to both questions. We only used the compass once and that was when we left the Azores. No one believed in it.

*Knott, Richard C., "Journey to Plymouth." *Naval Aviation News*, Washington, D.C.: November 1976.

The *NC-4*, which completed the first transatlantic crossing by air, has been fully restored and is now on display at the Naval Aviation Museum in Pensacola, Florida. (John Ficklen)

The crew of the *NC-4* is officially greeted at Plymouth, England, on completion of the last leg of their epic flight. (U.S. Coast Guard)

Q: After you climbed on top and couldn't see the station-ships, do I understand that the only thing you had to navigate with was dead reckoning and that's how you proceeded?

A: That was it. And I kept my eye on the lubbers point all the time.
    Read was a pretty good navigator and a wonderful fellow to work with, very conscientious. I don't know about the others, but he took his instruction from Byrd. He got out there and practiced at night and worked with Byrd. He tried out the sextant when we had moon.

At about 9:30 A.M., Azores time, shortly after passing USS *Philip* on station twenty, Read glimpsed the coastline of the island of Flores through a hole in the clouds. Hinton quickly descended and skirted the island at an altitude of 200 feet. Land was a welcome sight, but there was little opportunity for relaxation. Ponta Delgada was within reach, but the route could be treacherous. Between their present position and their destination, other islands rose abruptly from the sea, reaching a height of over 7,700 feet in the case of Pico Island. If the bad weather persisted or worsened, it would be a suspenseful homestretch.
    Shortly after 10:00 A.M. *Nancy Four* flew directly over the USS *Harding* on station twenty-two. Altitude was now about one hundred feet, and the

visibility was not improving. By the time it reached station twenty-three, the aircraft was skimming along only a few feet above the wave crests. At this point Read made a quick decision, and signalled Hinton to turn toward the island of Faial and its harbor at Horta where the base ship USS *Columbia* was anchored. It was not long before Faial loomed ahead. Flying close to the steep shoreline, they came upon a small harbor they believed to be Horta, and Hinton set the big aircraft down on the water. But in the poor visibility, they had made a mistake. This was not Horta, and moments later, they were airborne again, hugging the shore and peering ahead into the worsening weather. Luckily their destination was less than fifteen minutes away, and shortly after takeoff they sighted the harbor and made a necessarily low approach to the final landing. At 11:23 A.M., Azores time, about the same time that Towers and his crew were making their open-sea landing, *Nancy Four* splashed down at Horta. Minutes later a thick fog rolled in and completely blanketed the area.

And so it was that just before noon on 17 May 1919, after more than fifteen hours in the air, *Nancy Four* cut engines and came to rest in the harbor at Horta. The welcome here and at Ponta Delgada a few days later was lavish and emotional. There were crowds, dinners, speeches, and congratulatory telegrams. And this was only a sample of what was yet to come.

The flight from Ponta Delgada to Lisbon, Portugal, and the subsequent final leg of the epic flight to Portsmouth, England, were made without incident, and were in some ways rather anticlimatic. Nevertheless, when *Nancy Four* touched down at Lisbon at 9:00 P.M. on the twenty-seventh, completing the historic transatlantic crossing, the waterfront erupted with cheers, whistles, sirens, and twenty-one-gun salutes. The U.S. Navy and the flying boat had been the first to conquer the Atlantic by air. Back in the United States the news captured headlines across the country. Out in the midwest, a young Minnesota farm boy preparing to enter the University of Wisconsin that fall, learned of the historic flight with particular interest. His name was Charles A. Lindbergh.

CHAPTER FOUR

The Roaring Twenties

THEY CALLED THE YEARS immediately following the end of World War I the "Roaring Twenties," with good reason. There were motor cars, flappers, bathtub gin, and that marvelous new machine, the airplane. Americans were thrilled by the antics of the barnstormers who brought aviation up close to the average man. They were everywhere, stopping at cities, towns and whistle stops from coast to coast.

Flying boats too were a colorful part of the postwar era. A few imaginative entrepreneurs bought U.S. Navy surplus aircraft from the government at bargain prices, and hired Navy pilots newly released from service to fly them. The flying boats were ideally suited for both passenger service and air freight, because their large interiors provided comfortable room for passengers, while their power and unlimited runway length enabled them to lift heavy loads. They were also believed to be safer than aircraft designed to operate solely from land, provided of course, they did not stray too far from the water. They were ideal for sportsmen, who used them to fly to remote lakes or quiet bays for a few days of unsurpassed hunting or fishing. For sporting people of another sort, the flying boats provided transportation to the gambling casinos of Havana and the Bahamas, and were a popular means of circumventing the Volstead Act of 1919, which enacted Prohibition. Shoestring operators worked the summer crowds. Flying from bathing beaches and seashore resorts, they sold sightseeing rides to excited passengers, many of whom had never even seen an airplane, much less ridden in one. Flying boats were among the first to carry the mail. They set new aviation records, participated in goodwill flights, and enabled explorers to penetrate into areas where civilized man had never been before.

Hundreds of aircraft became available immediately after the war, and there were literally thousands of the new Liberty engines for sale at a fraction of their original cost. Some enterprising individuals with a flare for adventure discovered that the big Liberties installed in sleek motor-launches offered great advantage to those whose distilled cargoes were of considerable interest to the Coast Guard.

Unfortunately, the glut of surplus aircraft and engines which inundated the market dealt a crippling blow to American aircraft manufacturers. By 1922/23, many of those remaining in business were surviving by only a bare margin. Buyers simply could not be persuaded to pay thousands of dollars for a new aircraft, when they could buy a surplus machine in very good condition for considerably less. Notwithstanding this difficulty, there were still those spirited individuals who persisted in the attempt to establish a profitable business in the fledgling U.S. aviation industry.

Alan and Malcolm Loughead (later Lockheed) had formed the Loughead Aircraft Manufacturing Company at Santa Barbara, California, in 1916. One of their first aircraft was the F-1 Flying Boat, a large twin-engine biplane which featured a distinctive tail assembly with three vertical fins. The upper wing had a 74-foot span, while the lower one measured 47 feet. The hull was 35 feet in length, and it was considered a big aircraft for that time. The F-1

The Loughead F-1 featured a distinctive tail assembly, with three vertical fins. (Lockheed Aircraft Corp.)

was powered by two Hall-Scott 160-horsepower engines mounted in tractor fashion. These provided the Loughead aircraft with a cruising speed of about 70 miles per hour. John K. "Jack" Northrop, who would later become famous for his imaginative designs, including the Northrop Flying Wing, contributed much to the development of the F-1, and got his start in the aviation business with the Lougheads.

The F-1 with Alan Loughead at the controls made its first flight on 28 March 1918. It performed so well that on 12 April, he flew the aircraft from Santa Barbara to North Island, San Diego, California, for evaluation as a patrol plane by the Navy. In doing so, he covered the distance of 211 miles at an average speed of 70 miles per hour, which was an excellent accomplishment in 1918. The Navy, after considerable testing, declined to order any F-1s. The Loughead Aircraft Manufacturing Company did, however, build two HS-2L flying boats in 1918 under Navy contract.

The F-1 was subsequently converted to a land-based plane, and designated the F-1A. Unfortunately, this modified version crashed during a transcontinental flight attempt. It was salvaged and rebuilt in the original configuration as a flying boat, and used extensively for short passenger flights and as a camera-plane for the motion-picture industry. In October 1919, it was chartered by the U.S. government to entertain the visiting King and Queen of Belgium on a sightseeing flight off the California coast.

Another flying boat which came on the scene in late 1919 was William E. Boeing's B-1. It was intended to be the first of a line designed for the commer-

Grover Loening (left) stands alongside one of his Air Yachts, 1923. (Smithsonian Institution)

cial market, but because there were no buyers, it was the only one of its kind ever built. It did, however, serve as the inspiration for another smaller airplane designated the BB-1 built in 1920, as well as several other models of Boeing flying boats produced after 1928. The B-1 was a three-place pusher-type aircraft, with a single 200-horsepower Hall-Scott engine. It was turned over to Eddie Hubbard, and was used continuously on his Seattle-Victoria Air Mail Line until 1928, by which time the aircraft had logged over 350,000 miles in the air, and had undergone six engine changes.

An unusual flying boat that appeared in 1921 was Grover Leoning's Air Yacht, which won for him the Collier Trophy for that year. A monoplane, it was a departure from the contemporary flying boat design, and featured a roomy cockpit and cabin which gave it a rather unique profile. The Air Yacht had a wingspan of 43 feet, and was powered by a 400-horsepower pusher-type Liberty engine. It carried a pilot and four passengers when fully loaded, and had a top speed of 125 miles per hour. In August 1921 an Air Yacht, flown by David McCulloch, set an American altitude record for seaplanes, when it carried three passengers to an altitude of 19,500 feet. In April of the following year, Clifford L. Webster, a former Marine officer and naval aviator, flew it from Palm Beach, Florida, to New York City in an actual flying time of nine hours and fifty-six minutes. In June 1923, Loening began operating three of these strange-looking aircraft between New York City and Newport, Rhode Island. The service was well-patronized by New York businessmen who liked the idea of flying off to their summer homes after work on Friday, and arriving only an hour and a half later. Unfortunately, the popularity initially enjoyed by the service waned rapidly when later in the summer, one of the aircraft crashed while landing, seriously injuring a Mr. H. Carey Morgan, who later died of blood poisoning. According to the *Newport Mercury* of 28 July 1923, it was a peculiar accident. "The Loening seaplane had made a successful flight from New York [City] under the charge of Pilot H. H. Thorburn, having as passengers Mr. Morgan, and Mr. Harold Fowler. When making a landing on the water at the regular terminal in Newport harbor, the plane suddenly took a nose dive and turned completely over. Mr. Fowler was the first to escape from the wreckage and brought his companions to a place of safety on the floating plane, whence they were rescued by a naval boat."

In 1925, Kirkham Products Company produced a unique gull-wing monoplane flying boat to the order of Harold S. Vanderbilt. This too was a five-place pusher-type aircraft, powered by a 450-horsepower Napier "Lion" engine. It was one of the first all-metal flying boats produced in the United States and had a maximum speed of 145 miles per hour and a cruising speed of 125.

An important early contributor to the development of flying boats for commercial use was Inglis M. Uppercu's Aeromarine Plane and Motor Company of Keyport, New Jersey. Aeromarine was a first-rate operation. During the war, this company had established an excellent reputation as a manufacturer of aircraft for the Navy. After the signing of the Armistice, Aeromarine directed its emphasis toward the commercial market with great confidence. The Model 40, a two-place pusher type airplane originally designed for the U.S. Navy, had a 130-horsepower Aeromarine engine and was marketed as a sport-plane and a mail-carrier. A plush three-place version, the Model 50, mounted a 150-horsepower Aeromarine engine, and was offered as a "touring" aircraft.

Much of the company's efforts after the war went into conversions of Navy-surplus F-5Ls and HS-2Ls. The F-5Ls were remodeled into fourteen-passenger Model 75 Aeromarine Cruisers. The Cruisers were divided into two sections, a main cabin seating nine passengers, and a smaller smoking-compartment with seats for five. Governor Edwards of New Jersey christened the first of these on 22 June 1920; it was rumored that he performed his duties using a bottle of real champagne, an illegal commodity in the Prohibition era. The HS-2L was designated the Aeromarine Model 80, and carried a pilot and five passengers.

One of the major problems with early flying boats was a tendency for the wooden hull-planking to become waterlogged, when an aircraft was left in the water for any length of time. This phenomenon limited payloads, caused weight and balance problems in flight, and weakened the bottoms of the hulls. As early as 1923, Aeromarine offered a solution to this problem with its Model AMC, designed to replace the HS-2Ls then in service. It featured an all-metal hull constructed of aluminum alloy. The wings were made of conventional materials of the day, wood and fabric, and the aircraft mounted a single 400-horsepower Liberty pusher-type engine. The AMC could carry seven persons with sufficient fuel to last four hours, or five persons with fuel sufficient for seven hours of flight.

Aeromarine was an efficient, well-managed organization, but in the end it too succumbed to the deadly doldrums of the early 1920s. In 1924 the company produced its last aircraft, the Aeromarine EO Sport Flying Boat, an excellent two-place single-engine tractor-type aircraft with a seventy-horsepower Anzani engine. It was built to the order of a Mr. Earl D. Osborn, and featured staggered wings, the lower one of which was positioned aft of the upper, providing very good pilot visibility.

It was during this same postwar period that the air transport industry in the United States made its shakey start, and it was unquestionably the flying boat

The Aeromarine Model 40 was designed for the Navy, but was also marketed as a sport plane and mail carrier. (Curtiss Museum)

that led the way. Of the ten earliest commercial carriers, all operated flying boats, and nine did so exclusively.*

In the spring of 1919, Syd Chaplin, half brother of the famous comedian, began operating a Curtiss MF flying boat between San Pedro, California, and Santa Catalina Island, offering three round-trips a day. This service, inaugurated on the Fourth of July 1919, dwindled to sporadic flights by the end of September, and was discontinued completely by December. The following year Pacific Marine Airways was formed to reinstitute the Santa Catalina service, using two surplus Curtiss HS-2L aircraft flying out of Wilmington, California. This time the venture was successful, and Pacific Marine Airways continued in operation until it was taken over in 1928 by Western Air Express (later Western Airlines).

Back east, Rodman Wanamaker, whose aspirations of a transatlantic crossing had been frustrated twice by the war in Europe, persisted in his efforts to promote commercial aviation in the United States. In 1916, he formed the America Trans Oceanic Company, nicknamed A.T.O., and established bases of operation on Long Island, New York, and at West Palm Beach, Florida, from which he hoped to begin commercial airline service after the war. Shortly after hostilities ceased, A.T.O. went into operation with Curtiss HS-2L and H-16 flying boats. The company's general manager was a former naval aviator, Dave McCulloch, who had been one of the pilots of the *NC-3* during its unsuccessful transatlantic attempt in May 1919. Prohibition was now in full force, and A.T.O. did a lively business flying passengers to Cuba and the Bahamas, where alcoholic beverages were freely dispensed and temperance was clearly not in vogue.

One of the most popular trips made by A.T.O. was a regularly scheduled daily flight from Miami, Florida, to Bimini Island and back. Bimini, located only fifty miles offshore, was British territory, and a prime attraction there was an establishment known as the Bimini Bay Rod and Gun Club. A.T.O. was the official carrier for the club, and for the Bahama Development Company as well. The aircraft used regularly on the Miami-Bimini run was a crowd-pleaser, with a distinctively painted exterior that was perhaps the most unusual ever to grace the hull of a flying boat. The *Big Fish*, as it was called, was a Curtiss H-16

*The Seattle-Victoria Air Mail Line began operations with a Boeing CL-4S float-plane, but later switched to the model B-1 flying boat.

Table 4–1. The First U.S. Commercial Carriers

Company	Type Aircraft Flown	Route	Year(s) of Operation
St. Petersburg–Tampa Airboat Line	Benoist Type XIV	St. Petersburg–Tampa	1914
America Trans-Oceanic (A.T.O.)	Curtiss HS-2L Curtiss H-16	U.S. East Coast Miami to Bimini and Havana	1916–1921
Syd Chaplin Airline	Curtiss MF	San Pedro–Santa Catalina	1919
Aero, Ltd.	Curtiss HS-2L	New York–Atlantic City	1919–1920
Florida West Indies Airways, Inc.	Curtiss HS-2L	Miami–Key West–Havana	1919–1920
Seattle-Victoria Air Mail Line	Boeing CL-4S Boeing B-1	Seattle-Victoria	1920–1927
Aeromarine Airways Inc.	Curtiss F-5L Curtiss HS-2L	New York–Key West Miami-Havana or Nassau Cleveland-Detroit	1920–1924
Pacific Marine Airways	Curtiss HS-2L	San Pedro–Santa Catalina	1920–1928
New York–Newport Air Service, Inc.	Loening Air Yacht	New York–Newport, R.I.	1923
Gulf Coast Air Line Inc.	Curtiss MF Curtiss HS-2L	New Orleans–Pilottown, La.	1923–1927

adapted from the military configuration to carry a total of eleven passengers, with two forward in the old gunner's well, and nine aft in the main cabin. It was painted to resemble a huge fish, in deference to a popular local sport fisherman and club president who had once caught a gigantic whale-shark in those waters. The *Big Fish,* a popular photographic subject, operated between Miami and Bimini for two winter seasons. During the summers when the tourist flow languished, the *Big Fish* went north to operate between A.T.O.'s base on Long Island and the lake region of upstate New York. During the summer of 1921, a jarring night landing on the Hudson River cut short its colorful career. With its hull smashed like a broken eggshell, the aircraft was abandoned on the beach to face the elements. A.T.O. was one of the first international air passenger services operating on a regular basis from the United States.

There were other early airline companies that established their businesses in Florida to capitalize on the desire of many Americans to circumvent Prohibition. One of these was Aero Limited, which first began operating Curtiss HS-2L boats between New York City and Atlantic City, New Jersey, in the summer of 1919. Later the operation migrated to Florida, and joined with A.T.O. to satisfy the newly-developed demand for airline service to the Bahamas. Florida West Indies Airways Incorporated also began its operation flying Curtiss HS-2Ls between Miami and Key West, Florida, and Havana, Cuba. This was the first airline to receive a contract to fly the U.S. Mail to a foreign country.

At about this time, the energetic Mr. Uppercu and his Aeromarine Plane and Motor Company formed a subsidiary that moved into Florida as Aeromarine Airways. It promptly absorbed Florida West Indies Airways, including its airmail contract, and emerged as Aeromarine West Indies Airways. The future of this airline looked very promising. It was well capitalized, efficiently run, had well-maintained equipment, and employed some very proficient pilots. Edwin C. Musick, a former Marine Officer and Naval Aviator Number 1673, got his start in commercial aviation with Aeromarine. Later, he would pioneer the Pan American air routes across the Pacific Ocean.

Pacific Marine Airways used two Navy-surplus HS-2Ls on their Wilmington-Catalina route. (Western Airlines)

A.T.O.'s *Big Fish* was used between Miami and the Bahamas on what was probably the first U.S. international air passenger service. (Smithsonian Institution)

The Aeromarine Cruiser *Buckeye* carried a Model-T Ford auto from Detroit to Cleveland in 1922. (Smithsonian Institution)

Almost immediately, Aeromarine began to phase in the larger and more comfortable Aeromarine Model 75 Cruisers. Each aircraft was given its own identity in the form of a romantic name such as the *Nina,* the *Pinta,* and the *Santa Maria.* As the line expanded, Aeromarine aircraft made several record flights, all of which received enthusiastic coverage in the press. In May 1922, Aeromarine staged a carnival in New York City to open the flying boat season. On hand for the event were local and foreign dignitaries, both military and civilian. One of the more newsworthy events was a flight of the cruiser *Mendoza* with a record twenty-seven passengers stuffed aboard the fourteen-passenger aircraft. In those days there were no federal aircraft safety standards, and such ostentatious stunts were not uncommon.

By 1923, Aeromarine was operating up and down the east coast from New England to Key West, and internationally from Florida to Havana, Cuba, and Nassau in the Bahamas. Flights originating from New York City bound for one of these destinations outside the country were affectionately and appropriately called "Highball Expresses." Havana was only two days' journey from Manhattan, weather permitting.

Aeromarine had also expanded into the Great Lakes region for summer operations, and by the summer of 1922, it was scheduling two round-trips a day between Cleveland, Ohio, and Detroit, Michigan. On 15 August of that year the Aeromarine Cruiser *Buckeye,* flown by Captain Ed Musick, carried a Model-T Ford automobile from Detroit to Cleveland. By 17 September Aeromarine's Great Lakes operation had carried a total of 1,839 passengers and 2,574 pounds of freight. By November of that same year, Aeromarine was able to announce that in two years of operating its three divisions, it had carried more than 20,000 passengers without mishap. But for all its competence, innovation, and efficiency, Aeromarine could not bring in enough revenue to remain in existence as a viable business enterprise. It continued to operate until September of 1923, and then faded into oblivion. At the time of its demise, Aeromarine had carried more than 30,000 passengers, with only one serious accident.

There were those who found the flying boat uniquely suited to other tasks. Roy F. Jones, a former pilot in the Army Air Service, bought a surplus Navy MF-Boat, which he thought might be ideal for use in Alaska. He named it the *Northbird*, and in the summer of 1922, he and his mechanic Jerry Smith headed it north on one of the first flights from the United States to the Alaskan territory. The trip from Seattle, Washington, to Ketchikan, Alaska, took ten days because of foul weather and routine problems encountered along the way. He arrived at his destination on 22 July, with an actual flying time en route of slightly over nine hours. That summer and well into the next, Jones was kept busy hauling passengers, freight, and even fish, until one day *Northbird* crashed into a lake shortly after takeoff. Jones and a passenger survived, but *Northbird* was completely destroyed. Nevertheless, it had been a courageous effort. He and his Curtiss MF-Boat were the first to bring commercial aviation to Alaska and to demonstrate its utility in that harsh land.

Back in New York, Walter Hinton, who had piloted the *NC-4* on its epic flight across the Atlantic, was preparing for another long-distance aerial adventure, this time from the United States to Rio de Janeiro, Brazil. Hinton was a compulsive adventurer with a burning curiosity to experience everything the world had to offer. He had not been able to resist the challenge of this flight, which would span some 8,500 miles and had never been attempted before. The occasion was the celebration of Brazil's centennial, and the flight was to be a demonstration of American goodwill toward a southern neighbor. Hinton resigned his U.S. Navy commission, and launched himself on a new career in civil aviation. The trip was a significant undertaking, and was not without risk. There would be no station-ships along the way this time, and there would be long stretches of nothing but ocean and jungle wilderness. Repair facilities would range from extremely limited to non-existent, and finding fuel en route would be a recurrent problem.

Hinton set out from New York City on 17 August 1922 in his Navy-surplus Curtiss H-16 named the *Sampaio Correia*. His copilot was a Brazilian, Dr. E. Pinto Martins, and his mechanic, John Wilschusen, was an American. The flight was sponsored by *The New York World*, a newspaper which was known for its support of American aviation. They sent along photographer Thomas Baltzell and writer George T. Bye to record the story.

American and Brazilian newspapers followed the flight down the east coast of the United States, reporting every storm, every routine engine problem, and every unscheduled landing. To Hinton, a veteran flying boat pilot, these distractions were everyday occurrences, but to the people at home and those waiting in Brazil, they were high adventure.

On 22 August Hinton and company took off from Nassau bound for Port au Prince, Haiti, in the Caribbean Sea. Although the flight was uneventful, by late afternoon they had fallen behind schedule, and soon they were enveloped in the gathering darkness well short of their destination. Not wishing to proceed much further in the murky darkness characteristic of the area on a moonless night, Hinton decided to set down for the night at the U.S. Naval Station at Guantanamo Bay, Cuba, which was nearby at this point. As he approached the island, he began searching through the gloom to discover an identifyable navigation aid by which he could fix his position; he had spent considerable time in this area and knew it well. Finally he thought he had found his objective in the form of the Windward Point Light, and, using the light as a reference, he commenced his landing approach. Unfortunately, the light he had relied on was in reality the USS *Denver*, and in the darkness the big H-16 hit hard as it came down in the open sea instead of in the protected waters of Guantanamo Bay. The force of the landing tore the bottom out of the aircraft, and it settled in the water until only the upper wing was left afloat. The crew

Walter Hinton (second from left) and crew ready to set out from New York City in the *Sampaio Correia* on the flight from New York to Brazil. (Hinton Collection)

of the *Denver* had seen the lights of the *Sampaio Correia* plunge into the water. The last thing they expected out there that night was an airplane, and so they initially decided it must have been a shooting star. Fortunately, the ship's captain remembered reading that Hinton was on his way to Brazil, and the thought occurred to him that the strange sighting just might be Hinton. He ordered the searchlight trained on the area in question, and there they found the crew and the wrecked aircraft. Some sharks had discovered them also, and by the time the aviators were picked up, several of the big predators could be seen moving in close to the site. George Bye commented later, "Those sharks not only followed the lifeboat to the *Denver*, but even pursued the wrecked plane when it was towed into Guantanamo."

The five men survived the crash without injury, but the *Sampaio Correia* would never fly again. No one would have blamed the men if they had abandoned the project as a well-meant but futile effort and gone home. But Hinton, undeterred, immediately began contacting old Navy friends and associates in an attempt to borrow another aircraft in which to continue.

By law, the U.S. Navy could not loan Hinton an aircraft, but there were influential people in Washington who believed that the well-publicized flight should continue, and that its successful completion would pay dividends to the United States in goodwill as well as national prestige. Arrangements were made for the sponsors of the project to purchase another Navy H-16, which was declared surplus at Pensacola, Florida. The flight was underway again.

On 3 September 1922 Hinton and company left Pensacola in the *Sampaio Correia II* to recommence their long journey south. They flew first to St. Petersburg, Florida, then to Key West, then over the Atlantic to Cuba and Port-au-Prince, arriving there on 7 September. Here they remained for a month while the engines were exchanged for two others of the high-compression type, which

UNITED STATES

Pensacola

St. Petersburg

GULF OF MEXICO

Key West

Cuba

Santo Domingo

Puerto Rico

Port-au-Prince

Guadeloupe

Martinique

CARIBBEAN SEA

Trinidad

Georgetown

Cayenne

Sinnamary River

Maranhao

BRAZIL

Rio de Janeiro

ATLANTIC OCEAN

Track of the Sampaio Correia II from Pensacola, Florida, to Rio de Janeiro, 1922-1923.

would provide better performance and give the H-16 longer endurance. At 11:30 A.M. on 7 October 1922 the five departed for Santo Domingo and thence Puerto Rico, where upon arrival Hinton was unexpectedly arrested for failing to have a proper health certificate for the aircraft. A few words from the U.S. government resolved the misunderstanding, and on 10 October the group took off again and proceeded in stepping-stone fashion down the Windward Islands chain, stopping briefly at Guadaloupe and Martinique, and encountering severe buffeting storms before reaching Trinidad on 15 October. Here disaster was narrowly averted when the steamer *Viking*, near which the *Sampaio Correia II* was moored, caught on fire and burned to the waterline. Fortunately, the aircraft was quickly towed away from the inferno before it, too, caught on fire.

From Trinidad, Hinton and his four associates crossed over the water to the coast of South America, and made their way south along the shore-line, pausing briefly for scheduled stops in places like Georgetown in British Guiana, Paramaribo in Dutch Guiana, and Cayenne in French Guiana. As usual, there were unscheduled landings too. On one occasion they were obliged to land in the Sinnamary River in French Guiana for engine repairs, and there the aircraft became entangled in the trees and heavy undergrowth along the river bank. It took several hours of hacking and cutting before they were able to extricate the big flying boat from the jungle and proceed on their way.

Leaving Cayenne on 30 November, the intrepid group once again headed south and into Brazil. They spent ten days in the state of Maranhao for a complete overhaul of the engines. Then they continued east and south around the shoulder of Brazil toward their destination. Finally, at 11:32 A.M. on 9 February 1923, the *Sampaio Correia II* landed at Rio de Janeiro. The Brazilians who had been waiting a long time for their arrival now vented their enthusiasm. Guns were fired from the forts around the harbor, ships blew their whistles and sirens, and churches throughout the city rang their bells. An eager crowd gathered to welcome the *Sampaio Correia II* and its crew. It had taken nearly six months to make a flight that now takes only a few hours, but in those days it was a significant feat. Hinton had left New York City with full confidence that he could complete the record journey. Eighty-five hundred miles, six months, and one wrecked airplane later, he not only achieved his objective, but he was also the first to do it.

The complete adventures of Walter Hinton would fill several volumes. Today, this old gentleman lives quietly in Pompano Beach, Florida, savoring a thousand memories of his colorful deeds and numerous personal achievements.

CHAPTER FIVE

Lean Years—Good Years

At the end of World War I, the flying boat was the operational mainstay of naval aviation. Most U.S. Navy pilots, in fact, had never flown an aircraft designed to operate only from land. The Americas and the HS-boats had established an enviable record in the war, and were the only American-built aircraft to be used extensively in combat against the enemy. The U.S. Congress authorized the conversion of the collier *Jupiter* into America's first aircraft carrier in 1919, but it would be 1924 before she would join the fleet, and several years thereafter until the carrier would develop its potential as a practical weapon system. Meanwhile, many U.S. Navy planners believed that the big seaplanes with their proven war record were destined to play a key role in any future wartime operations involving naval aviation. This philosophy was reflected in many of the developments in naval aviation which occurred in the decade following the war.

As early as 23 May 1919, while the *NC-4* was in the Azores waiting for good weather to complete the historic transatlantic crossing, *The New York Times* reported that the U.S. Navy was making plans to build an even bigger and better flying boat. On 2 October the Manufacturers Aircraft Association optimistically predicted that the Navy would have a giant seaplane by the following spring capable of crossing the Pacific. In February 1920 the Naval Committee of the U.S. House of Representatives was told of plans to construct two giant seaplanes larger than any ever built.

The Navy's *Giant Boat*, designated the GB-1, was designed as a triplane, similar in some respects to the NCs, but considerably larger. One major innovation was its nine engines mounted in three nacelles. Each nacelle housed three Liberty twelve-cylinder engines, and these transmitted power through clutches, pinions, and a single shaft to a mammoth propeller having an arc 18 feet in diameter. The hull was 65 feet long, 10 feet 6 inches high, and 14 feet 6 inches in width of beam. The wingspan was 150 feet, with the wings featuring steel spars and Duralumin ribs covered with cotton fabric. A gunner's station was the uppermost point of the aircraft, 41 feet above the keel. The overall length was 96 feet 3 inches. When it was completed, it would weigh 7,000 pounds maximum gross weight. The GB-1 was designed to cruise at 80 miles an hour for 1,800 nautical miles.

The Naval Aircraft Factory was authorized to begin construction of the GB-1 in July 1920, and the Gallaudet Company, which had been awarded the contract to build the unique nacelle assemblies, had already started the project. The hull was originally planned to be of metal construction, since the state of the art had advanced to the point where this was now possible, but cost constraints ultimately forced a revision in favor of wood.

While all appeared to be going reasonably well at the outset for a project of this complexity, Navy planners were becoming increasingly concerned over developments on the political scene. President Woodrow Wilson, attempting to force Congress to act on the issue of membership in the League of Nations, had publicly warned that the United States must either look to the League to keep world peace, or maintain an extensive military establishment, especially a navy

A single nacelle of the Navy's GB-1 *Giant Boat* housed three Liberty twelve-cylinder engines. (U.S. Navy)

second to none. Congress chose to do neither, and the American people themselves turned inward in a mood of isolationism. By the spring of 1921, it had become apparent that funding for naval aviation was not going to be authorized at anywhere near the level of expenditures desired. The resulting alternatives were to go ahead with the *Giant Boat* at an estimated cost of two hundred thousand dollars, or to shelve the project and spend the money on operational needs. Reluctantly the painful decision was made in favor of the latter choice, and work on the big seaplane ground to a halt. In January 1922 the hull and some of the wing components were placed in storage, and the three nacelles completed by Gallaudet were shipped to the Naval Aircraft Factory for safekeeping.

Nineteen twenty-one was also the year of the Washington Naval Disarmament Conference. It dealt primarily with international limitations on numbers of surface combatant ships, but domestic support generated for the disarmament concept was a clear indication of the public attitude in the United States on military spending in general. Interestingly, the Washington Conference did not impose limitations on either aircraft or submarine strength. Perhaps the international conferees did not consider naval aviation well enough developed to be of any significant consequence. Submarines, on the other hand, got considerably more attention, and several proposals to place limitations on them were considered. The final draft of the treaty issued by the conferees prohibited their employment as "commerce destroyers," but this unrealistic document was never ratified by France, and consequently never became operative. The concept of the submarine as a weapon against shipping was thus implicitly sanctioned.

Ironically, it was to be the flying boat and other long-range patrol aircraft which would one day prove to be among the more effective countermeasures against the submarine.

In the postwar period, the F-5L, an American version of the British F-5 developed during the war, became the workhorse of U.S. naval aviation. A primary objective of the U.S. Navy in the early 1920s was to adapt the capabilities of this aircraft to the needs of the fleet. The F-5L had already proven itself to be a worthy replacement for the highly-regarded H-16 in many ways. In April 1919, an F-5L based at NAS Hampton Roads, Virginia, and flown by Lieutenant H. B. Grow, had established a world endurance record with a flight of twenty hours and nineteen minutes. During the last months of the war, F-5Ls performed scouting missions, laid smokescreens for fleet units, acted as gunnery spotters, and conducted bombing exercises and test drops of some of the first aerial torpedoes. In September 1922, an F-5L from NAS Hampton Roads became one of the world's first airborne ambulances, when it was instrumental in saving the life of a critically ill woman by airlifting her from Cape Hatteras, North Carolina, to a hospital in Norfolk, Virginia.

Several ships were converted into seaplane tenders to provide mobile bases for the flying boats; among these ships were the *Aroostook, Sandpiper, Wright,* and *Shawmut.* This latter ship, originally a minelayer, deployed to Guantanamo Bay, Cuba, with a squadron of H-16 flying boats in February 1919 to participate in fleet exercises. She is considered to be the U.S. Navy's first seaplane tender.

In December 1920, a group consisting of two NC flying boats under the command of John Towers, and twelve F-5Ls, took off from San Diego, California, under the overall command of Captain H. C. Mustin, with the objective of reaching the Panama Canal Zone. Both the NCs became casualties en route. The *NC-5* was badly damaged in the course of an open-sea landing and had to be sunk by naval gunfire from a destroyer. The *NC-6* was also damaged and later abandoned on the beach north of San Juan Del Sur, Nicaragua. The poor performance of these two aircraft was attributed to the fact that they, unlike their sister-aircraft *NC-1* through *-4* designed for the transatlantic effort, had only three engines. The remaining four aircraft built in the series, *NC-7* through *-10,* were also originally configured with only three engines, but later they were provided with a fourth. The F-5Ls completed the 3,200-mile trip in twenty days, with an actual flying time of less than fifty-two hours.

Upon reaching NAS Coco Solo in the Canal Zone, Mustin's group of twelve F-5Ls was joined by an Atlantic coast squadron from NAS Hampton Roads, commanded by Lieutenant Commander Harry Cecil. It consisted of nine F-5Ls and the *NC-10.* The *NC-7* had also started the trip with the group, but had been forced to drop out en route due to an engine failure. It was hoisted aboard the tender *Sandpiper,* only to later break loose and be lost in heavy seas. The *NC-8* and *-9* were delivered to Cecil's squadron when they returned to the United States.

Mustin's squadron of F-5Ls left Panama to return to the west coast of the United States on 23 February 1921, and arrived in San Diego on 10 March, after losing one aircraft along the way in an open sea landing. Cecil's squadron departed the same day and proceeded to Guantanamo Bay, Cuba, via Nicaragua, Honduras, and Mexico.

Never before had so large a flight of aircraft as Mustin's negotiated such a distance. Despite the loss of three aircraft, Mustin declared the venture a complete success, asserting that it had irrefutably demonstrated the ability of large numbers of seaplanes to operate with fleet units. The operation certainly established the durability of the F-5L type, and it is not surprising that further design improvements of the flying boat by the Navy during the next several years incorporated many of the basic design characteristics of this aircraft.

The New York Times, commenting editorially on the Panama flight, decried the prevailing attitude in Washington toward naval aviation. ". . . It is

The F-5L, here shown operating with fleet units at Guantanamo Bay, Cuba, became the workhorse of naval aviation. (U.S. Navy)

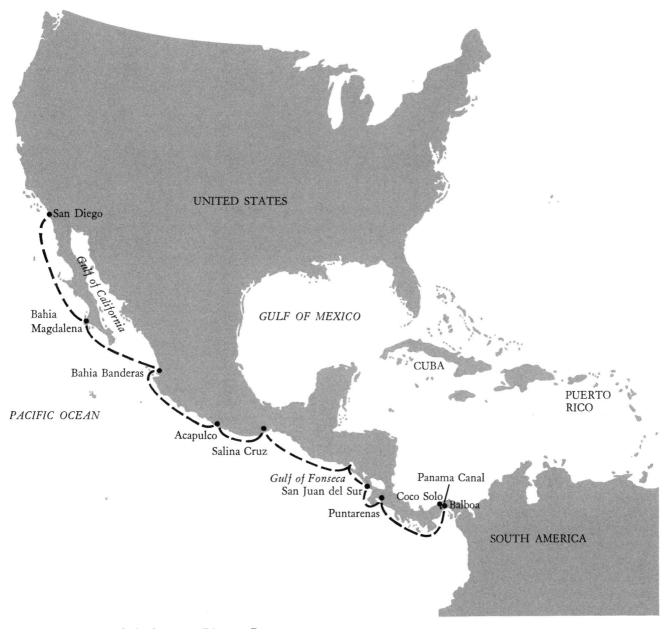

Track of the Mustin flight from San Diego to Panama, 1920–21.

like pulling teeth," the *Times* stated, "to get adequate appropriations from Congress for a service that in the opinion of reputable specialists should prove more effective in a sudden emergency of war than the battle-fleet itself." But Congress was unimpressed. Its members reflected the mood of the country in favor of isolationism, and against military spending. Congress was determined to have peace, and much of its membership felt that the best way to achieve that goal was to limit the means of making war.

Naval aviation was greatly affected by the austere funding program. The number of naval air stations dwindled to six, while the large numbers of surplus aircraft still on hand from World War I provided Congress with a ready excuse to keep appropriations for the development of new aircraft to a minimum. Even though both models were obsolete by 1920, HS-2Ls remained in service until 1926, and some H-16s were used until 1928. Only the F-5Ls provided the Navy with any real aviation capability during the early 1920s.

In the summer of 1921, F-5Ls participated in the controversial bombing exercises staged off the Virginia Capes, in which German warships acquired after World War I were used as targets to demonstrate the effectiveness of aircraft attacks on naval vessels. On 21 June F-5Ls destroyed the target submarine *U-117*, and the following month, they were employed along with Army aircraft in successful bombing demonstrations on the light cruiser *Frankfurt* and the battleship *Ostfriesland*.

It was during that same summer that the Bureau of Aeronautics was established under Rear Admiral William A. Moffett. He would be the new voice of naval aviation, speaking on the same level with other bureau chiefs. Moffett was aware, however, that he would have to temper his enthusiasm with caution and diplomacy, especially since a new "gag law" had gone into effect in 1921, prohibiting unsolicited requests for increases in appropriations. Those who disregarded this dictum risked dismissal. There were also internal problems resulting from the confrontation within the Navy between the proponents of naval aviation and the traditionalists, who saw the Navy only in terms of ships of the line. The issue had become a major source of interservice friction as well. Outspoken Brigadier General William "Billy" Mitchell fanned the flames of controversy with statements that challenged the existence of not only the Navy air arm, but also the Navy itself. Ironically, it was Mitchell's comments which caused the Navy to close ranks in opposition to his views. In all fairness it cannot be denied that it was he who brought the case for aviation before the American people in a most dramatic way.

Despite the scarcity of funds, the twenties were not without significant technological achievements in the field of aviation. Perhaps the most significant progress occurred in the area of engine design, a particularly remarkable development in view of the negative influence of thousands of surplus engines then available. Most of these surplus motors were Liberties, Curtiss OX-5s, and Hispano-Suizas, the latter being a European engine manufactured in quantity in the United States during World War I. But these were all fairly heavy water-cooled engines. The U.S. Navy needed a lighter alternative, capable of both powering carrier aircraft and providing longer range and better performance for its flying boats.

Charles L. Lawrance had experimented with a two-cylinder 28-horsepower air-cooled engine as early as 1916, but because of its low power output, it had little practical use. Later he produced a three-cylinder 60-horsepower engine, and, with considerable Navy encouragement, he developed this into a nine-cylinder, 200-horsepower radial, designated the J-1. In 1922, Lawrance's small organization merged with the Wright Aeronautical Corporation, and his engine with further improvements became known as the Wright Whirlwind. It represented a significant development in aircraft engines; a Whirlwind engine powered Lindbergh's *Spirit of St. Louis* across the Atlantic in 1927, and won the Collier Trophy for Lawrance that same year.

While the Whirlwind was being developed at the Wright Aeronautical Corporation, Fred B. Rentschler, then president of the company, and two of its more talented engineers, left the organization and joined the Pratt and Whitney Tool Company of Hartford, Connecticut. With Navy backing, they too developed a powerful air-cooled radial engine with a built-in supercharger, called the "Wasp." It developed 425 horsepower, and weighed less than 650 pounds.

The U.S. Navy placed substantial orders for both Whirlwind and Wasp engines, and by the late 1920s, the air-cooled radials were specified for virtually every new Navy aircraft. These engines and their descendants played important roles in both military and commercial aviation, from their initial development until the appearance of modern turboprop and jet engines years later.

There were other important technological developments in the early 1920s as well. In 1921, American metallurgists produced an aluminum alloy that was even better than that developed earlier by the Germans. At first most of this alloy made available to the U.S. Navy was used in dirigibles, but later it became a common material for the hulls of Navy flying boats. During the years 1923 and 1924, the metal propeller was first introduced. It later became standard equipment on all U.S. Navy aircraft. Tetraethyl leaded gasoline also appeared on the scene about this time, but it was not used to any appreciable degree because of its corrosive effects.

In 1922, the U.S. Navy adopted a new aircraft designation system, in which standard letters were used to indicate aircraft type and manufacturer, and numbers were suffixed to identify the model. Thus the F-5L became the PN-5, with P standing for patrol, N for Naval Aircraft Factory, and 5 for the fifth model. The F-6L with larger vertical stabilizers and balanced rudders was redesignated the PN-6.

An unusual flying boat developed during the early 1920s was the Tandem Fighter or TF. This aircraft was not a fighter-plane in the strict sense, but was instead a compact patrol aircraft, which, it was hoped, could successfully engage enemy aircraft in an aerial melee if necessary. The TF carried a crew of four, and was armed with three Lewis machine guns. Relatively little information is available on this aircraft. Only four were built by the Naval Aircraft Factory by 1923. The first three mounted 300-horsepower Hispano-Suiza engines, and the fourth utilized twin Packards. The hull looked much like a scaled-down NC-Boat, with the tail assembly being supported by a structure protruding from the aft end of the short hull. Unlike the NCs there were no longitudinal support-members running from the upper wing to the tail. The overall length of the TF was 44 feet 5 inches, and the wingspan was an even 60 feet. The maximum speed was 107 miles per hour. It had a gross weight of 8,846 pounds, and could remain aloft at cruising speeds up to nine hours under optimum conditions.

It was also in 1923 that, despite a limited budget, the U.S. Navy began work on a new generation of long-range flying boats to succeed the F-5Ls (PN-5s). A phased development program was undertaken by the Naval Aircraft Factory, and in the first phase two PN-7s were produced. In general appearance these aircraft were very similar to their predecessors. The wooden hulls were almost identical, but the wings, although still covered with fabric, utilized metal structural members which provided increased strength and permitted the use of fewer bracing struts between the upper and lower airfoils. The wings were also thicker, a design feature which provided greater lift with a reduction in wingspan. The PN-7s each mounted two 525-horsepower Wright T-2 liquid-cooled engines. The performance of these aircraft was in general satisfactory, and the PN-7 saw some service with the fleet. Still, there was much in the design of this aircraft which could be improved.

The next two flying boats in the PN series were originally intended to be PN-8s, each powered by two Wright T-2 engines. They were built with Duralumin hulls, thus eliminating the water-logging problem which had plagued

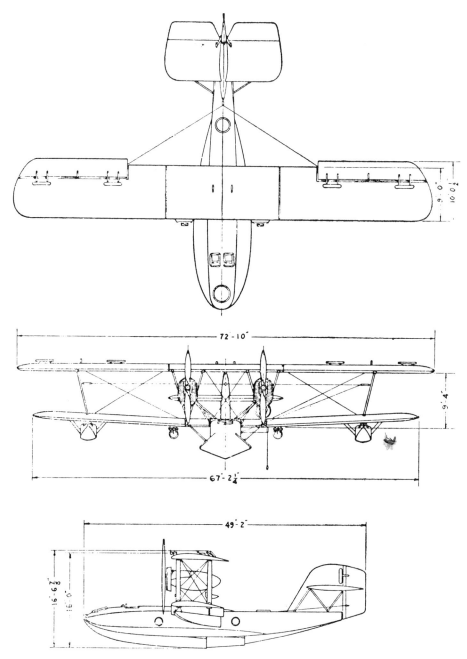

The PN-9, produced at the Naval Aircraft Factory.

water-based aircraft since the first practical seaplanes made their debut at Hammondsport. The aluminum alloy was also lighter and much stronger than wood, enhancing both fuel capacity and seaworthiness.

At about this time, however, the 475-horsepower Packard 1A-1500 engine became available, with a reduction gear ratio which turned the propeller at half the speed of the engine. This facilitated the use of large efficient propellers for long distance flights. One of the PN-8s was fitted with these Packard engines and designated the PN-9. On 1 and 2 May 1925 this aircraft, flown by Lieutenants C. H. "Dutch" Schildhauer and K. R. Kyle, set a world endurance record at Philadelphia, Pennsylvania, by remaining aloft for 28 hours, 35 minutes, and 27 seconds, without refueling. Impressive as this was, the Navy had an even more demanding test in store for the PN-9: a nonstop flight from California to Hawaii.

A flight of three aircraft, two PN-9s* and one PB-1, was to be led westward over the Pacific Ocean by Commander John Rodgers. A graduate of the U.S. Naval Academy, Class of 1903, the Navy had sent him to Dayton, Ohio, in March 1911 to learn the art of flying from Orville and Wilbur Wright. He soloed in the Wright B-1 airplane the following month, to become Naval Aviator Number 2. Now, fourteen years later, he was still leading the way, showing the doubters what naval aviation could accomplish.

William E. Boeing's PB-1 was designed especially to meet the U.S. Navy's requirements for an aircraft which could make grueling long-distance over-water flights. It was somewhat larger than the PN-9, with the lower hull constructed of metal and the upper part of wood. The wing spars and ribs were of tubular metal construction and covered with fabric. Two Packard 2A-2500 engines which developed 800 horsepower each were mounted in tandem, back to back on the center line of the aircraft, providing optimum single-engine performance in the air should one engine fail.† As Rodgers pointed out, however, in an article appearing in the 21 September issue of *The New York Times*, a disadvantage of the tandem configuration is that the pusher propeller in the rear operates in the wash of the tractor propeller in front, and is thus less efficient. Furthermore, the tandem arrangement on a twin-engine aircraft is less than ideal for maneuvering on the water. In contrast, an aircraft like the PN-9, with one engine on each side of the center line, had better water-handling characteristics, because differential power could be applied to effect a smaller turning radius.

On 26 August 1925 John Rodgers set out with the PN-9 *Number 1* and the PN-9 *Number 3* from NAS San Diego, California, for San Francisco, California, the starting point for the record flight.‡ At San Francisco the two PN-9s rendevouzed with the Boeing PB-1, which had been flown there from Seattle, Washington, under the command of Lieutenant Commander J. H. Strong. The flight to Hawaii had been scheduled for the twenty-eighth, but because the PB-1 was experiencing difficulties with the engine foundations, Rodgers rescheduled the flight for the thirty-first, hoping to begin with all three aircraft. Despite efforts to correct the problem, the PB-1 failed to attain an "up" status, and, requests for further delay by the PB-1's commander notwithstanding, the two heavily-laden PN-9s laboriously took off on the afternoon of 31 August 1925 and headed out over the Pacific, bound for Hawaii.

The crew of the PN-9 *Number 1* was as follows:

Commander John Rodgers, Aircraft Commander and Navigator
Lieutenant B. J. Connell, Pilot
Aviation Pilot S. R. Pope, Copilot
Chief Radioman O. G. Stantz
Aviation Machinists Mate First Class W. H. Bowlin

As with the flight of the Nancies across the Atlantic six years before, the Navy had stationed ships along the planned route, this time at 200-mile intervals. Neither of the aircraft carried radio-compasses, but they planned to obtain reciprocal bearings to the ships from the aircraft radio transmissions by the use of shipboard radio-direction-finding equipment.

---

*Naval Aircraft Factory records indicate that only one PN-9 was built. The other aircraft was the PN-8, which apparently had been fitted with Packard engines at some point, transforming it into a PN-9.

†In 1928, the PB-1 was fitted with two Pratt and Whitney GR-1690 Hornets of 475 horsepower each also mounted in tandem. The aircraft was redesignated PB-2 at that time. No additional aircraft of this type were ever produced.

‡The two PN-9s were labeled *Number 1* and *Number 3* because three aircraft were originally scheduled to take part. Lieutenant Commander J. H. Strong in the PB-1 was the next senior aircraft commander to Rodgers, and consequently his aircraft was *Number 2*.

The crew of the PN-9 that made the historic first flight to Hawaii in 1925. Left to right: Pope, Connell, Rodgers, Stantz, and Bowlin. (C. H. Schildhauer Collection)

PN-9 *Number 1* experienced difficulty getting airborne on the first try, and had to make a second takeoff run. PN-9 *Number 3*, however, took off on the initial attempt, and for a short while maintained a position about fifteen minutes ahead of the group commander in *Number 1*. At 5:30 P.M. it passed over the first station-ship, the destroyer *William Jones*, and headed for the next ship in line. Unfortunately, after proceeding about a hundred miles further, an oil-line rupture caused the PN-9 to make an emergency landing in the open sea. A few hours later the *Jones* rescued the crew and took the hapless PN-9 *Number 3* in tow.

PN-9 *Number 1* was having somewhat better luck and was proceeding on course. One matter of concern, however, was excessive fuel consumption, about six gallons per hour more than had been anticipated. To further complicate matters, the expected tailwind had not been encountered, and instead the winds remained calm throughout the night. Shortly after daybreak, radio contact was made with the aircraft carrier *Langley* at the 1,200-mile station. Winds at this point were still less than three knots, and Rodgers began to fear that he would have to land and refuel from one of the station-ships.

However, upon reaching the USS *Reno* about two and a half hours later, the aircraft began to be assisted by more favorable winds, and Rodgers estimated that he could make it to the *Aroostook* with some fuel to spare. This would put him a little more than 200 miles from Maui, Hawaii. The PN-9 would thus give a good accounting of its range, even if it could not make it all the way without making a fuel stop. As the day progressed, they passed USS *Farragut*, and soon radio contact was made with the *Aroostook*. Radio-bearings transmitted from the ship indicated that the PN-9 was to the south, while Rodgers' own computations placed him to the north of the ship. By that time the situation was becoming serious. All the fuel in the hull tanks had been consumed, and the gravity-feed tank in the upper wing would soon be empty as well. Rodgers decided that the radio-bearing lines of position from the ship were probably more accurate than his estimated position, and he therefore began to head the aircraft down the last bearing-line, with hopes of sighting the ship before the fuel was completely gone. Unfortunately, the bearings were in error, and the distance between the aircraft and the *Aroostook* was actually increasing.

Shortly after 4:00 P.M. on 1 September, the steady drone of the Packard engines ceased, to be replaced by a deafening silence. Lieutenant Connell pushed the nose over, and dead-sticked the big flying boat into the swells without mishap. Now there was nothing left to do but wait. Connell's skillful landing had left the airplane intact, and there was food aboard for two or three days. No one expected a wait of more than a few hours before they would be located by *Aroostook* or one of the other ships. Then they would refuel and be on their way.

But as the hours went by, no ships appeared. The batteries had enough voltage to power the radio receiver, but not enough to transmit. They could, therefore, listen to the ships conducting the search, but could not tell them where they were. Rodgers plotted the search area, and soon realized that the station ships had also been misdirected by the erroneous bearings, and were orienting the search to the south. Something had to be done.

Projecting the track of the drifting aircraft by dead-reckoning, Rodgers calculated that if he could direct the path of the aircraft with the rudder to even a few degrees off the wind-line, the combination of wind and current would set them very close to the island of Oahu, Hawaii. The crew cut the fabric off the lower wings and fashioned it into crude sails, which they hung between the upper and lower wings on each side of the hull. Then they steered their make-shift sailing vessel tail-end first as best they could toward a relatively small piece of land in a very large ocean.

The food ran out quickly, but man can survive for weeks without it. Potable water, on the other hand, was a more urgent problem. They rigged a catch-basin with part of the fabric from the wings, but they were not able to get very much rain the first few days. Their hopes were buoyed on the third day when a merchant ship passed within five miles of them, but the ship continued on without stopping. At one point, five submarines which had joined the search came to within thirty miles, but then they turned and went off on another leg of the search pattern. A few days later, they ran completely out of drinking water, and the effects of dehydration began to be felt. Relief came a day and a half later in the form of a hard rainstorm, which refreshed them and filled their makeshift fabric reservoir.

On the morning of 8 September they saw the profile of Oahu above the horizon, but it soon became apparent that their course would not allow them to come ashore there. On Connell's suggestion, they tore up the flooring and made leeboards, which they attached to the hull to reduce movement sideways to enable them to make headway towards Oahu. The leeboards provided con-siderably more control, but not much more movement toward the island. At that point Rodgers decided to change course for Kauai, Hawaii, further to the west. If they missed that, they would be swept westward past the Hawaiian chain into the vastness of the world's largest ocean. The crew of the PN-9 watched Oahu slip by, as they deliberated this sobering thought.

On the morning of 10 September Kauai was sighted dead ahead. The tired airmen now had another problem to contend with—how to get the aircraft to a safe anchorage without its being torn apart. Fortunately, about ten miles from Kauai, this concern was made moot when they were sighted by the submarine *R-4* commanded by Lieutenant Donald R. Osborne. After some discussion as to whether they would sail the rest of the way, they reluctantly agreed to accept a tow into Nawiliwili Harbor on the other side of the island. They had made it all the way.

The following day aboard the destroyer *Macdonough*, they steamed into Pearl Harbor, Hawaii, to a hero's welcome. They had officially broken a world record by flying 1,841 statute miles without refueling, and they had completed the journey by sailing the remaining 450 miles to Kauai. Moreover, the PN-9 had landed safely in the open sea, and survived without mishap for nine days. Except for the damage inflicted by the crew to the wings and the floor boards, the PN-9 *Number 1* was essentially intact, and in just over a week, was in the air again.

It had been a magnificent achievement, and the new airport at Honolulu, Hawaii, was named for John Rodgers in recognition of it. Perhaps more important to Rodgers, though, was his new assignment as Assistant Chief of the Bureau of Aeronautics. Naval aviation had come a long way since 1911, and now he would have an opportunity to have a direct influence on its future.

Unfortunately, a tragic accident was to result in Rodgers' untimely demise. In the early afternoon of 27 August 1926, a U.S. Navy aircraft was making its approach to the field at the Philadelphia Navy Yard. The pilot, Assistant Chief of the Bureau of Aeronautics Rogers, was coming to inspect two new PN-10s at the Naval Aircraft Factory. These were improved versions of his PN-9, and it is probable that Rogers had something more than a routine interest in their development. As the aircraft began its final approach to the field, observers were startled to see it suddenly fall into a spin, and plunge convulsively into the Delaware River. It took some time to extricate the badly injured Rodgers from the wrecked aircraft and rush him to the nearby Naval Hospital. At 5:02 P.M. that summer afternoon, almost one year after his record-breaking adventure, John Rodgers passed into history.

The two PN-10 aircraft began service in late 1926, and proved to be very satisfactory additions to the PN-family. In August 1927, Lieutenant B. J. Connell, veteran of the 1925 PN-9 adventure, used one to shatter several Class-C world seaplane records for distance covered, endurance, and load-carrying capacity.

The last of the PN-series were the PN-11s and PN-12s. Four twin-tailed PN-11 models were built, all longer with wider hulls and no sponsons. The XPN-11 was powered by two Pratt and Whitney R-1690 radial air-cooled Hornet engines of 525 horsepower each, while a second PN-11 mounted 500-horsepower Wright R-1750 geared radials. The final two PN-11s were ultimately fitted with Wright 1820-64 radial engines of 575 horsepower each, and redesignated XP4N-2s. One other twin-tailed model also mounting Wright R-1820s was designated the XP4N-1.

Two PN-10s already under construction in 1927 were completed with Wright R-1750 air-cooled radials, as PN-12s. They differed structurally from the earlier PNs in that, with the exception of the tail and control surfaces, they were built entirely of metal, including even the wings. Since at least one PN-12 was completed before the PN-11s, it was actually the first U.S. Navy flying boat to use the new air-cooled engines; one was fitted with Wright 1750-D Cyclones, while the other had Pratt and Whitney R-1850 Hornets. According to Commander W. W. Webster, then Chief Engineer at the Naval Aircraft Factory, the PN-12 had the latest flying boat design features. During May, June, and July of 1928, these aircraft set several Class-C seaplane records for payload, distance covered, speed, and endurance. The U.S. Navy had the airplane it wanted.

The record-setting performance of the PN-12s in the summer of 1928 fully justified the production contract for the model, which had been awarded to the Douglas Aircraft Company the previous December. Douglas built twenty-five of these aircraft, designated PD-1s. Unlike the PN-12s, the PD-1s had fabric-covered wings, probably because of the cost of metal ones. They were slightly

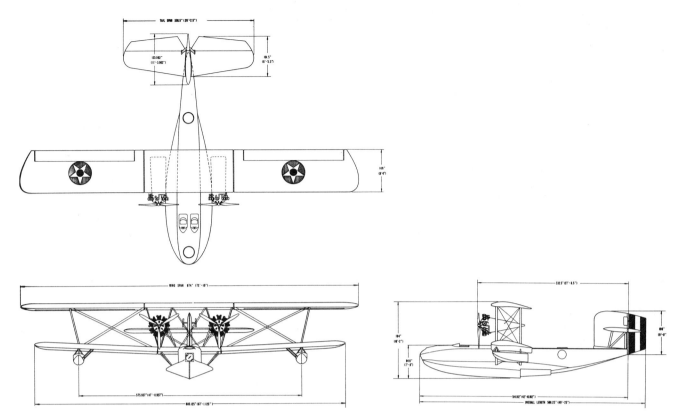

The Douglas PD-1. (McDonnell Douglas Corp.)

heavier and faster, and were powered by 525-horsepower R-1750 Wright Cyclone engines, which were replaced in 1934 by newer and more powerful R-1820 Cyclones. The PD-1s were welcome additions to the operating forces, since by that time the aging F-5Ls and H-16s were overdue for retirement. The first PD-1 was delivered to Patrol Squadron Seven (VP-7) on 6 June 1929. They were also used by VP-4, VP-6, and VP-10. These aircraft remained in operational service until 1936, when they were relegated to a training role at NAS Pensacola, in which capacity they served until final retirement in 1938.

In the spring of 1929, as the first PD-1s were being flight-tested at San Diego, California, before being delivered to VP-7, a second contract was awarded to the Glenn L. Martin Company for twenty-five of their version of the PN aircraft. The result was the PM-1, an aircraft very much like the PD-1 in most respects. Although the wingspan was identical to the PD-1 at 72 feet 10 inches, the total wing area was 74 square feet greater, which increased the payload by about 500 pounds, but decreased the speed by about 3 or 4 miles per hour. Later, the Navy awarded Martin an additional contract for five more PM-1s, bringing the total number built to thirty. Toward the latter part of 1929, the Keystone Aircraft Corporation was given a contract for eighteen PK-1s, and the following spring, Martin was awarded a contract for twenty-five PM-2s. The PK-1s and the PM-2s, both of which became operational in the spring and summer of 1931, were fitted with Wright R-1820-64 engines of 575 horsepower each. The distinguishing design characteristic of both these aircraft was their twin tail assembly, modeled on the original PN-11 type. The PK-1 was slightly faster than the PM-2, with a top speed of 120 miles per hour versus 116 in the case of the latter. Complete cowlings were featured on both aircraft.

A noteworthy but infrequently mentioned figure in the post World War I development of naval aircraft was Charles Ward Hall. His father, Charles Martin Hall, was vice president of the Aluminum Company of America, and he had developed the electrolytic process used to produce aluminum inexpen-

The Martin PM-1 in flight. (U.S. Navy)

The Keystone PK-1 with its twin fins, on a takeoff run. (U.S. Navy)

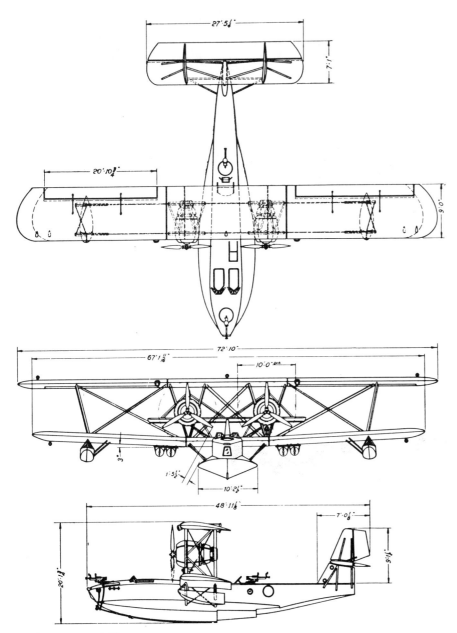

The Keystone PK-1.

sively. The younger Hall, quick to grasp the potential of the lightweight metal in aircraft construction, entered into an agreement with the U.S. Navy to fabricate aluminum wings for the HS-2L on a limited experimental basis. This endeavor produced a stronger and significantly lighter wing, which influenced Navy thinking toward future designs. Hall's first aircraft was a two-place biplane flying boat made entirely of aluminum, except for the upper wing. This aircraft, called the *Air Yacht*,* was powered by a three-cylinder, sixty-horsepower Wright engine, which could keep it airborne for about one hour at seventy-five miles per hour. The hull was covered with a light application of grease to prevent corrosion. Although never produced commercially, the *Air Yacht* provided Hall with the experience he needed to continue.

In December 1929, the Hall Aluminum Aircraft Corporation unveiled a second model which was based on the PN-series. This XPH-1 mounted two

*Hall's *Air Yacht* should not be confused with Grover Loening's aircraft of the same name, built in 1921–23.

The Hall aluminum PH-1 shortly after being launched. (U.S. Navy)

The Hall aluminum XP2H-1 set a nonstop flight record between Norfolk and Panama in 1935. (U.S. Navy)

535-horsepower Wright GR-1750 engines, and, like the PD's and PM-1s, it had a 72-foot 10-inch wingspan. A unique feature of the XPH-1 was its tapered hull, wide at the bottom and narrow at the top, without any sponsons. Following evaluation of the prototype, nine production aircraft were ordered by the U.S. Navy in June 1930, and Patrol Squadron Eight (VP-8) began receiving them as replacements for their PM-1s in July 1932. The production model, the PH-1, mounted two 620-horsepower Wright R-1820-86 engines, and had a completely enclosed cockpit. It boasted a top speed of 134 miles per hour, 10 miles per hour faster than the prototype, and was noteworthy particularly for its handling characteristics on the water. Its short takeoff capability and superior performance in rough sea conditions were of particular interest to the U.S. Coast Guard, which agency ordered five of the following model PH-2s in 1936, and seven PH-3s in 1938.

A little-known but no less impressive contribution of Charles Ward Hall was the XP2H-1, which was contracted for by the U.S. Navy on 30 June 1930. Powered by two sets of 600-horsepower Curtiss V-1570-54 Conqueror engines mounted back to back in tandem between the wings, the XP2H-1 with a wingspan of 112 feet was the Navy's largest flying boat in active service at the time.*

*The NCs had a greater wingspan (126 feet), but these had all been destroyed or retired from service by this time.

The Sikorsky XP-2S-1 on land. (Sikorsky Aircraft Corp.)

It could carry 3,360 gallons of fuel, and had a maximum range of 4,560 miles. For endurance purposes, either the two forward or two aft engines could be shut down in flight. The Navy took delivery of this aircraft in October 1932, and on 15 and 16 January 1935 it made a record nonstop flight from Norfolk, Virginia, to Panama in 25 hours and 15 minutes, piloted by Lieutenant John S. Thatch. The aircraft, the only one of its kind ever built, later sank during an open-sea landing attempt.

In 1928, the U.S. Navy began to acquire a few Sikorsky aircraft, which were adaptations of the popular Sikorsky S-38. In 1932, Sikorsky built the XP2S-1, a flying boat with conventional design very unlike other Sikorsky models of the day. Smaller than the PD/PK/PM aircraft, the XP2S-1 was powered by two Pratt and Whitney R-1340-88 engines of 450 horsepower each, mounted in tandem along the center line, which gave it a top speed of 124 miles per hour. Contrary to Sikorsky's expectations, the Navy did not award a contract for this model, and the XP2S-1 became a one of a kind aircraft. This company also produced the XSS-2 in 1933, a one of a kind amphibian aircraft designed for scouting with the fleet.

The PD, PM, PK, and PH types of aircraft, all inspired by the PN-series, served the Navy well during the 1930s. But in the increasingly fast-moving world of aircraft design, these flying boats were obsolete even before they became operational. Looking into the future, U.S. Navy planners had begun as early as 1927 to conceptualize a new generation of flying boats. Their thinking was prompted in large measure by a desire to establish air links with U.S. holdings in Hawaii, the Canal Zone, Alaska, Guam, and the Philippines. What they wanted was a large flying boat with a 100-foot wingspan, a monoplane designed to make optimum use of the powerful new air-cooled radials that were becoming available, and capable of a 2,000-mile range. They began searching for a company that could produce such an aircraft.

CHAPTER SIX

Coming of Age

Reuben Fleet was a man who knew what he was about. Forceful and outspoken, he must be counted as one of the more successful of the early aviation entrepreneurs. Unlike many innovators who tried to make a profit with the airplane, Fleet was a businessman well acquainted with the economic realities of aircraft manufacture long before he sold his first airplane. He was a pragmatist and a fierce competitor, in an age when competition took its deadly toll of marginal operators and dreamers. In some ways Reuben Fleet was a dreamer too, but his unshakable belief in the future of American aviation was based on a keen understanding of its enormous potential for both military and commercial exploitation. A U.S. Army aviator during World War I, he later served as the First Officer-in-Charge of the U.S. Airmail, then as Business Manager at McCook Field in Dayton, Ohio, and finally as Contracting Officer for the Army Air Service. With this valuable experience and numerous contacts in the aviation industry, he left the Army, and with $25,000 cash, formed the Consolidated Aircraft Corporation at East Greenwich, Rhode Island, on 29 May 1923. Major Fleet, as he was known for the rest of his life, quickly established himself as a respected and responsible member of the aviation business community, and a leading manufacturer of training aircraft for both the U.S. Army and the U.S. Navy.

In 1927, Fleet hired aircraft designer Isaac M. (Mac) Laddon, a civilian employee of the Army Air Service Engineering Division, whom he had known at McCook Field. Laddon's specialty was large multi-engine aircraft, and his credentials included experience in flying boat design. This addition to the engineering staff was fortuitous, because Fleet had decided to enter the competition to design the U.S. Navy's new long-range flying boat that would become the replacement aircraft for those then in service.

The Navy had formulated the general specifications, with Captain Dick Richardson providing the basic hull design. But it was left to Laddon to draw up the detailed plans, and to solve a myriad of problems to meet the Navy's stringent requirements.

On 28 February 1928, the Consolidated Aircraft Corporation, then located in the old Curtiss factory at Buffalo, New York, was awarded a $150,000 contract to build the prototype. The result was an aircraft whose progeny would play a significant role in the early development of U.S. overseas airlines, and whose military line would culminate in the PBY Catalina of World War II fame. For Consolidated this was a move into large-scale operations, which would eventually give that company world leadership in flying boat production.

The new aircraft was dubbed the *Admiral*, in honor of Rear Admiral William A. Moffet, then Chief of the Bureau of Aeronautics. Designated the XPY-1, the *Admiral* was a monoplane, and therefore represented a significant departure from traditional Navy design philosophy. Construction began in March 1928 and progressed rapidly, despite the necessity of developing new techniques for working the newly-available aluminum sheet to form the long, sleek Richardson-designed hull. The big flying boat was powered by two Pratt and Whitney R-1340-38 Wasp engines of 450 horsepower each. A third engine

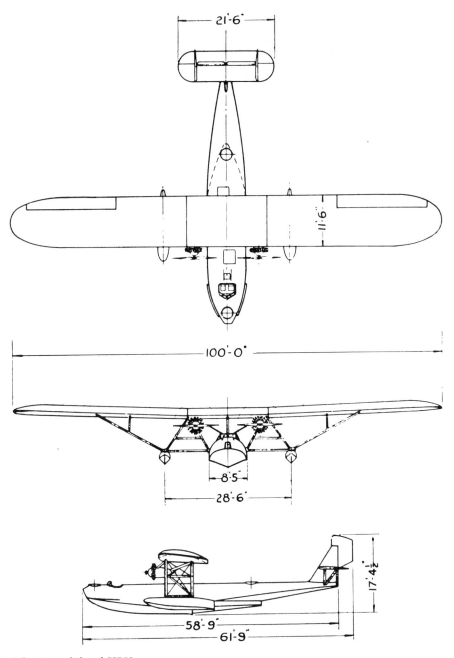

The Consolidated XPY-1.

was also installed over the wing in an attempt to increase speed, but this innovation was unsuccessful, and the engine was removed. The large parasol wing had a metal frame with fabric covering and a span of 100 feet, in accordance with Navy requirements. It had a single-step hull, and was balanced on the water by two pontoons slung under the wing outboard of the metal hull on long struts, one on each side. The XPY-1 cruised at 110 miles per hour, had a service ceiling of over 15,000 feet, and a maximum range of 2,620 miles. By the end of the year the aircraft was ready for flight. Unfortunately, the winter season interposed a natural obstacle to testing, rendering both Lake Erie and the Niagara River icebound.

Reuben Fleet was not disposed to wait until spring to fly his company's new creation, so he loaded it in sections aboard railroad flatcars and shipped it to Washington, D.C. There it was reassembled at the naval air station on the Anacostia River, where it was again made ready for flight on 10 January 1929.

The XPY-1 Admiral was a monoplane, representing a radical departure from traditional Navy design philosophy. (U.S. Navy)

The first of a series of test flights took place on that day, with Lieutenant A. W. Gorton at the controls. Later, on the 22nd of that month, Lt. W. G. Tomlinson made a demonstration flight, with Assistant Secretary of the Navy for Air Edward P. Warner and Captain Dick Richardson aboard. Their satisfaction was evident; the aircraft was clearly a success.

The next event lends an ironical twist, but illustrates one of the more frustrating hazards which can befall an aviation manufacturer. Consolidated had incurred a half million dollar loss on the development of the XPY-1, but had done so willingly in anticipation of the handsome profit which would be reaped when the aircraft went into production. The Navy, always searching for ways to trim its costs, surprised Consolidated by putting the production contract up for bid. The Glenn L. Martin Company, which had no developmental costs to cover, underbid the unhappy Consolidated firm, and was granted the production award for nine P3M-1s on 29 June 1929. To add insult to injury, Martin was also awarded a contract at about the same time to develop a new prototype to be designated the XP2M-1.

The P3M-1s were very much like the XPY-1. Many of the engineering drawings had to be derived from the specifications or taken from the aircraft itself, since Consolidated was neither obliged nor disposed to turn over its drawings to Martin. Only three P3M-1s were built, and the first of these was not test flown until February 1931. The remaining six aircraft of that contract were built as P3M-2s, with the Pratt and Whitney R-1340 engines being replaced with Pratt and Whitney R-1690-32s of 525 horsepower each. The P3M-2s also featured enclosed cockpits, which helped to reduce pilot fatigue. They were used operationally for a short time by Patrol Squadron Ten (VP-10) in 1931 and 1932, and were then relegated to a training role at Annapolis, Maryland.

The Martin XP2M-1 prototype, featuring some interesting changes, made its debut in June 1931. The hull incorporated external longitudinal stiffeners, which gave the aircraft a pinstripe appearance. The wing was built somewhat closer to the fuselage, with two 575-horsepower Wright R-1820-64 engines set into the leading edge for greater streamlining. A third engine was mounted over the wing as had been tried with the XPY-1, with essentially the same result. This engine too was finally removed, and the aircraft was redesignated the XP2M-2. Only one XP2M model was ever built. The three-engine version of the aircraft had a top speed of 143 miles per hour, which was reduced to 128 with the removal of one engine.

Consolidated, in the meantime, had not wasted time brooding over its setback. Considerable foresight and shrewd planning had gone into the design

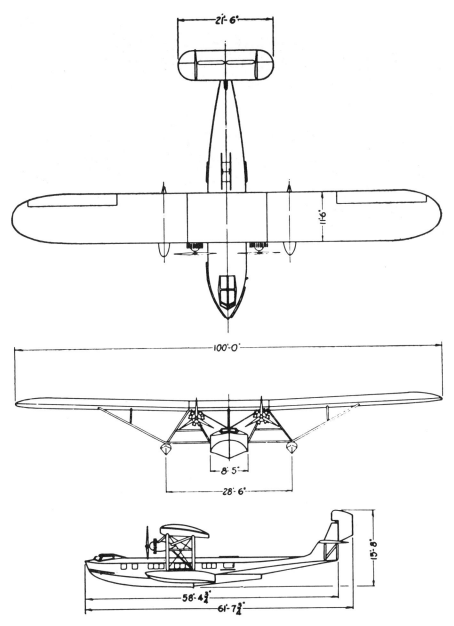

The Consolidated Commodore.

NYRBA contracted to buy fourteen Consolidated Commodores. (Smithsonian Institution)

The Consolidated XP2Y-1, originally built and flown as a three-engine aircraft. (General Dynamics)

of the XPY-1, and it had been purposely built with an intent to offer it for commercial as well as military use. Even before Martin had won the Navy's production contract, Fleet was buttonholing potential buyers and extolling the virtues of the commercial version, which was called the Commodore. In January 1929, he carried his idea to fruition, when he joined with James H. Rand Jr. of the Remington Rand Corporation and former Army Captain Ralph O'Neill, a World War I ace, to form an airline to operate between North and South America. He then sold fourteen of his Commodore flying boats to the new company, known as the New York, Rio and Buenos Aires Line (NYRBA). By this bold stroke, Fleet recovered his half million dollar loss, and ultimately realized a $280,000 profit.

Consolidated had not given up on the Navy, however, and Fleet immediately began work on new ideas for an improved Navy flying boat using the XPY-1 as the base design. On 26 May 1931 Consolidated was awarded the developmental contract for the XP2Y-1, and shortly thereafter, on 7 July, it was granted a production contract for twenty-three of these aircraft.

The new Navy flying boat, called the Ranger, was a sesquiplane, so named because, in addition to the 100-foot parasol wing, it had a smaller lower wing of slightly less than half that span attached directly to the fuselage. This mini-wing provided extra lift as well as support for the two stabilizing floats. Two 575-horsepower R-1820-E Wright Cyclone engines compensated for any speed loss which may have been caused by the added resistance of the lower wing.

The XP2Y-1 was originally built and flown as a three-engine airplane, with the third engine mounted on the centerline above the wing, as had been the case with the XPY-1 and the XP2M-1. Again, added fuel consumption and maintenance troubles outweighed any advantage in increased speed, and the third engine idea was abandoned permanently. The twin-engine version of the XP2Y-1 had a top speed of 126 miles per hour.

The first flight took place from the Niagara River on 26 March 1932, despite a problem with floating ice which continued to plague the testing operations of the Consolidated Aircraft Corporation. This difficulty notwithstanding, the XP2Y-1 was delivered in Washington, D.C., on 18 April 1932.

The twenty-three production P2Y-1s were built as twin-engine aircraft, the first of which was delivered to VP-10 at Norfolk, Virginia, on 1 February 1933. By the summer of that year, all aircraft authorized by the contract had been completed.

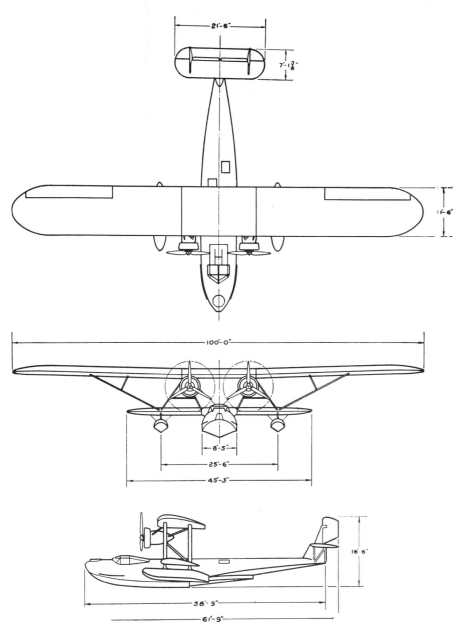

The Consolidated P2Y-1.

On 7 September 1933 a contingent of officers and men from Patrol Squadron Five (VP-5) took off from Norfolk, Virginia, in six newly-acquired P2Y-1s, bound for Coco Solo in the Panama Canal Zone. Lieutenant Commander Donald M. Carpenter led the group south. One aircraft, *5-P-12*, developed fuel-line problems along the way, and was obliged to put into Miami, Florida, for minor repairs. This accomplished, *5-P-12* was soon back in the air, trailing its squadron mates by only about 150 miles. Except for some uncooperative weather, no other problems were encountered en route, and the five-plane formation arrived in Coco Solo 25 hours and 19 minutes after their Norfolk departure. The *5-P-12* arrived approximately an hour later to make the endeavor a complete success. This nonstop mass flight of 2,059 miles (1,788 nm) established a new world flying boat record, exceeding the mark set by General Italo Balbo and his twelve Savoia Marchetti flying boats in 1931.

But this was to be only the preliminary event for these new aircraft in which everyone seemed to have so much confidence. They would soon have a

The personnel of VP-10, commanded by Lcdr. Soc McGinnis (fourth officer from left), at Coco Solo on 6 October 1933, the day prior to their departure for San Diego. (U.S. Navy)

chance to prove themselves further, for the Navy was already planning a more stringent challenge. VP-10, then based at Coco Solo, had been flying the first batch of P2Y-1s that Consolidated had delivered at the beginning of the year. That squadron was now directed to trade these for six of the latest P2Y-1s, which had recently been flown down from Norfolk by a second contingent of VP-5. Patrol Squadron Ten was about to be home-based in Hawaii, and they were going to fly there in their new aircraft. This would mark the end of the era in which patrol planes had to be crated and loaded aboard ship for such a journey.

It had been eight years since John Rodgers had made his historic near-miss flight to Hawaii in the PN-9. While aircraft had improved considerably, there were still the uncertainties of weather and the absence of navigation aids to cope with. Long-distance overwater mass flights like the one contemplated were hardly an everyday occurrence. This one would add significantly to the role of naval aviation, at a time when the United States was assuming an increasingly more active role in the Pacific theater.

Having made the exchange of aircraft, VP-10 departed Coco Solo on 7 October 1933 for San Diego, California, via Acapulco, Mexico, under the command of Lieutenant Commander Knefler "Soc" McGinnis. At Acapulco, one aircraft was unable to take off, because of the combined effect of its heavy load and the fact that several inches of the propeller tips had been ground off to eliminate ragged ends and restore balance. This aircraft was hoisted aboard the seaplane tender *Wright* for the remainder of the trip to San Diego, once again demonstrating the value of these vessels to seaplane operations. The other aircraft flew to their destination without incident.

As a result of the takeoff problem at Acapulco, a so-called "blow off" procedure was initiated to assist heavily laden aircraft to get up onto their step. This was a useful technique which could be utilized when there was little wind, and the water was calm and glassy. To execute a "blow off," a second flying boat was employed to conduct a high-speed taxi run in front of the departing aircraft. This not only created some wind, but it also served to break up the slick surface of the water, thus reducing suction. It appears to have been helpful, and was used on numerous occasions.

Soc McGinnis and his P2Y-1 arrive over Hawaii. (U.S. Navy)

The six planes of VP-10 remained in San Diego three months for overhaul and fine-tuning. Then on 9 January 1934, they flew to San Francisco, California, and anchored for the night in Paradise Cove, just north of the city.

The long jump across the eastern Pacific began the following day, with favorable weather conditions predicted. As with other long overwater ventures, ships were stationed along the route, this time at 300-mile intervals. Even though this was to be the longest mass flight ever attempted, Navy officials insisted that it was merely a routine transfer of aircraft. The *New York Herald Tribune*, commenting on the event two days later, noted "A virtual absence of fear for the safety of the men participating." This comment notwithstanding, there was definitely not a lack of public interest in the flight. It was simply that by 1934 aviation was coming of age, with airplanes no longer considered contraptions for the foolhardy. The public was becoming accustomed to the rapid pace of aviation progress, and skepticism was giving way to confidence in the reliability of aircraft and the cool competence of the men who flew them.

Perhaps the greatest problem encountered on this particular flight occurred during departure. The first aircraft, *10-P-4*, under the command of Lieutenant T. D. Guinn, broke free of the water at 12:04 P.M. Pacific Standard Time, and was followed into the air at 12:43 by *10-P-1* flown by Lieutenant Commander McGinnis. Commander Marc Mitscher, who had piloted *NC-1* in the 1919 transatlantic attempt, was aboard *10-P-2* as an observer and pilot. While the first two aircraft had become airborne with relatively little difficulty, the remaining four experienced problems. The heavy fuel loads, coupled with light winds and a calm sea, made takeoff troublesome, and it was almost two hours before the last plane laboriously struggled into the air to join the others circling overhead. It was 2:22 P.M. by the time all had joined up and headed out over the new Golden Gate Bridge then under construction.

At 5:52 that evening the flight passed over the USS *Sandpiper*, the first station-ship located 300 miles off the coast, and at 2:20 the next morning they over-flew USS *Breese* at the halfway point. The planes maintained formation throughout the trip, flying at altitudes which varied from 500 to 5,000 feet due to cloud conditions en route. Average speed was 98.4 miles per hour. The *10-P-5*, flown by Lieutenant J. Perry, became separated from the formation briefly on two occasions due to poor visibility, but joined up again both times with little difficulty. Twenty-four hours after departing San Francisco, the six planes of VP-10 flew over Diamond Head, Oahu, Hawaii, and made a pass at an altitude of 1,000 feet over the city of Honolulu, to the delight of waving people in the streets below. As ships in the harbor blasted out a welcome on their whistles, the planes commenced their approach to Pearl Harbor, passing over John Rodgers Municipal Airport prior to landing. The *10-P-1* touched down at 12:29 P.M., and the last of the six was on the water by 12:37.

Some fifteen hundred people greeted the tired crews, whose voices were broadcast by commercial radio on the mainland coast-to-coast. McGinnis expressed pleasure with the squadron's accomplishment. "It was a tough trip over," he said, "with low clouds and fog in our path from seven o'clock last night until early morning. But it was no worse than night-flying we have experienced off the coast of Mexico and around San Diego." One crew member commenting on the flight said, "[he] would be willing to turn around and fly back again." Another felt differently and remarked, "All I want to do is go home—or somebody's home—and sleep." Admiral Ernest J. King sent them the following message: "The Chief and Officers of the Bureau of Aeronautics heartily congratulate Commander VP Squadron 10 and his officers and men on the successful and workmanlike accomplishment of the nonstop flight from San Francisco to Honolulu, which is the longest formation nonstop flight in the history of aviation." President Roosevelt wired McGinnis, "Heartiest congratulations to you and all associated with you in preparing for and successful completion of the greatest undertaking of its kind in the history of aviation, the formation flight from San Francisco to Honolulu, Hawaii, a magnificent accomplishment." Major Reuben Fleet saw in the flight a portent of the future. "The flight of the Navy's VP boats," he said, "offers ample proof that we are not far from transoceanic air transport commercially. I believe that such airlines to Europe will be in use within two years." Ironically, a Japanese Navy spokesman had this to say: "It shows," he said, "what increased powers this development has placed at the disposition of mankind. It remains to be seen whether these powers will be used beneficently or destructively."*

These were good years for the flying boats. The Navy continued to develop their utility and effectiveness in fleet exercises at Guantanamo Bay, Cuba, and gradually expanded the scope of their operations in both the Caribbean and the Pacific. In 1933, thirty flying boats from Pearl Harbor, Hawaii, made their first deployment to French Frigate Shoal, a desolate reef situated about 780 miles west-northwest of Oahu, in a chain of small islets and reefs leading to Midway Island. Then in the summer of 1934, twelve PM-1s made the Navy's first mass flight to Alaska, where they encountered some of the worst flying conditions they had yet experienced. Three squadrons from Coco Solo operated from tenders throughout the Caribbean during the first two months of 1935, and in April of that same year, VP-7 and VP-9 made their second assault on Alaska, this time operating as far west as Dutch Harbor in the Aleutians. Some wondered about the usefulness of these deployments to such remote regions, but in a few years the Navy's judgment on this matter would be fully vindicated. In

*All quotations from the *New York Times*, 12 and 13 January 1934, p. 4 and 3, respectively.

A PM-1 of VP-9 in flight over Resurrection Bay, Alaska, in May 1935. (U.S. Navy)

May 1935, the Pearl Harbor squadrons deployed to Midway Island, this time extending their patrol and reconnaissance capabilities across the central Pacific in the direction of Japan. Seven years later, flying boats would operate from Midway under much different circumstances in a fleet support role, which would greatly influence the survival or elimination of the U.S. Navy in the Pacific.

Nineteen thirty-six began with a thirty-one plane flight from Coco Solo to the Galapagos Islands, 1,200 miles southwest of Panama. There the squadrons conducted bombing practice, and investigated the feasibility of establishing a seaplane base from which aircraft could operate to provide early warning of the approach of an enemy task force signifying an impending attack on the Panama Canal.

During these years, the mission of the flying boats, particularly in the Pacific, became more clearly defined. They were to extend the U.S. defense perimeter far out to sea, away from U.S. coasts and island possessions, and to provide support to the fleet by seeking out enemy naval forces hundreds of miles distant.

But much remained to be accomplished. Even in the early 1930s, the expansionist tendencies of Japan were being viewed with concern by many in the Navy. In 1931 the Japanese had occupied Manchuria, adding that piece of Chinese real estate to Korea, Formosa, and several other Pacific islands already under their control. By the end of 1934, Japan had abrogated the Washington Treaty of 1922 and the subsequent agreements of 1930, the terms of which specified that Japan should maintain an inferior position to the United States and Great Britain in numbers of major combatants in the ratio of 5:5:3. There-

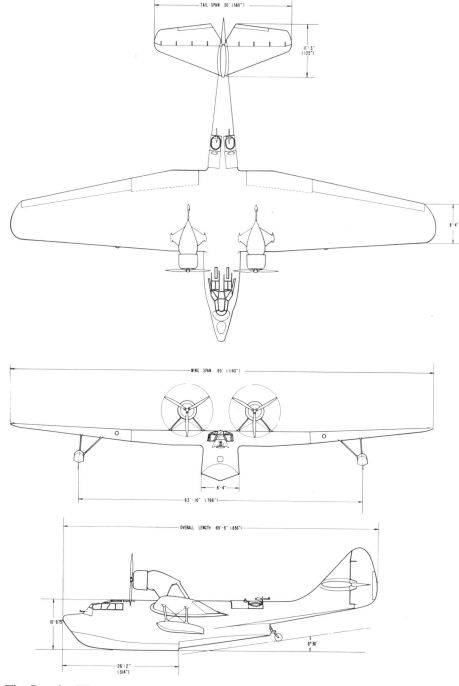

The Douglas XP3D-1. (McDonnell Douglas Corp.)

after she initiated a major ship-building program, having as its goal the creation of a Japanese Navy that would be second to none in the Pacific theater. The rumblings were ominous.

Much of the progress of U.S. naval aviation in these years of development and maturation can be credited to Rear Admiral Moffett. His untimely death aboard the ill-fated airship *Akron* in April 1933 was a tragic loss, but he left his successor an impressive legacy. The old *Langley* had given birth to a new kind of naval aviation, and at the time of Moffett's death, the carriers *Lexington*, *Saratoga*, and *Ranger* were already in commission. The flying boats had also fared well under Moffett. In the spring of 1933 the aircraft inventory of Commander Aircraft, Base Force was as follows:

The Consolidated P2Y-3 had engine nacelles faired into the leading edge of the wing. (U.S. Navy)

VP-1   Twelve Keystone PK-1s
VP-2   Nine Martin PM-2s
VP-3   Twelve Douglas P2D-1s (Float seaplanes)
VP-4   Twelve Douglas PD-1s
VP-5   Eight Consolidated P2Y-1s
VP-6   Six Douglas PD-1s
VP-7   Six Martin PM-1s
VP-8   Six Hall Aluminum PH-1s
VP-9   Six Martin PM-1s
VP-10   Six Consolidated P2Y-1s
VJ-1   Three Martin PM-2s
VJ-2   Two Martin PM-2s

Rear Admiral Ernest J. King became the new Chief of the Bureau of Aeronautics on 3 May 1933. King was determined that the momentum established by Moffett would not be allowed to dissipate. He was convinced of the value of patrol aviation to any Pacific war, and set about acquiring for the Navy the most advanced, long range monoplane flying boat which could be designed using contemporary technology. On 28 October 1933 a prototype XP3Y-1 was ordered from the Consolidated company, with hopes that Reuben Fleet could produce another successful breakthrough like that represented by the earlier P2Y. In the meantime, Donald Douglas and his company had been working under Navy contract to design a similar aircraft, the XP3D-1, which showed excellent potential. On 11 February 1934 the Navy also ordered a prototype of the Douglas version, thereby setting the two aircraft manufacturers in competition for the production contract.

Meanwhile, the last aircraft produced under the Navy's P2Y-1 contract with Consolidated was modified by the substitution of R-1820-88 Wright Cyclone engines, which were raised and faired into the leading edge of the upper wing as with the Martin XP2M. The result of this change was an approximate 10 miles per hour increase in airspeed, a 432-gallon increase in fuel capacity, and more than a 900-mile increase in maximum range. The modification proved so successful that on 27 December 1933 the Navy awarded a contract to Consolidated for twenty-three more of these aircraft, to be designated P2Y-3s. These were all delivered in the first half of 1935. Consolidated also produced a conversion kit, which enabled VP-5 and VP-10 to modify their P2Y-1s to the P2Y-2

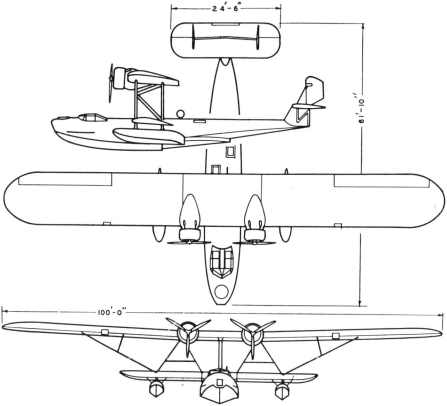

The Consolidated P2Y-3.

configuration. Six P2Y aircraft were sold to Argentina, one to Colombia, and another to Japan. Altogether, forty-eight P2Ys were built for the U.S. Navy. These were some of the most reliable aircraft ever procured; they continued to give satisfactory performance throughout their service, which lasted into the early 1940s.

The new Consolidated and Douglas prototypes made their appearances in early 1935. Douglas was first with the XP3D-1, which made its initial flight on 6 February 1935. This was a mid-wing aircraft with two Pratt and Whitney Wasp R-1830-58 engines of 825 horsepower each, mounted above the wing. The aircraft hull was metal, as was most of the wing. It had a top speed of 161 miles per hour, and a maximum range of over 3,500 miles. A similar amphibian version with 930-horsepower R-1820-45 Wright Cyclone engines had been built for the Army and designated the YOA-5. The only one of these built was delivered in 1934.

The Consolidated entry, designated the XP3Y-1, was completed at Buffalo, New York, shortly after the Douglas aircraft was presented, and it was transported to Norfolk, Virginia, by railroad as was customary for Consolidated flying boats in the winter season. There it was assembled and flown by test pilot Bill Wheatley on 21 March 1935. The XP3Y-1 design clearly showed its P2Y lineage, but it was significantly different in several ways. Gone was the profusion of struts and wires. A single metal parasol wing spanning 104 feet was cantilevered above the hull on a pylon-like structure, braced on each side by two sturdy struts running diagonally from the midsection of the hull. Gone too was the twin tail assembly of the P2Y, with its external bracing. Electrically activated retractable floats provided an additional streamline feature, becoming wing-tips after takeoff. An important weight reduction was obtained by sealing off sections of the wing as fuel cells, thus saving the weight of separate fuel tanks. Other innovations included a thermal deicing system which directed hot exhaust gases from the engines to the leading edges of the wing.

The Consolidated model P2Y-3 was one of the most reliable aircraft ever procured for the U.S. Navy. (John Ficklen)

While the Consolidated entry was undergoing evaluation by the U.S. Navy at Norfolk, the Douglas contender was being put through its paces at Santa Monica, California. Both aircraft performed to full expectations, and were similar in most aspects of performance. The final decision, as it turned out, was based primarily on cost. Douglas offered the XP3D-1 for $110,000 each, while Consolidated priced the XP3Y-1 at $95,000, a figure which was later pared down to $90,000 per aircraft.

The production contract was awarded to Consolidated on 29 June 1935, for sixty P3Y-1s. Meanwhile, Reuben Fleet had decided to move his entire operation to a more hospitable climate. He chose San Diego, California, which city had offered an attractive site at Lindbergh Field, together with a new seaplane ramp nearby. Throughout August and September the Consolidated Aircraft Corporation, with over 400 employees and their families and about 150 freight cars, moved across the United States to their new home. Lawrence D. Bell, Vice President and Sales Manager, stayed behind and formed the Bell Aircraft Corporation.

On 9 October Lieutenant Commander "Soc" McGinnis took off in the XP3Y-1 from NAS Norfolk, bound for Coco Solo, Panama Canal Zone, arriving the next day. On the fourteenth he left Coco Solo and flew nonstop to San Francisco, covering 3,281 statute miles in 34 hours and 45 minutes, establishing yet another new world seaplane record. Commenting on the flight, Admiral King said, "This has been a year of notable accomplishments by all wings of the aircraft squadrons, but by far the most striking feat is Lieutenant Commander Knefler McGinnis' flight in the XP3Y-1. . . ." On 20 October this aircraft was placed on display at San Diego for the dedication of the new Consolidated plant.

Reuben Fleet wasted no time getting production started. He had contracts totaling about nine million dollars to complete, the most important of which was the Navy's order for sixty new flying boats. He began his new operation with over 800 employees, and within six months had increased that number to 2,000. Mac Laddon, the creative genius behind Consolidated's successful line of flying boats, became one of three new vice presidents of the company, and, with Fleet continuing as the driving force, the organization began large-scale operations.

The XP3Y-1, despite its triumphs, went back into the shop for modification. During takeoff attempts at Coco Solo on 14 October for the record-breaking flight to San Francisco, the tail assembly had tended to sink into the water under full power, because of the heavy fuel load. This caused the pilot to lose directional control, and inevitably resulted in an aborted takeoff run. McGinnis was finally obliged to take off with less than the designed maximum amount of fuel, and so was forced to terminate at San Francisco rather than Seattle, Washington, as originally planned. This idiosyncrasy was eliminated by extending the hull all the way back beneath the rudder, and by redesigning the rudder itself. New Pratt and Whitney R-1830-64 engines were installed, which delivered 900 horsepower for takeoff and 850 horsepower at 8,000 feet, and provided the aircraft with a top speed of 184 miles per hour. Maximum weight was 25,276 pounds with 1,750 gallons of fuel, which gave the aircraft a maximum range of over 4,000 miles without bombs or torpedoes. The modified XP3Y-1 had a rotating nose turret equipped with a 30-caliber machine gun, which was removed and stowed when not in use. As in the original version, there was also one 30-caliber gun for each of the two waist positions, and another for an opening in the rear accessed by a tunnel, just aft of the second step. Later, 50-caliber machine guns would be used at the waist positions with adapters. The aircraft was capable of carrying a maximum external ordnance load of four 1,000-pound bombs, or two 1,435-pound torpedoes. By May 1936 it was in the air again, after having received the new patrol bomber designation, XPBY-1. The modifications were also incorporated into the sixty production aircraft still

The Consolidated XPBY-1 over San Diego. (General Dynamics)

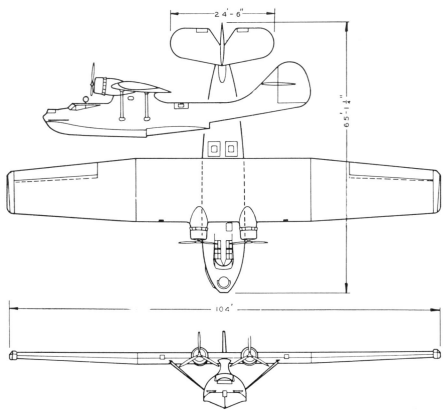

The Consolidated PBY-1.

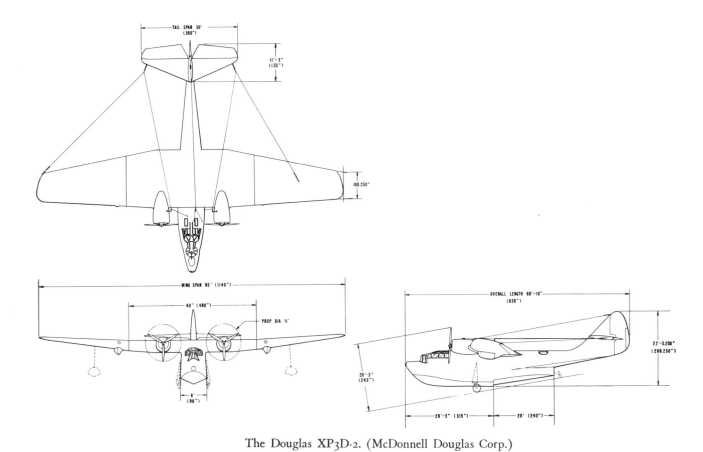

The Douglas XP3D-2. (McDonnell Douglas Corp.)

under construction, and their designation was similarly changed to PBY-1. These were the first of what was to become one of the U.S. Navy's best-known aircraft.

It was fortunate for Consolidated that the modification effort was made, because the Douglas contender also reappeared that same month as the XP3D-2. This aircraft had also undergone significant improvements, with the wing raised to rest on top of the fuselage, and the engines lowered and faired into the leading edge. It too boasted the new Pratt and Whitney R-1830-64 engines, and a top speed of 183 miles per hour at 8,000 feet. Its maximum weight was 27,946 pounds, but its fuel load and consequently its maximum range were both slightly less than the XPBY-1. Like its competitor it featured a bow turret, and had hydraulically-operated floats which recessed into the underside of the wing when retracted. Still, the Consolidated model appears to have retained the advantage, because two months later, on 25 July 1936, the Navy awarded an additional contract to Fleet's organization for fifty follow-on PBY-2s. Douglas used the experience gained from the XP3D to design a transport flying boat known as the DF-151, which was unveiled in 1936. This aircraft had Wright Cyclone R-1820-G2 engines which developed 1,000 horsepower on takeoff, and 850 horsepower at 5,800 feet. It carried approximately thirty passengers, and had a cruising speed of 164 miles per hour (maximum speed was 178). Two of these were sold to Japan and two to the Soviet Union.

During King's tenure, the Vinson-Trammel Treaty Navy Bill was signed into law. This legislation authorized the building of ships which would bring the U.S. Navy's strength up to the limits allowed by the naval treaties of 1922 and 1930. Even more significant for naval aviation, it authorized procurement of aircraft in numbers commensurate with the new ship strength. Under King, a tentative program was developed to bring aviation strength up to 1,910 air-

The Douglas DF-151 at its mooring. It was a twin-engine transport flying boat. (McDonnell Douglas Corp.)

craft by 1940 to 1942. During 1935, President Roosevelt made almost thirteen million dollars available to the Navy under the Emergency Appropriations Act to purchase aircraft under the new law. More than two million dollars of this money was used to expand the facilities of the Naval Aircraft Factory at Philadelphia, so that at least ten percent of the new planes could be produced by the Navy itself. In addition, funds allocated by the National Industrial Recovery Administration and Public Works Administration were used to upgrade naval air stations.

The procurement of increased numbers of aircraft caused a manpower problem, with not enough regular U.S. Navy officers available for flight training. Admiral King eliminated this shortage with the Aviation Cadet Training Program, which, after authorization by Congress and the President in July 1935, began training pilots who, upon earning their wings, were commissioned as officers of the Naval Reserve on active duty.

King completed his tour as Chief of the Bureau of Aeronautics in June 1936, and relieved Admiral F. J. Horne as Commander Aircraft, Base Force. This post gave him an opportunity to become directly involved with the operations of the flying boats under his command. Like his predecessors, he deemed it important for his squadrons to receive maximum operational training in areas and under conditions in which they might have to operate in time of war.

Ernest J. King had a reputation for being a demanding taskmaster, and if there were any lingering doubts, they were quickly dispelled. Upon assuming command, he announced that he would deploy to Alaska the following month in his flagship USS *Wright* with Patrol Squadrons Seven, Nine, and Twelve. Several smaller tenders accompanied the force, and were stationed at intervals along the way. At Sitka, Alaska, a base was established at an abandoned Navy coaling station, and from there the squadrons fanned out with supporting tenders. One was dispatched to survey the Alaskan Peninsula as far west as Dutch Harbor, while another was sent to operate between Kodiak Island and Seward, Alaska. The third squadron stayed on at Sitka to explore the coastal areas to the north and south, as well as the nooks and crannies of the Chatham Strait. All three found the weather unpredictable and treacherous, but by such deployments the store of knowledge on Alaskan flying boat operations was slowly accumulating, and a nucleus of experienced personnel was being trained for the future.

The first production PBY-1 was accepted in September 1936, and delivered to the newly-formed Patrol Squadron Eleven on 5 October. A few days later, King left for Hawaii to operate with the Pearl Harbor squadrons, and to investigate basing possibilities in the central Pacific. Thirty-one PK, PH, and P2Y aircraft from Patrol Squadrons One, Four, Eight, and Ten participated, along with the tenders *Wright*, *Swan*, *Avocet*, and *Pelican*. They departed Hawaii and proceeded first to French Frigate Shoal. One squadron remained there in an attempt to recover an aircraft which had broken loose in high winds, and sank in the lagoon in thirty or more feet of water (the aircraft was never recovered). The remaining squadrons were dispatched with supporting tenders to reconnoiter several small islands, to determine if they were suitable for seaplane operations. Most of these locations were found to be inhospitable, because of menacing coral formations and lack of deep channels by which the tenders might navigate through the reefs that surrounded the lagoons. Johnston Island, located approximately 700 miles southwest of French Frigate Shoal, was of particular interest to King, as were Palmyra and Baker Islands even farther to the South. These, he hoped, might provide base sites from which the flying boats could project the U.S. warning perimeter in the direction of the Marshall Islands then held by Japan under a League of Nations mandate. Investigating aircraft reported that neither Baker nor Palmyra were suitable prospects.* In the case of Johnston, however, King had sent an advance party there by ship some time before, with a quantity of dynamite, to blast an opening through the reef and to ensure that the lagoon was cleared of coral heads. As a result, tenders and aircraft were able to operate from Johnston with little difficulty. King and his squadrons remained in the central Pacific for about three weeks, before returning to Pearl Harbor.

On 27 November 1936 the Navy placed a third order with the Consolidated Aircraft Corporation for sixty-six PBY-3s with the newer, more powerful Pratt and Whitney R-1830-66 engines. VP-6, in the meantime, began to receive PBY-1s, and the skipper, Lieutenant Commander William H. McDade, put his pilots and crews through a rigorous training program in anticipation of deployment. By January 1937 they had taken delivery on all their new aircraft and were ready for assignment. On 28 January the squadron took off from San Diego Bay, rendezvoused over Point Loma, California, and headed west on the first direct flight from North Island to Pearl Harbor. No longer was it deemed necessary to go via San Francisco to gain the small mileage advantage for the trip across the ocean. The twelve planes comprising the squadron covered the distance of 2,553 miles without incident in 21 hours and 43 minutes. During that same month two new patrol squadrons, VP-16 and VP-17, were formed with six PM-1s each, and based in Seattle, Washington, at a new naval air station there.

On 2 February 1937 King embarked on board the USS *Wright* and set out for the Caribbean for exercises in the Virgin Islands. After traveling as far as Acapulco aboard *Wright*, he intended to proceed ahead of the ship in the Douglas XP3D-2, which he had selected as his flag aircraft. Because the harbor of this Mexican port is small and surrounded by hills, the pilot was obliged to taxi out into the open ocean to obtain the necessary room for takeoff. There he encoun-

---

*This survey notwithstanding, Palmyra Island was used as a seaplane base in World War II.

King's flag plane, the Douglas XP3D-2, in 1936 before its demise. (McDonnell Douglas Corp.)

tered heavy swells, and as he increased power for the takeoff run, the right float separated from the aircraft's wing. The XP3D-2 did a flat cartwheel, split open, and sank in deep water. Fortunately no one was injured, but the plane which had given the PBY such tough competition was lost.

The Virgin Islands exercise was eminently successful, with squadrons participating from the east and west coasts of the United States and Coco Solo. Part of the time was spent working with U.S. submarines, simulating attacks and developing hold-down tactics. There were as yet no sophisticated sensors, but the human eye was found to be reasonably effective in spotting periscopes and even the submerged submarines themselves running at shallow depths in the clear Caribbean waters. Even then, it was generally understood that the real value of the aircraft as an antisubmarine countermeasure was not necessarily in making a kill, but rather in preventing the submarine from getting in position to attack friendly shipping, or in causing her to break off an attack for fear of being depth-bombed by the aircraft.

With the exercise completed, the squadrons headed home. Those proceeding to Coco Solo were engaged on arrival in a prearranged simulated attack by Army fighters based in the Panama Canal Zone. King was going to be certain that his pilots and crews were ready for any eventuality.

In April, the flying boats participated in Fleet Problem XVIII in the central Pacific, and on the twelfth and thirteenth, the twelve PBY-1s of VP-11, under Lieutenant Commander L. A. Pope, made the flight from San Diego to Pearl Harbor in 21 hours and 25 minutes. The *New York Times* remarked that the flights were now considered so routine that the Navy had not even bothered to make an official announcement of the squadron's safe arrival. By May VP-11 had received the first of the PBY-2s, and the following month, all sixty aircraft on the original PBY-1 contract had been delivered to Patrol Squadrons Three, Six, Eight, Eleven, and Twelve. It was also in June that VP-3, under Lieutenant Robert W. Morse, set a new mass-flight distance record, flying its PBY-1s 3,085 miles nonstop from San Diego to Coco Solo in 27 hours and 58 minutes.

On 1 July 1937 Patrol Squadrons Seven, Nine, and Twelve left San Diego and flew north to join Admiral King, who was waiting at Seattle aboard his new flagship USS *Langley* (AV-3), now designated a seaplane tender. Once

A VP-11 Consolidated PBY-2. (U.S. Navy)

again the flying boats headed north to Alaska, and again, because of the high probability of bad weather en route, ships were stationed along the way to provide RDF fixes. VP-7 proceeded directly to Kodiak Island, and upon arrival, found the weather so bad that a landing in the harbor was impossible. A small tender previously assigned there was requested to put to sea and take station about ten miles out, to provide radio-fix positions from which the pilots could descend through the fog and fly into port underneath the weather. The fog proved to be so thick and close to the surface that after descending, some of the pilots elected to land in the open sea and taxi into the harbor. At Sitka the weather was not much better, and *Langley*, which had left Seattle on the tenth and arrived at Sitka on the thirteenth, gave similar radio assistance. This deployment lasted three weeks, during which time the flight crews continued to familiarize themselves with the geography and to work out ways to cope with the harsh Alaskan environment.

A reorganization of the U.S. Navy's air arm took place on 1 October 1937, resulting in the flying boat squadrons and their tenders being distributed among five patrol wings under Commander Aircraft Squadrons, Scouting Force, with Admiral King assuming that title. The implication of this move was that patrol aviation was now recognized as a working branch of the U.S. Fleet.

Rear Admiral King relinquished command of the flying boats in December to become Commander Aircraft, Battle Force, and to receive a third star for a job well done. Much had been accomplished since he had become involved with the big seaplanes in 1933, and his direction was in evidence everywhere. He had influenced everything, including procurement, basing, mission development, and doctrine, and he had worked his pilots and crews hard under all imaginable conditions. It would return much in the form of performance and confidence born only of experience. At the time of his departure, there were over 150 operational flying boats. Long-distance flights which would have been thought foolhardy only a few years before, were now being made by large groups of aircraft as a matter of routine. As if to emphasize the point, fourteen new PBY-2s made the flight from San Diego to Coco Solo on 8 December 1937, under the command of Lieutenant Commander B. E. Grow, cutting the transit time to 22 hours and 20 minutes.

CHAPTER SEVEN

The Great Clippers

Advocates of commercial aviation had been predicting since before World War I that scheduled airlines would soon be established, and that international and transoceanic flights would follow shortly thereafter. Indeed, there were several hardy pioneers who labored mightily to make that prediction a reality. But even the energy and enthusiasm of men like Uppercu, and the wealth and dedication of others like Wanamaker, were not enough to make commercial aviation a going concern. For the most part, people still believed that flying was inherently dangerous, and that aviators were possessed of overactive adrenal glands and underactive thought processes. There was no escaping the fact that in the early days of aviation, there was an element of risk involved. The press did nothing to allay public apprehension, and as a result of journalistic hyperbole, the most routine flights were too often characterized as colorful struggles against death in the clouds.

There were other reasons why flying as a mode of commercial transportation was not readily accepted in the United States. A major one was simply that it was not reliable. Travelers, especially businessmen, could not afford to be held up for hours and sometimes days as a result of weather or mechanical difficulties. Further, aircraft passenger accommodations were cramped, noisy, and uncomfortable, and the amount of baggage a passenger could bring with him was severely restricted. In contrast, the U.S. railway system was the finest in the world, and for the average traveler, a much more practical alternative.

But while commercial aviation in the United States remained virtually dormant during most of the 1920s, Europe was making steady progress. The French were particularly quick to recognize the special advantages of the airplane, and several small airlines were formed to link French colonial holdings and to expand French influence into other areas, including South America. Some of these early air services were later brought together to form Air France, one of the giants of international air transport. The Dutch were not far behind with Royal Dutch Airlines (KLM), and Great Britain eventually followed suit with Imperial Airways. All these airlines were subsidized by their governments, which partly accounts for their ability to survive and develop.

The Germans too were active. Several airlines, ostensibly South American but financed by German capital and operated by German nationals with dual citizenship, appeared in Brazil, Bolivia, Colombia, and Peru. They exercised increasing influence in South American affairs, both commercial and political. Sociedad Colombo-Alemana de Transportes Aeros (SCADTA), the national airline of Colombia, headed by Dr. Peter Paul von Bauer, was particularly aggressive, and had plans to expand its Dornier Wal flying boat service throughout the Caribbean and into the United States. This was viewed with concern by some Americans, and particularly by the U.S. Navy, which saw all such developments in that area in terms of potential threats to the Panama Canal.

In the late 1920s, two Americans came upon the scene to give the Europeans some competition in international commercial aviation. Both were competent aviators, and both were obsessed with the dream of building a great American overseas airline. Their names were Juan T. Trippe and Ralph A. O'Neill. It was inevitable that they would eventually come into fierce competition with each other.

Juan Trippe was born into a prominent family whose ancestry went far back into colonial America. His father presided over the firm of Trippe and Company, members of the New York Stock Exchange. Juan Trippe's early development was normal for a young man of his social class. He attended private schools, and later went on to Yale University. In December 1917, he left Yale to enlist in the U.S. Navy as a Seaman Second Class for training in the Naval Reserve Flying Corps. On 17 June 1918 he was commissioned an Ensign at Pensacola, and became Naval Aviator Number 1806. By that time, however, World War I was in its final stages, and after serving for a time at the Rockaway Naval Air Station, he left the Navy and returned to Yale to complete his education. While he did not distinguish himself as a scholar, he was active in sports, and became a member of some of the more exclusive campus social organizations. But like so many other young men, his experience in naval aviation had changed the course of his life. An idea was forming in his imaginative mind. He founded the Yale Flying Club, and participated in one of the first intercollegiate air meets at what would later be called Mitchell Field, New York. Writing for the May 1919 issue of *The Yale Graphic*, he speculated on the success of the impending flight of the NC boats, and asserted that if they were successful they would not only be the first across, ". . . but also the first to demonstrate that a flight across the Atlantic Ocean is a perfectly sane commercial proposition. . . ," a contention which he would prove twenty years later.

After graduating from Yale in 1922, he put his interest in aviation aside, and went to work for the New York banking firm of Lee, Higginson and Company, but soon tired of that pursuit. In 1923 he organized Long Island Airways with a modest number of flying boats, purchased from Navy surplus at $500 each. He ran sightseeing flights from Long Island beaches and charter flights up and down the coast, but could not seem to make a steady profit. By 1925, Long Island Airways had gone the way of so many others of that period. Yet, this disheartening experience only seemed to sharpen his interest.

Trippe now turned to his wealthy friends from the Yale Flying Club, John A. Hambleton and Cornelius Vanderbilt "Sonny" Whitney. Together they formed Eastern Air Transport, but before this company got started, its backers decided to merge with a New England organization called Colonial Airways, to form Colonial Air Transport. This new company, with an assist from the Kelly Air Mail Act of 1925, began operations in December of that year. Trippe was finally tasting success. But his impatience to expand led to a rift between Trippe and his supporters on one hand, and the other stockholders of Colonial on the other. The Trippe group sold their holdings, and formed the Aviation Corporation of America on 2 June 1927. At this point the group was enlarged to include W. Averill Harriman, William A. Rockefeller, William H. Vanderbilt and other individuals of similar status and influence. As a result of negotiations with Cuba's President Machado, Trippe was granted an exclusive permit to fly into Havana. He then joined forces with Atlantic Gulf and Caribbean Airways Incorporated and Pan American Airways Incorporated to form the Aviation Corporation of the Americas (AVCO). Pan American had a contract to fly airmail to Cuba, but Trippe held the landing rights on that island. AVCO became the holding company, and Pan American Airways Incorporated became the operating branch of the organization.

The aircraft used by Pan American for its early flights between Florida and Cuba were land-based Fokker trimotor airplanes. But as the company began its expansion throughout the Caribbean and into South America, flying boats became the preferred aircraft because of their special attributes. There were few suitable airfields in the cities served by Pan American, but plenty of rivers, harbors, and quiet lagoons ideally suited to the flying boat. Moreover, airports cost money, not only for the large amount of land involved, but also for con-

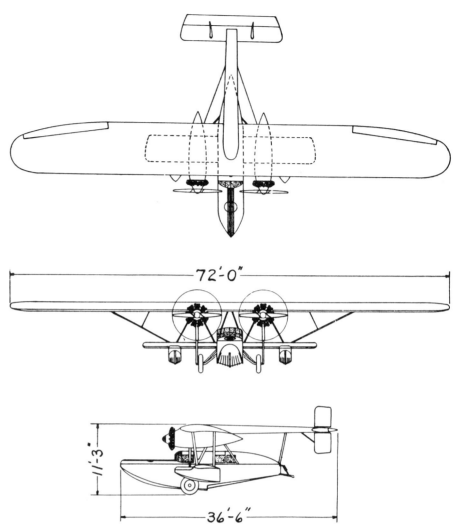

72'-0"

11'-3"

36'-6"

The Sikorsky S-36

struction of runways and airport facilities. Suitable sites close enough to the cities were usually either nonexistent or prohibitively expensive. On the other hand, it was a relatively simple matter to buy or lease modest waterfront facilities, which often permitted passengers to disembark in downtown areas. Moreover, the flying boat was considered much safer, and gave hesitant passengers an extra measure of confidence. A forced landing in the jungle by a land-based airplane was likely to be fatal, whereas an unscheduled stop in a sheltered cove by a flying boat was apt to be no more than an inconvenience. As Pan American's Chief Engineer, Andre Priester, astutely observed, "A seaplane carries its own airport on its bottom."

Pan American acquired its first flying boat, an S-36 amphibian, from Igor Sikorsky on 7 December 1927. The Russian genius had fled to France as a result of the Russian revolution, and eventually emigrated to the United States, where in 1923 he founded the Sikorsky Aero Engineering Corporation. In 1926, this company produced a twin-engine open-cockpit flying boat designated the S-34. This aircraft had a short life, and was wrecked while landing during a test flight. But it gave rise to an improved version, the S-36 sesquiplane amphibian, which carried eight persons including the pilot, and performed reasonably well. It was in fact the first American-built amphibian of significance designed for commercial use. Although it was somewhat underpowered with two Wright Whirlwind J5 engines of 220 horsepower each, five were built, with one going to Pan American. Meanwhile, Sikorsky was hard at work developing the follow-on S-38.

The Kelly Foreign Air Mail Act of 8 March 1928 provided a sizable subsidy, which was a boon to Juan Trippe's plans for expansion. Pan American bid on and won Foreign Air Mail Routes (F.A.M.) Numbers 5 and 6. F.A.M. Number 5 ran from Key West, Florida, across to Cuba, thence to the Yucatan Peninsula, and south to the Panama Canal Zone. F.A.M. Number 6 also started at Key West and crossed to Cuba, then it ran eastward to Haiti and Puerto Rico, then south to Trinidad. The Postmaster General came under criticism for favoring Pan American in awarding these and other routes, but the Kelly Foreign Air Mail Act permitted such discrimination on the basis of ability to "satisfactorily perform the services required to the best advantage of the government." The Postmaster General was determined to establish an American carrier that could successfully compete with the growing European airlines. He was known to believe that a single airline would best serve this purpose, and Pan American was to be the "chosen instrument."

Moving into Central America, Trippe expanded his operation down the western coast of South America, persuading, cajoling, compromising, and buying out competitors, and forming new companies to mask his developing air empire where political expediency made such ploys necessary. By the summer of 1929, Pan American had penetrated all the way to Santiago, Chile. But now a new obstacle confronted Trippe, in the form of a rival U.S. company known as the New York, Rio, and Buenos Aires (NYRBA) Line Incorporated, headed by Ralph O'Neill.

NYRBA was a formidable opponent. It had the backing of influential men such as James H. Rand of Remington-Rand, Lewis Pierson of Irving Trust, and William B. Mayo of the Ford Motor Company. Reuben Fleet was also a principal stockholder, providing NYRBA with Consolidated Commodore Aircraft, probably the finest commercial flying boat of its day. O'Neill, the president and driving force behind this venture, like Juan Trippe, had set his sights on the creation and development of a great American flag airline.

O'Neill was well known in aviation circles, having established his reputation as a fighter pilot in World War I and one of America's first aces. Returning to civilian life after the war, he found to his disappointment that there was little interest in commercial aviation. Somewhat reluctantly he took a job as an engineer for a firm which required him to travel extensively throughout Mexico and Central America. But aviation lured him like an irresistible magnet, so that by 1920 he was back in its pursuit, organizing an air force for the government of Mexico. He spent about five years in this capacity, during which time he expanded his experience and his contacts in the aviation business. Then in early 1928, he became the exclusive sales representative of the Boeing Airplane Company in South America. He also had contracts to represent Pratt and Whitney and the Hamilton Propeller Company. O'Neill was ideally suited for this role. He was a competent aviator, as well as an engineer. Furthermore, he had an outgoing personality, considerable experience in dealing with Latin Americans, and spoke their language fluently. But O'Neill had more in mind than peddling airplanes, engines, and propellers. His real goal was the establishment of an airline between North and South America, and during his travels throughout the vast southern continent, he spent considerable time promoting his idea and gathering information for the time when it would become a reality. Like Trippe, he had concluded that large flying boats would be best suited for the job. In contrast, however, he believed that the most profitable route would run down the east coast of South America, ultimately linking the major population centers from New York City to Buenos Aires, Argentina. By July 1928 O'Neill was back in New York City, armed with extensive data to support his proposals to potential investors. For additional persuasion, he produced airmail contracts from the governments of Argentina and Brazil.

NYRBA was born in the summer of 1929, and made rapid progress. The Commodore aircraft were not quite ready for service, but O'Neill, aware that time was a critical factor, decided to make the first survey flights with an interim flying boat which might later be used for feeder line operations. He settled on the Sikorsky S-38 sesquiplane amphibian.

The S-38 was clearly not designed with an eye toward aesthetics. Its fuselage had a long banana-shaped nose, and the blunt aft end looked as though the hard-pressed Sikorsky firm had run out of materials. It had a high upper wing with a span of 71 feet 8 inches, from which protruded a twin boom structure much like that used on the Nancy boats. This was supported toward the tail by struts anchored to a single point on the aft end of the cut-off hull. There was also a 36-foot 1-inch lower wing, which provided additional lift and support for two stabilizing wing floats. Two 410-horsepower Pratt and Whitney Wasp engines were slung under the upper wing on struts. With two pilots and eight or nine passengers, it had a range of about 600 miles at 103 miles per hour cruising speed.*

While the S-38 could hardly be called a beautiful airplane, it was well engineered, and extremely functional. Its immediate success probably saved the struggling Sikorsky organization from extinction; it was so popular that the Russian engineer was swamped with orders. Accordingly, he was obliged to inform Ralph O'Neill that S-38 aircraft could not possibly be made available to NYRBA for a proposed survey flight in June or July. O'Neill had run up against a major obstacle, but not for long. Contacting Admiral Moffett, who had suggested the S-38 to him, O'Neill asked that the Navy defer taking delivery on its order of S-38s so that NYRBA might have the first production model. Admiral Moffett, who seems to have taken an interest in NYRBA and the indefatigable O'Neill, was agreeable to the delay. On 11 June 1929 O'Neill began the survey flight south in NYRBA's first S-38, the *Washington*. The competition was joined.

NYRBA began its scheduled operations on 21 August 1929 between Buenos Aires and Montevideo, Mexico, and the following month, initiated the first regular air service over the Andes mountains from Buenos Aires to Santiago. These latter flights were made with the venerable trimotor Fords, while the former made excellent use of the S-38s. But back in the United States, the Commodore flying boats were now nearing completion. On 3 October the first Consolidated Commodore Model 16 was christened *Buenos Aires* at NAS Anacostia, Washington, D.C., by Mrs. Herbert Hoover. On 18 February 1930 it would initiate the first weekly scheduled direct flights from Miami, Florida, to Santiago, Chile.

The Commodore, like the PY-1 Admiral, was a parasol-winged monoplane, and in 1929, it was the ultimate in luxury among the commercial flying boats. There were two passenger compartments forward, each designed to seat up to eight passengers, and either two three-passenger compartments or one four-passenger compartment aft. All were tastefully decorated in pastel shades. The floors were carpeted, and the seats were upholstered. The exterior color combination was particularly striking, with coral wings and a cream fuselage. The underside of the hull was black.

The second Commodore to come off the Consolidated production line was flown to the seaplane base at Port Washington, New York, in early November, where it was disassembled and trucked to Madison Square Garden for a huge air show, which featured the latest and best that the aircraft industry could produce. On 10 November, the opening day of the show, Mrs. Jimmy Walker, wife of the colorful mayor of New York City, christened the big aircraft *Rio de Janeiro*, with a bottle of bootleg champagne. The Commodore was easily

*See Chapter 11 of this book for a further discussion and illustrations of the S-38 and its follow-on models.

Consolidated Commodore Airliners being built for NYRBA. (General Dynamics)

The interior of the Commodore, the latest word in passenger luxury in 1929. (Smithsonian Institution)

the largest and most impressive airplane of the show, and the crowds lined up for a chance to walk through the spectacular machine.

Ultimately, a total of fourteen of these aircraft were built. The *Buenos Aires* had an open cockpit as in the military version, but this was later enclosed, as were the cockpits of all subsequent Commodores, for greater pilot comfort and reduction of fatigue. The first three to come off the production line were designated Model 16, which had designed accommodations for eighteen passengers and a crew of three, made up of two pilots and a radio operator doubling as a steward. In actuality, the number of passengers which could be carried was determined by the cargo and fuel load. For example, a Commodore flying boat with 450 gallons of fuel could accommodate eighteen passengers and about 500 pounds of cargo, including baggage. With a full fuel load of 650 gallons, however, the number of passengers was limited to ten, plus approximately 600 pounds of cargo. In this configuration the Commodore had a maximum range of 1,000 miles, cruising at 108 miles per hour.

Nine of these aircraft were built as Model 16-1s, which had seating arrangements for as many as twenty-five persons. The *Buenos Aires* was also later converted to a 16-1, for a total of ten. Two were built as Model 16-2s, with a seating capacity of up to thirty-three. The limiting factor for all three models, however, remained gross weight (17,600 pounds), and additional passengers translated into less fuel or cargo and more frequent refueling stops along the way. All fourteen Commodore aircraft mounted two 575-horsepower Pratt and Whitney engines with three-bladed propellers.

NYRBA hired ex-Navy pilots almost exclusively, because of their extensive experience with flying boats. Admiral Moffett had apparently furnished O'Neill with a list of former Navy aviators who might be interested in pursuing a career in commercial aviation. This was a natural source of flying boat pilots in the early days for both NYRBA and Pan American. They were the dedicated professionals who made U.S. air operations in South America possible, and who would later use even bigger flying boats to establish commercial air routes across the oceans of the world.

Airlines need passenger terminals and logistics facilities as well. NYRBA first used the famous Dinner Key facility in Miami as a departure point for Commodore aircraft flying to the Caribbean and South America. Later, this installation, known as the "gateway between the Americas," would become a familiar landmark to north and southbound travelers flying in the great Pan American Clippers. To provide essential services along the route to Buenos Aires, NYRBA turned barges into floating bases, some of which, like one in Havana, Cuba, were quite elaborate. For the most part, however, these strategically placed way-stations were relatively inexpensive to build and maintain, and were an important factor in eventually making the long-range flying boat operation economically feasible. But it was the Consolidated Commodore itself which transformed the idea into a workable concept. Not only did the big flying boat have the necessary carrying capacity and range to make air travel a credible alternative to surface transportation, but it cut New York City to Buenos Aires transit time from twenty days to seven or eight. Furthermore, the Commodore proved to be a reliable and safe machine, which imparted a sense of well-being as well as elegance to its passengers. Mr. Forrest Wilson, in the August 1933 issue of *Cosmopolitan* magazine, said of the Commodore:

> It is pulled by twin Pratt and Whitney Hornet engines whirling three-bladed propellers and developing 575 horsepower each. More than once, if you go on this voyage, you will feel and exult in the might of these eleven hundred and fifty horses dragging you upward out of some tight position for takeoff. It is mechanical, the whole thing—though surely it was a happy coincidence that from the engineering calculations of streamlines emerged a hull as low and long and rakish as that of this flying boat. A fit craft in which to fly the ancient Spanish Main!

The NYRBA *Havana* in flight over the Statue of Liberty. (General Dynamics)

All this is not to suggest that the Commodore fleet was free from mechanical malfunction or mishap. On the contrary, on one early trip down the coast of South America, a fuel line ruptured in flight and caught on fire. The pilot, Captain Robin McGlohn, landed and taxied the burning aircraft up onto a river bank, so the passengers could make a hasty exit through a rear hatch. The fire was extinguished and the aircraft saved. On another occasion, the structural soundness of the Commodore was amply demonstrated, when Captain Herman E. Sewell was obliged to land one with eighteen passengers aboard in a field of Cuban sugar cane. The big flying boat came down smoothly among the cane stalks and slid neatly to a stop, as though it belonged there. No one was injured, and the aircraft was virtually undamaged. It was disassembled, trucked out, quickly repaired, and was soon in the air again.

These were but some of the trials and tribulations associated with running an airline in the late 1920s and early 1930s. During its short life, NYRBA took such difficulties in its stride, and overcame other more serious challenges through the dogged determination of its creator, Ralph O'Neill. Despite his herculean efforts, however, NYRBA finally succumbed to internal dissension, commercial and political intrigue, and the effects of the Great Depression. In the fall of 1930, it became a part of the Pan American Airways empire of Juan Trippe.

With the acquisition of NYRBA assets, and bolstered by several lucrative U.S. foreign airmail contracts, Pan American looked ahead to new opportunities. This American flag airline, chosen carrier of the U.S. Post Office Department, now encircled the entire South American continent. Foreign competition had been effectively checked, and while the French and Germans remained active, they posed no significant threat to the operations of the expanding U.S. company. Pan American acquired ten Commodore aircraft from NYRBA, and purchased the remaining four of the vanquished company's order directly from Consolidated. No more of these aircraft were built, because by this time Pan American had already challenged Igor Sikorsky to design and build a larger flying boat with a significant increase in both passenger and cargo carrying capacity.*

The new aircraft, designated S-40, was to be the first of the great fleet of Pan American Clippers, so named because they would one day link the United States and the port cities of the world with fast, efficient commercial service, much as the sailing clipper ships had done during the golden age of sail.

Large aircraft were Sikorsky's forte. In 1913, while then a young engineer in Russia, he had designed and flown the world's first successful four-engine aircraft, the *Russikiy Vitiaz* (Russian Knight), also known as *Le Grand* because of its enormous size. The wingspan of this impressive machine was 92 feet, and the landing gear was made up of no less than 16 wheels. It was therefore somewhat surprising that in designing the S-40, he eschewed the chance to put forth the kind of bold new concept for which he was noted. Instead, the first of the great Clippers was essentially a scaled-up version of the highly successful S-38. Sikorsky's decision to stay with a proven design may have been conditioned by hard years of struggle just to keep his company alive. His autobiography indicates, however, that the safety of the large number of passengers who would entrust their lives to this aircraft was a primary consideration:

> Too much novelty in design, which already included serious departures from the conventional, represented a great risk. That was the reason why we took as a model for the S-40 the reliable S-38 amphibian, which had been thoroughly tested and was known to possess excellent safety and control characteristics.†

---

*Pan American ordered the first S-40 on 20 December 1929.

†Igor. I. Sikorsky, *The Story of the Winged-S* (New York: Dodd, Mead & Company, 1938), p. 194.

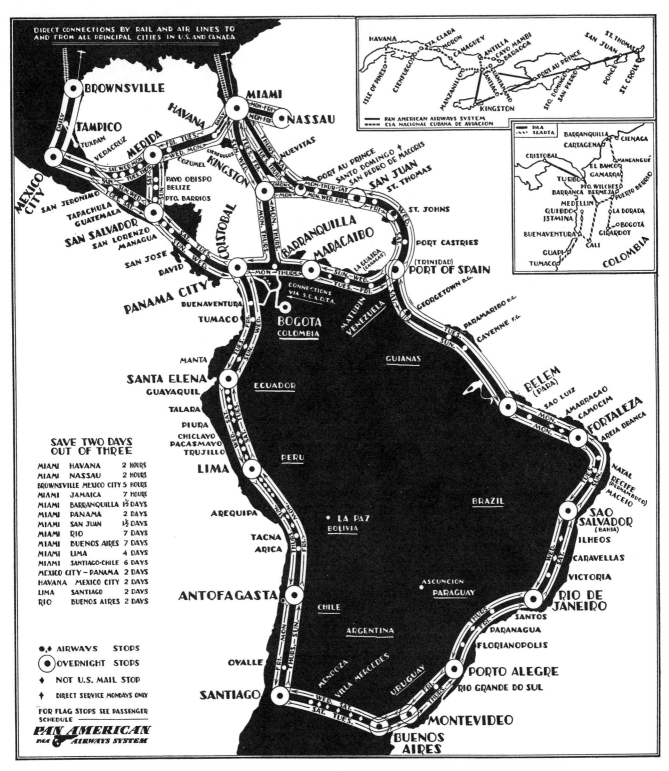

The Pan American Clipper Latin American routes, 1932, as shown on a contemporary brochure. (Pan American World Airways)

He seemed to feel that the tremendous size of the new aircraft would be engineering challenge enough. And indeed it was. When the S-40 was completed in the spring of 1931, its gross weight was more than seventeen tons. Sikorsky himself relates the difficulty encountered in finding springs heavy enough to use in the landing gear for the huge amphibian. The problem was finally resolved by obtaining them from a supplier of heavy-duty railroad car springs.

Igor I. Sikorsky with a model of his S-40 Clipper. Note the landing gear on the original version. (Sikorsky Aircraft Corp.)

Although the S-40 was originally designed as an amphibian, it was used almost exclusively as a flying boat. Three were built, and the first was christened *American Clipper* by Mrs. Herbert Hoover on 12 October 1931. In November the *American Clipper* made its first passenger flight from Miami to the Panama Canal Zone with stops at Cienfuegos, Cuba, Kingston, Jamaica, and Barranquilla, Colombia. The pilots were Colonel Charles Lindbergh* and Pan American's Captain Basil Rowe, while Igor Sikorsky rode as a passenger on the solidly booked flight.

Although a close relative of the S-38 the S-40 Clipper was somewhat more appealing to the eye. Unlike its ungainly progenitor, the S-40 was a monoplane, with four 575-horsepower Pratt and Whitney Hornet B engines protruding from a jungle of struts and wires beneath a big parasol wing which spanned 114 feet. The banana-nose appearance of the smaller amphibian had been eliminated, and from a bow aspect in flight, the S-40 was as spectacular as a square-rigged ship under full sail. Inside, the plush compartments with 8-foot overheads and large picture windows were designed to seat up to forty passengers, but like the Commodore, the actual capacity depended more on distance to destination, cargo, and fuel load. The aircraft carried a crew of five, generally consisting of two pilots, an engineer, a radio operator, and a purser/steward.

In 1935, all three S-40s were converted to the S-40-A configuration, which entailed replacing the Hornet B engines with 660-horsepower Hornet T2D1s. The landing gear was also removed, and henceforth this aircraft was operated solely as a flying boat. The combination of added power and reduced weight

*Lindbergh had been engaged as a consultant by Pan American some time before; he made several survey flights in the S-38, lending his personal prestige to the airline.

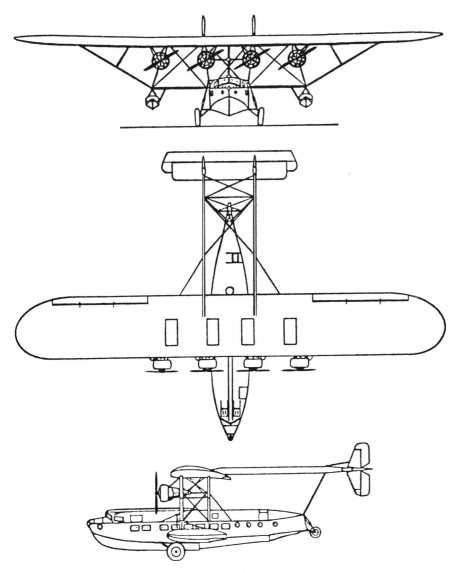

The Sikorsky S-40 Clipper. (Charles Cooney)

increased both the payload by over 1,500 pounds, and cruising speed by 5 miles per hour. As Sikorsky had intended, the S-40 Clippers provided safe, reliable service for many years, until they were rendered obsolete by more advanced models. During World War II, the *American Clipper*, the original flagship of the Pan American Clipper fleet, continued to give dependable service as a flying classroom for military navigators. It was finally dismantled and scrapped in 1943.

Although the S-40 proved itself many times over on the Caribbean and South American routes, the aircraft was not capable of making profitable flights across the oceans. Yet, potential transoceanic operations began to receive increasing attention from the dynamic chief of Pan American. In December 1929 Trippe entered into discussions with the British concerning a cooperative effort to provide transatlantic airline service. As a result of these discussions, Pan American-Imperial Airways was created on 14 May 1930, to function as a jointly-owned subsidiary of the two sponsoring organizations. The preferred route ran from New York City to Bermuda, the Azores, and finally to Lisbon, Portugal, but the French airline Compagnie Générale Aéropostal possessed the exclusive rights to the Azores-Lisbon segment. In the fall of 1930, the chief

The Sikorsky S-40 Clipper in flight, after the landing gear was removed. This aircraft operated exclusively as a flying boat in its later years of service. (Pan American World Airways)

executives of Aéropostal, Imperial, and Pan American met in New York City, and negotiated an arrangement wherein the two European carriers would each provide twenty-five percent of the service, while Pan American would provide the remaining fifty percent. It was an attractive agreement from an American point of view. One bad feature which would cause difficulties later, however, was the stipulation that transatlantic service had to be initiated simultaneously by the three parties. This was not a particular problem in 1930, because none of the parties to the agreement possessed the equipment to put such a venture into operation. It simply did not exist.

The energetic Mr. Trippe did not neglect this aspect of the problem for long, and on 15 August 1931 a letter went out from Pan American to the major American aircraft companies, soliciting designs for a long-range flying boat capable of meeting rather stringent performance requirements. It had to have a range of at least 2,500 miles at a cruising speed of 145 miles per hour, and it had to be capable of carrying at least sixteen persons (including a crew of four), and about 300 pounds of mail. Two companies took up the challenge, and on 30 November 1932, Pan American announced that contracts for such an aircraft had been signed with the Sikorsky Aviation Corporation of Bridgeport, Connecticut, and the Glenn L. Martin Company of Baltimore, Maryland.

For Igor Sikorsky and his engineers, this represented a most interesting challenge, one which would require all their engineering skill and considerable innovative thought. Sikorsky felt that the S-40 had conclusively demonstrated the feasibility of giant four-engine passenger flying boats. Now he could concentrate on new ideas to improve the breed. In his own words,

> The size, weight, power, and various other design and operating elements could be considered as well known. It appeared safe to make as large a step forward as we could in refinement of design.*

The result was the Sikorsky S-42.

The first of these new Clippers was completed in December 1933, and incorporated several new ideas. The familiar cut-off Sikorsky hull had been extended to full length, and provided direct support of the tail assembly with its twin vertical fins and rudders. The S-42 was powered by four 700-horsepower S5D1G Pratt and Whitney Hornet engines. These provided maximum effec-

*Sikorsky, p. 71.

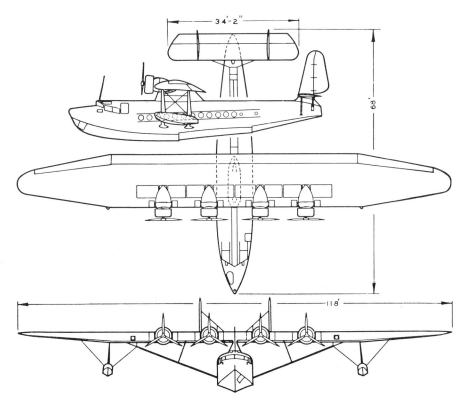

The Sikorsky S-42.

tiveness by mating with the new Hamilton Standard variable pitch propellers recently perfected. The engines themselves were equipped with synchronization indicators, an advanced carburetion system, and electric starters. They were aerodynamically faired into a large 114-foot 2-inch parasol wing, mounted on a pylon a few feet above the fuselage, and supported by struts braced against the sides of the hull just above the chine.* The skin of the S-42 was "Alclad" aluminum, with flush riveting cutting down considerably on surface drag. But it was the efficient wing design which made the big difference. Loading was some 30 pounds per square foot, about double that of most aircraft of its time; it was not until the early 1940s that this wing-loading capability was surpassed. To add to the efficiency of the advanced airfoil, large high-lift flaps were installed on its trailing edge, permitting slower landing speeds, smoother touch-downs, and increased safety.

The S-42 was a true seaplane. Wheels were attached only for beaching, and did not encumber the aircraft with heavy, bulky landing gear. The spacious hull was sectioned into nine watertight compartments. These included an unusually large flight deck and cockpit, and four comfortable passenger compartments, each accommodating eight persons. There was also a bow mooring compartment, two cargo compartments, and one steward's compartment.

In early test flights the S-42 performed beyond expectations, and on two occasions, 26 April and 17 May 1934, it established world weight-carrying records. These records, and calculations made during the extensive test program, convinced Sikorsky that he had produced another excellent airplane, and he decided to use it in an attempt to bring additional world records to his adopted country. The record attempts were made in a single flight on 1 August 1934, over a predetermined measured course, with the aircraft flown by Captain Edwin C. Musick, Pan American's Chief Pilot, and Sikorsky Test Pilot Cap-

*Angular joint between the sides and bottom surface of a flying boat hull, usually but not always at the waterline.

tain Boris Sergievsky. Colonel Lindbergh, representing the Pan American technical committee, was also a participant. When it was over, Sikorsky's S-42 had captured for the United States no less than eight additional world records, previously held by France and Germany. When asked to comment, the Russian immigrant shyly acknowledged these and the earlier two as "proving the superiority of American aircraft."

The first S-42 was delivered to Pan American at Dinner Key in August 1934. Shortly after its arrival, it began scheduled operations over the South American route. Stopping at Rio de Janeiro, Brazil, on its inaugural flight south, the aircraft was christened *Brazilian Clipper* by Señora Getúlio Vargas, wife of the President of Brazil. Three S-42s were built for Pan American. They were followed by three S-42-A Clippers, mounting 750-horsepower Hornet S1EG engines and a redesigned airfoil, which increased the wingspan by 4 feet. These changes, plus a stronger, lighter aluminum skin, permitted an increase in gross weight from 38,000 to 40,000 pounds. The improved model also included convertible sleeping accommodations for fourteen passengers. The last four in the 42-series were S-42-B aircraft incorporating certain aerodynamic modifications, and Hamilton Standard constant-speed propellers. This latter feature was a quantum improvement over the two-position variable pitch propellers used on the S-42 and the S-42-A, because the pilot could select the desired RPM for a given flight condition, and propeller pitch would automatically adjust to maintain the proper RPM. The increased efficiency of the S-42-B brought about a further increase in gross weight, this time to 42,000 pounds.

With the S-42 operational, Juan Trippe had an airplane which might be used for transatlantic service. But at this point a series of complications arose concerning the preferred route. The French arrangement with Portugal for the Azores-to-Lisbon segment expired due to the inability of Aéropostal to provide service. The British, whose Bermuda Islands were a key refueling point, had no aircraft with a transatlantic capability, and therefore exercised their option under the previous agreement that prohibited one participant from initiating service until the others were ready. The northern route, from Newfoundland, Canada, to Denmark via Greenland, Iceland, and the Faroe Islands, had been successfully surveyed by Colonel Lindbergh and his wife in 1933. Unfortunately, Trippe was prevented from pursuing this route by political unrest in Newfoundland.

Finding himself temporarily thwarted in his attempts to establish transatlantic service, Trippe began to concentrate his efforts in the Pacific. He had already probed this area to some degree. In 1931, the Lindberghs had surveyed a route along the Aleutians, across the Bering Sea to Siberia, and south to Japan. This time Trippe's way was blocked by a lack of diplomatic relations with the Soviets, and a deteriorating situation with the Japanese concerning China. Undaunted, he turned his attention to the Central Pacific.

The route chosen ran from San Francisco, California, to Hawaii, and thence to Midway and Wake Islands, Guam, and Manila in the Philippines. All were under U.S. control, and permission was readily granted by the U.S. Navy to establish bases at Midway, Wake, and Guam. The longest segment of the route lay between San Francisco and Honolulu, and Lieutenant Commander McGinnis' P2Ys had already demonstrated that flying boats could safely negotiate that part.

On 16 and 17 April 1935 an S-42 flown by Captain Musick and a crew of five made the first commercial survey flight between the two cities, arriving in Honolulu after some 18 hours. On 15 June the S-42 made the flight from Hawaii to Midway Island; in August, the Midway to Wake Island segment was surveyed; and in October, the Sikorsky Clipper extended operations from Wake Island to Guam. The first transpacific airmail was carried by the *China Clipper* in November. Regular passenger service across the Pacific began in October 1936.

The S-42 was truly a pioneer of transoceanic flight. In March 1937, Captain Musick, in the *Samoan Clipper*, surveyed a South Pacific route to New Zealand via Kingman Reef and American Samoa. In the Atlantic an S-42-B made the first commercial flying boat survey flights over both the northern and southern routes to Europe. The British also ran a transoceanic survey flight at the same time, but on the basis of this experience, decided that they were not yet ready to initiate regular commercial transatlantic service.

In April 1937, Juan Trippe concluded an agreement with Portugal for landing rights at Horta in the Azores. Pan American aircraft were capable of flying nonstop from New York to the Azores on their way to Europe, but because of the prevailing westerly winds, they required a fueling stop at Bermuda on the way home. The British refused to concede landing rights until they could develop a competing aircraft, and the transatlantic route was again postponed.

Meanwhile, in the South Pacific regularly scheduled mail service was inaugurated between Hawaii and New Zealand in December 1937. The first trip was made without incident, but on the second flight south, the S-42-B *Samoan Clipper* and its crew of seven came to an untimely end. Early on the morning of 11 January 1938, the big seaplane took off from Pago Pago, the capital of American Samoa, on the final leg of the journey to New Zealand. At 6:08 A.M. Captain Musick reported by radio that he was returning to Samoa. His number four engine had developed an oil leak, and he was shutting it down. Since the clipper had been airborne only a short time, it was still heavy with fuel, and Captain Musick elected to jettison some of it. At 8:24 A.M. he transmitted again to say that he was still dumping fuel and would be landing shortly at Pago Pago. There were no further transmissions.

The following day the U.S. Navy seaplane tender *Avocet* located the remains of the *Samoan Clipper* just fourteen miles northwest of the island. The bits and pieces of debris suggested that a tremendous explosion had occurred in flight, and it has since been speculated that sparks from the engine exhaust ignited the trailing fuel. The loss of the *Samoan Clipper* and its experienced crew was a great blow for Pan American, and service to New Zealand was discontinued until 1940. The company would especially miss the forty-four-year-old Chief Pilot who had contributed immeasurably to the development of transoceanic aviation. Ed Musick had begun his flying career as a Second Lieutenant, U.S. Marine Corps Reserve, and Naval Aviator Number 1673. He was one of the most highly regarded of the airline pioneers, a pilot's pilot, and one of the first real professionals in the industry.

While Sikorsky was finishing the S-42 Clipper, the Glenn L. Martin Company began work on its contender, designated the M-130. Martin was not a newcomer when it came to flying boats. The founder of the firm had been one of the earliest experimenters with waterborne flying machines, and the company had more recently gained considerable expertise from its experience with the PMs, P3Ms, and the XP2M built for the Navy. Not everyone in the Martin Company was happy with the idea of building Clippers for Pan American, and C. A. Van Dusen, whose job it was to keep the organization solvent, advised Martin that the project would "bankrupt the company." But Glenn L. Martin was a determined individual, who had already set as his goal the production of the finest and most advanced flying boat the world had yet seen. And indeed, it was the Martin aircraft which began the great love affair between the American public and the romantic Clippers.

Only three of these fine flying boats were built. Their successful design, which was a significant improvement over the older S-42, can be largely attributed to the work of Martin's Chief Engineer Lessiter C. Milburn, Project Engineer L. D. McCarthy, and Engineer and Test Pilot William K. "Ken" Ebel. Pan American's Chief Engineer, Andre Priester, was also a major contributor to its development.

The *China Clipper* in flight. In its years of service, this aircraft flew more than three million miles, and stirred the imagination of the nation. (Pan American World Airways)

The Pan American *China Clipper* moored to a receiving barge at Apra Harbor, Guam, 1940. (Pan American World Airways)

The *China Clipper* was the first of the three to be completed, and was test flown by Ebel on 30 December 1934. It was perhaps the best known and most widely acclaimed individual aircraft in the history of commercial aviation. There was something about the graceful giant that lifted American spirits even during the depths of the Great Depression. The *China Clipper* and its sisters the *Philippine* and *Hawaii Clipper*s, stirred the adventurous soul of the nation, and conjured up visions of the exotic east.

Tickets to Hawaii and points further west were sold to those who possessed the means as much as a year in advance. For those who could only dream, the big flying boat provided flights of fancy—and the price was right. Delivered to Pan American on 9 October 1935, the *China Clipper* was extensively test-flown before being put into regular service. Then at 3:46 P.M. on 22 November 1935, before a crowd of twenty-five thousand people, the *China Clipper* took off from

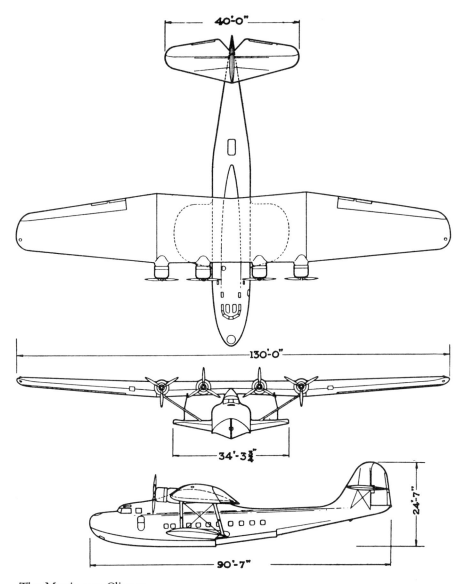

The Martin 130 Clipper.

the Pan American base at Alameda, California, under the command of Captain Musick, flew under the cables of the Golden Gate Bridge then under construction, and headed outbound on the first airmail run across the Pacific. Proceeding in stepping-stone fashion via the carefully surveyed path of Hawaii, Midway and Wake Islands, and Guam, the *China Clipper* landed at Manila on the afternoon of 29 November 1935. The 8,210-mile flight had been made in 59 hours and 48 minutes actual flying time, and the arrival was within two minutes of scheduled touchdown.

The *Philippine Clipper* was the second M-130 to be delivered to Pan American, on 24 November 1935, and followed the *China Clipper* across the Pacific on 9 December 1935. On 28 April 1937 the *Philippine Clipper* made the first survey flight from Manila to Hong Kong, opening the last segment of the transpacific route.

The *Hawaii Clipper* was the last to be delivered, and has the distinction of initiating the first transpacific passenger service. Leaving Alameda on 21 October 1936 with nine passengers aboard, it arrived at Manila on 27 October after an uneventful flight. The *Hawaii Clipper* was also the first M-130 to be lost. This occurred on 28 July 1938 during a flight from Guam to Manila under the command of Captain Leo Terletsky. The circumstances of the accident are

One of four Sikorsky VS-44 Excalibers built for American Export Airlines. (Sikorsky Aircraft Corp.)

unknown. After the last position report placing the aircraft about 560 miles east of Manila, the *Hawaii Clipper,* crew, and passengers disappeared without a trace.

When the M-130s were first assembled at the Martin plant in Little River, Maryland, they were each powered by four R-1830 Pratt and Whitney Twin Wasp engines, which developed 830 horsepower at 2,400 RPM at an altitude of 6,000 feet. Power was a necessity, for the big airplane had a wingspan of 130 feet and a gross weight of 51,000 pounds, almost 26 tons. In 1938, these aircraft were refitted with 950-horsepower Twin Wasp engines with "hydromatic" propellers which changed pitch automatically, and the maximum gross weight rose to over 52,000 pounds. The M-130 carried up to 32 passengers, with sleeping accommodations for eighteen, plus a crew of eight. Like other commercial flying boats, the actual passenger load was dependent on other factors. With maximum fuel, a minimum mail and cargo load, no passengers, and a cruising speed of 130 miles per hour, it had a range of 4,000 miles. This decreased to just over 3,000 miles with twelve to fourteen passengers, 30 pounds of baggage per person, and a mail and cargo load of 2,000 pounds. There were three sleeping compartments aboard, each comfortably accommodating up to six passengers.

One unusual feature of the M-130 was its sponsons, which helped to lift the airplane off the water, provided additional lift when airborne, and carried some 1,900 gallons of fuel. Maximum speed was about 180 miles an hour, with a cruising speed of over 150. With a full load, a customary speed was 130 miles per hour at 10,000 feet.

Shortly after the outbreak of World War II, the Navy acquired both the *China* and *Philippine Clipper*s, and used them extensively with Pan American crews in the Pacific.

On 21 January 1943 the *Philippine Clipper* met its end on a trip from Pearl Harbor, Hawaii, to San Francisco. The flight was commanded by Pan American Captain Robert M. Elzay, with Rear Admiral R. R. English and his staff as passengers. When the Clipper arrived at its destination, it found high winds, low visibility, and rain, and Elzay elected to fly a holding pattern over the ocean until the weather improved. After a time, he apparently decided to descend to investigate conditions near the surface of the water over which they were supposedly flying, a customary procedure for seaplanes in those days. Unfortunately, they were considerably further east than Elzay realized, and the

Cut-away view of the Sikorsky VS-44. Note the sleeping compartments. (Sikorsky Aircraft Corp.)

Philippine Clipper struck a mountain northwest of San Francisco. All aboard perished.

The *China Clipper* continued to provide reliable service to the U.S. Navy until returned to Pan American in October 1943. Shortly thereafter, it began service on an African route between Miami and Leopoldville in the Belgian Congo.* Then on 18 January 1945 during a night landing at Port of Spain, Trinidad, it crashed, killing nine crew members and fourteen passengers. The circumstances surrounding this accident suggest that the copilot, who was flying the aircraft at the time, may have misjudged the altitude and failed to slow the rate of descent for touchdown. Depth perception can be significantly distorted at night over the water, particularly when the surface is calm and glassy. It appears that he inadvertently flew the big flying boat into the water, where it broke apart on impact and sank. By the time of this tragedy, the *China Clipper* had flown more than three million miles, and endeared itself to Americans everywhere.

Martin produced only one other Clipper-type aircraft during this period, the M-156. It was very much like the M-130 in appearance, except for twin vertical stabilizers and rudders. It was also larger, with a wingspan of 157 feet, and a gross weight of 62,000 pounds. Built for the Soviet Union in 1937, the M-156 was known as the *Soviet* or *Russian Clipper*. Its disposition is unknown.

Toward the end of the great Clipper era, the steamship company American Export Lines Incorporated, challenged the Pan American flying boat empire with its subsidiary known as American Export Airlines (A.E.A.). This company came into being in 1937, and began laying out transatlantic routes the following year. By 1942, A.E.A. was operating its first Vought-Sikorsky VS-44A Excalibur aircraft under contract to the newly formed Naval Air Transport Service. In total A.E.A. purchased four VS-44 flying boats for transatlantic service.

The Vought-Sikorsky VS-44 was a commercial version of the U.S. Navy's PBS-1 discussed in Chapter 8. It was powered by four 1,200-horsepower Pratt and Whitney R-1830-S1C3-G engines. The wingspan was 124 feet, and the overall length was 79 feet 3 inches. The Excalibur had a gross weight of 57,500 pounds, a maximum speed of 235 miles per hour, and a cruising speed of 160.

*Now Kinshasa, Zaire.

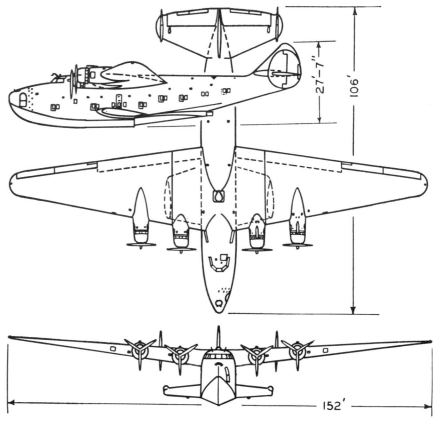

The Boeing 314.

The maximum altitude at which it could sustain flight, or service ceiling, was 19,000 feet. This airplane had sleeping accommodations for sixteen passengers, but could carry up to forty-two plus crew for relatively short flights. The VS-44 had a maximum range of 3,800 miles, cruising at 150 miles per hour, with a 5,000-pound payload. When specially configured, however, it was capable of flying a distance of more than 6,000 miles.

On 22 June 1942 Chief Pilot Charles Blair flew one of these planes on the first westbound nonstop transatlantic flight with passengers and mail aboard, crossing in 25 hours and 40 minutes from Foynes, Ireland, to New York City. In July 1945 American Airlines gained a controlling interest in A.E.A., and the company's name was changed to American Overseas Airlines. A few months later, the VS-44s were replaced by land-based aircraft. In the late 1940s, Blair acquired one of these four-engine Sikorskys for use by his own company, Antilles Air Boats. In 1977, he presented this sole surviving VS-44 airplane as a gift to the Naval Aviation Museum in Pensacola, Florida.

The last and grandest of the Pan American Clipper flying boats was the Boeing 314. It was developed from a concept originated by Wellwood Beall, a Boeing engineer. Beall worked up a sketch using the wing design of the Boeing XB-15, a large bomber which the company was then developing for the Army, and which would eventually lead to the design of the B-17 Flying Fortress of World War II. Under this wing he suspended a cavernous flying boat hull, and submitted the design to Chief Engineer Robert Minshall. Boeing's premier designer liked the idea, and on 21 July 1936 Pan American contracted for six of the sky giants.

The first of the 314s was completed and test flown on 7 June 1938. It was assembled in the open air, because there was not a hangar large enough to accommodate its massive bulk. During the first test flight, it was discovered that the single vertical stabilizer and rudder were too small, making it difficult

The Boeing 314 Pan American Airways *Yankee Clipper*. It was the last and perhaps the grandest of the Pan American flying boat Clippers. (Pan American World Airways)

to turn the aircraft in flight. After the installation of triple stabilizers and rudders, however, the problem was resolved.

The M-314 had a wingspan of 152 feet, a gross weight of over 82,000 pounds, and a designed capacity of seventy-four passengers and a crew of ten. It was powered by four GR-2600 Wright Double Cyclone engines that delivered 1,200 horsepower each at 2,100 RPM and 5,400 feet of altitude, and 1,500 horsepower for takeoff. This gave it a maximum speed of 193 miles per hour at an altitude of 10,000 feet, a cruising speed of 183, and a range of some 3,500 miles. With this airplane Pan American was in a position to bypass Bermuda, stop in the Azores where they already had landing rights, and go on to Europe. This time both the French and the British granted landing authority.

On 3 March 1939 Mrs. Eleanor Roosevelt christened one of these airborne luxury-liners the *Yankee Clipper*. It departed Baltimore on the twenty-sixth of March to conduct a survey flight to Europe via the Azores, stopping at Bermuda on the return trip.

On 20 May this airplane, under the command of Captain Arthur E. La Porte, made the first regularly scheduled mail flight to Europe, returning to New York City a week later. Then on 28 June the *Dixie Clipper*, an airplane piloted by Captain R. O. D. Sullivan, inaugurated the first regular transatlantic passenger service. The *Yankee Clipper* opened the northern transatlantic route to passengers on 8 July.

The original six 314s were all delivered to Pan American by 16 June 1939. Two went to the Pacific coast, where they were used on the San Francisco to

Interior view of the Boeing 314 Clipper. (Pan American World Airways)

Hong Kong run, and four were assigned to the east coast, for employment in transatlantic service. By March 1941 the first of an improved version, designated 314-A, had been successfully test flown. This newer model, of which six were built, had more powerful Double Wasp engines which developed up to 1,600 horsepower for takeoff. Power was enhanced further by installation of larger more efficient propellers, and the gross weight limit was increased to 84,000 pounds. The original six 314s were also fitted with the new engines and converted to 314-As.

World War II interrupted the development of commercial transoceanic travel. On 7 December 1941 the Boeing 314 *Anzac Clipper* avoided the Japanese attack on Pearl Harbor by landing at the island of Hilo instead of at Honolulu. Others were not so fortunate. The Martin M-130 *Philippine Clipper* was caught refueling at Wake Island by Japanese fighter-bombers. Although hit by machine gun fire in several places, it somehow escaped serious damage, and made a quick trip home a short time later. The Sikorsky S-42-B *Hong Kong Clipper* was surprised on the water in Hong Kong harbor by Japanese planes and destroyed. The *Pacific Clipper* had just completed a flight to New Zealand, and proceeded home the long way, via Australia, the Dutch East Indies, India, Africa, and South America.

The Boeing 314s served with distinction during the war. Some were taken over by the U.S. Army, some by the U.S. Navy, and some continued to function as commercial airliners. Three were acquired by the British airline BOAC, and given the names *Bristol, Berwick*, and *Bangor*. *Berwick* had the honor of transporting Winston Churchill home from a meeting with Franklin Roosevelt in early 1942. The British Prime Minister even tried his hand at piloting the big flying boat, and seemed to enjoy it immensely. Roosevelt made personal use of one of these reliable machines, when he flew in the *Dixie Clipper* to the Casablanca Conference in January 1943.

After the war, Pan American abandoned the flying boats in favor of faster and more convenient land-based airliners. These too were called Clippers, but somehow the magic was gone, and public interest faded. The 314s were sold, and a few found new employment with some of the small airlines that proliferated in the late 1940s. By 1952, all had been sent to the junk yard, or had been otherwise destroyed. The era of the great Clippers had ended.

CHAPTER EIGHT

The Warboats

By 1937, it had become evident even to casual observers that U.S. policy was on a collision course with the ambitious designs of Japan in the Pacific. Hitler's Germany had also become a matter of grave concern. While there were many Americans who insisted that war could be avoided by strict isolationism, there were others who were convinced of the futility of this posture, and quietly set about preparing for the nation's defense as best they could. The U.S. Navy already had a reliable flying boat patrol bomber in the PBY, but lead times of two years or more made it prudent to develop new design concepts for projected requirements. The Consolidated Aircraft Corporation had already started to assemble a new four-engine flying boat for the Navy, and contracts for other models had also been awarded to Sikorsky, Martin, and Boeing.

There was a popular belief among flying boat enthusiasts that bigger was necessarily better, and Igor Sikorsky had begun work on a large four-engine seaplane as early as 1935. Designated the XPBS-1, this large patrol bomber featured a tail turret with a 50-caliber machine gun, the first of its kind to be mounted in an American aircraft. It had another 50-caliber machine gun in a nose turret, and two 30-caliber guns in waist positions. The XPBS-1 was powered by four Pratt and Whitney XR-1830-68 engines, each of which developed 1,050 horsepower on takeoff. Maximum gross weight was set at 48,540 pounds, and with a full fuel load, the aircraft could fly a distance of 4,500 miles. With a 4,000-pound load of bombs and ammunition, its range was reduced to just over 3,000 miles.

The XPBS-1 was first flown on 13 August 1937, and, although it was considered to be a successful design, it was never ordered into production. Instead, the Navy turned its attention to another four-engine aircraft being developed by Consolidated at about the same time. The prototype Model 29, designated the XPB2Y-1 by the Navy, was contracted for in May 1936 and completed in December 1937. The Coronado, as it was later called, was powered by the -72 version of the 1830 Twin Wasp engines, and boasted a maximum gross weight of almost 53,000 pounds. Maximum range was 5,000 miles, which decreased to approximately 3,500 miles with a 4,000-pound bomb load. The big seaplane was 79 feet 3 inches in length, with a wingspan of 115 feet. The top speed was 230 miles per hour. Like the Sikorsky model, 50-caliber machine guns were mounted in the nose and tail, but 50-caliber weapons instead of 30s were featured in the waist positions, and a 30-caliber machine gun was carried in a tunnel hatch. The bomb bays, which were built into the wings, could carry a bomb load of up to six tons. The floats were retractable, as in the PBY, and became wing tips after takeoff.

The XPB2Y-1 was originally designed and built with a single large vertical stabilizer and rudder. When the aircraft was first test-flown by Consolidated's Chief Test Pilot Bill Wheatley on 17 December 1937, it became immediately apparent that there were serious directional control deficiencies. In an attempt to correct this problem, Consolidated's engineers installed elliptical fins on the horizontal stabilizer, but these were not effective. Unusual flight attitudes would sometimes result in hazardous spins, from which recovery could be made only

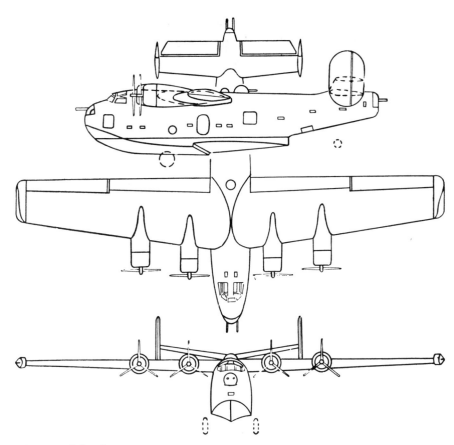

The Consolidated PB2Y-2.

with full power. Concerned over the performance of his new airplane, Reuben Fleet himself climbed into the cockpit with Wheatley for a test flight to see what could be done to resolve the problem. As a result of his observations, the horizontal stabilizer was redesigned with a 7 1/2-degree dihedral, to accommodate two large round endplates which constituted the vertical stabilizers and rudders. This solved the problem of lateral stability, but other modifications were necessary, and the Navy did not take final delivery until October 1938. This particular aircraft was subsequently assigned as flag plane to Rear Admiral A. B. Cook, Commander Aircraft, Scouting Force.

Partly because of the modifications, but mostly because of budgetary constraints, the Navy did not enter a production order for the Coronado until 31 March 1939. The prototype had cost a million dollars to build, and the six follow on PB2Y-2s were to be delivered at $300,000 each. In 1939 this was a lot of money, roughly three times the cost of the proven PBY.

The first of six PB2Y-2s were delivered to the U.S. Navy in December 1940. They were provided with the newer, more powerful -78 Twin Wasp engines, which developed 1,200 horsepower for takeoff and provided a 25 mile per hour increase in top speed, to 255. Significant design departures from the prototype included a deeper hull, large oval-shaped vertical tail surfaces, and a ball turret in the nose. The PB2Y-2 carried a total of six 50-caliber guns.

Patrol Squadron Thirteen (VP-13) was the first to receive the Coronados. The last aircraft in the original series of six was modified to become the prototype for the PB2Y-3s. This model used -88 Twin Wasp engines, and had self-sealing fuel tanks, armor plating, and power-operated turrets in the nose and tail positions, with 50-caliber twin mounts. Another 50-caliber twin mount powered turret protruded from the top of the fuselage just aft of the wing. These modifications increased the gross weight to 68,000 pounds, and reduced maximum speed to 224 miles per hour. Still it performed reasonably well against

A PB2Y-2 Coronado of VP-13. (General Dynamics)

the Japanese. A VP-13 report of an action involving a PB2Y-3 flown by Lieutenant J. B. Wheatley, and a Japanese Mitsubishi G4M Betty aircraft on 11 May 1944, provides a vivid account of the lethal qualities of the 50-caliber twin mounts:

> While at 5,000 feet on a course of 205°T in the vicinity of 13-03N, 154-37E, a BETTY was sighted 4 miles distant on the starboard bow approaching on a course of 075°T and flying at about 1,000 feet altitude. When the BETTY crossed the bow of the CORONADO and was about two miles ahead, the CORONADO made a left turn and started a dive which took it through a small cloud. Emerging from the cloud, the CORONADO was a mile directly astern of the BETTY and doing an estimated 220 knots while the BETTY was making an estimated 170 knots. The enemy apparently still had not seen the CORONADO.

> LT. WHEATLEY swung his plane to the right and made a low quarter approach and fire was opened by the bow turret at 200 yards; at this time the BETTY top turret gunner returned fire although it is believed his guns were unable to bear. He was quickly silenced by the top turret gunner of the CORONADO, who then turned his guns toward the bomb bays. Meanwhile, the bow turret concentrated fire in the fuselage aft of the wing root, then shifted to the port engine and continued to fire until it was ablaze. With the range closing to within 50 yards, concentrated fire was poured into the starboard engine of the BETTY.

> Within 15 seconds after the initial burst was fired, the BETTY was ablaze from nose to tail and fell off on the left wing. There were no survivors.

In all, 217 Coronados were built. They functioned throughout World War II as patrol planes, transports, search and rescue aircraft, and in a variety of other roles. Ten were designated PB2Y-3Bs and delivered to the British Royal Air Force, where they were ultimately used as cargo aircraft by Number 231

Squadron of the Air Transport Command. Thirty-one were configured as forty-four-passenger transports, PB2Y-3Rs, and used in both the Atlantic and Pacific. One was outfitted with Wright R-2600 Cyclone engines and designated PB2Y-4, while others received -92 Twin Wasp engines and became PB2Y-5s. The Coronados served as bombers against the Japanese during the Marshall Islands campaign, and in a similar role in other actions during the final months of the war, as the U.S. pushed closer and closer to the Japanese homeland. A PB2Y-5H hospital plane configured to carry twenty-five stretchers evacuated wounded marines from the bloody fighting on Iwo Jima.

Consolidated learned much about deep-hulled flying boats from its experience with the Coronado, and applied some of that knowledge to a smaller twin-engine Model 31, designated XP4Y-1 by the U.S. Navy, and known as the Corregidor. This was a fine aircraft with considerable potential, but unfortunately it never went into production. The prototype was a somewhat portly looking machine, with a deep stubby hull supported in the air by a 110-foot narrow-cord wing designed by David R. Davis. Outwardly it appeared that such a wing could not lift the weight and bulk of the Model 31 hull. In wind tunnel tests at the California Institute of Technology, however, this unique airfoil not only demonstrated its capability to do just that, but confounded the experts by exceeding what was then thought to be the maximum possible wing efficiency.

The Model 31 was designed to function as either a fifty-two-passenger commercial amphibian, or as a Navy patrol plane capable of carrying an effective weapon load over 3,500 miles at respectable speeds. Part of the XP4Y-1's outstanding performance characteristics can be attributed to the two double-row 18-cylinder Wright R-3350 engines, which produced up to 2,000 horsepower, and propelled the aircraft in flight at a top speed of more than 230 miles per hour, with a cruising speed of 136. In the military configuration, it was designed to accommodate a 37-millimeter cannon in the nose, with 50-caliber twin mounts in the tail and in the dorsal position on top of the fuselage. The normal gross weight was 46,000 younds, with 48,000 the maximum.

When the Corregidor was first test flown on 5 May 1939, it virtually leaped into the air after a surprisingly short takeoff run. The airplane handled well in flight, and Consolidated engineers felt that they had developed a worthy successor to the PBY. But the transition from the development to the production stage is often lengthy and replete with problems. The threat of war was coming ever closer, and the Navy, anxious to increase the tempo of its preparations, elected to spend the bulk of its production funds on the proven PBY. The Corregidor, with its radical wing design, was still an unknown quantity to some extent, and was therefore sidetracked for further development. In 1943 it was scheduled for production in a facility at New Orleans, Louisiana, but prior to start-up priorities shifted, and the decision was made to divert the Wright R-3350 engines intended for the Corregidor to the production of the B-29 Superfortress. The P4Y-1 project was scrapped. But despite its inglorious fate, this twin engine flying boat had served as a proving ground for the high aspect-ratio Davis wing, and had pioneered its use for such distinguished Consolidated aircraft as the B-24 Liberator bomber and the PB4Y Privateer flying boat.

During this prewar period, the Glenn L. Martin Company had been working on some new design concepts of its own. Recognizing that even the venerable PBY must give way to improvement and innovation, Martin began designing its own twin-engine flying boat patrol bomber. The result of this effort was the deep-hulled, gull-winged Martin 162. To test the design and at the same time to decrease costs, Martin built the prototype of this aircraft to one-quarter scale, and flew it as a single-seat model (162-A) in early 1937. By 30 June of that year, the Navy had affirmed its approval of the design by contracting for a full-scale prototype, designated the XPBM-1. The Navy apparently placed considerable confidence in the potential of this design, inasmuch

The Martin 162-A was a quarter-scale prototype of the PBM Mariner. (Martin Marietta)

as six months later, while the prototype was still in the early stages of testing,
a production contract was awarded to the Martin Company for twenty PBM-1s.

The XPBM-1, like its miniature predecessor, had gull wings and a horizontal tail plane. It was also equipped with retractable wing floats which folded
into the underside of the wing. A 30-caliber single mount in the nose, and one
50-caliber in each of the top, waist, and tail positions, comprised the armament,
and at 40,814 pounds gross weight, it could carry 1,000 pounds of bombs 3,450
miles. The XPBM-1's two R-2600-6 Wright Cyclone engines each developed
1,600 horsepower for takeoff, and provided for a maximum speed of 213 miles
per hour at 12,000 feet. Early tests begun on 18 February 1939 were not completely satisfactory and necessitated several changes, the most striking of which
was the addition of a distinctive dihedral to the tail-plane.

The first of the production PBM-1s was delivered to Patrol Squadron
Fifty-five (VP-55) in September 1940, and the last of this order was accepted
in May 1941. These aircraft, called Mariners, were very similar to the prototype
in most respects, and were capable of carrying up to 4,000 pounds of bombs in
bomb bays which were aft extensions of the engine nacelles. A single XPBM-2,
also completed in May, had an increase in fuel capacity of more than 1,000
gallons. This version was designed for launching by catapult. Although early
tests were successful, no more examples of this type were built.

On 1 November 1940 a contract was awarded to the Martin Company for
379 PBM-3s. These and aircraft from a subsequent order of PBM-4s actually
appeared as PBM-3C and -3D patrol bombers, PBM-3R transports, and PBM-
3S antisubmarine aircraft. They were delivered to the Navy between April 1942
and June 1944. The -3C and -3R models had R-2600-12 Cyclone engines. The
-3R was unarmed and carried twenty passengers, while the -3C patrol bomber
version featured twin 50-caliber power turrets in the nose and dorsal positions.
The -3D version was powered by -22 Cyclone engines with four-bladed propellers. Self-sealing fuel tanks, and more than 1,000 pounds of armor plate were
featured in this aircraft, and it carried eight 50-caliber machine guns in power
turrets in the nose, dorsal, and tail positions. The PBM-3S was configured for
use in antisubmarine warfare, and had no power turrets and little armor plate.
As a result of the reduced weight, however, its range was significantly in-

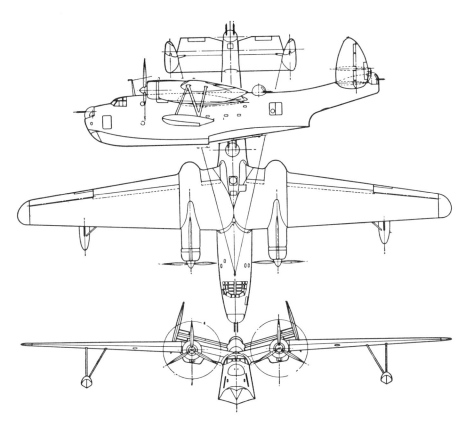

The Martin PBM.

creased, enabling it to remain on station over a patrol area for extended periods of time. Airborne radar became available early in the war, and greatly enhanced the search capability of the PBMs. This new electronic search device was used extensively in the PBM-3C and -3D models, and later proved to be particularly useful on the PBM-3S aircraft against the submarine threat. The Mariners were used exclusively in the Atlantic for antisubmarine operations until late in 1943. They established an impressive record, as indicated by the following U-boat credits:*

30 June 1942	U-158 sunk off Bermuda by a PBM-1 piloted by Lt. Richard E. Schreder of VP-74. This was the first submarine sunk by a U.S. Navy seaplane, the third by a U.S. Navy aircraft, and the fifth by U.S. forces.
17 May 1943	U-128 sunk off Brazil by two PBM-3Cs piloted by Lts. Hoyland Davis and H. C. Carey of VP-74, with the assistance of two destroyers.
15 July 1943	U-159 sunk in the Caribbean south of Haiti by a PBM-3S flown by Lt. R. C. Mayo of VP-32.
19 July 1943	U-513 sunk off Florianopolis, Brazil, by a PBM-3C commanded by Lt. j.g. R. S. Whitcomb of VP-74.
26 July 1943	U-759 sunk in the Caribbean east of Jamaica by a PBM-3C piloted by Lt. R. W. Rawson of VP-32.
28 July 1943	U-359 sunk south of Puerto Rico by a PBM-3S of VP-32.
31 July 1943	U-199 sunk off Rio de Janeiro, Brazil, by a PBM-3C piloted by Lt. j.g. William F. Smith of VP-74, with the assistance of Brazilian aircraft.
3 August 1943	U-572 sunk north of Dutch Guiana by a PBM-3S flown by Lt. j.g. Clifford C. Cox of VP-205. It was a night attack: the plane did not return.

*Office of the U.S. Naval Aviation Historian.

A Mariner making a JATO takeoff. (U.S. Navy)

6 August 1943   U-615 sunk north of Aruba by PBMs of VP-204 and 205, assisted by other aircraft from VB-130 and the U.S. Army Air Force. Seven PBMs were involved; some of the pilots were, Lt. j.g. J. M. Erskine, Lt. A. R. Matuski (shot down), Lt. L. D. Crockett, Lt. j.g. J. W. Dresbach (killed) and LCdr. R. S. Null.

27 Sept. 1943   U-161 sunk off Bahia, Brazil, by a PBM-3C of VP-74.

A number of Mariners were sent to Great Britain in late 1943 as PBM-3Bs. These were earmarked for use by the RAF Coastal Command, but they were underutilized and were eventually returned to the United States. It was during this period that the PBM began to appear in the Pacific, where it remained in operational service until mid-1958. All PBM-3 aircraft and subsequent models were equipped with larger non-retractable wing floats.

The Mariner did not perform particularly well on one engine, especially with a heavy load. On one occasion during the summer of 1944, a PBM-3 experienced a break in an oil line while flying over southeastern Arizona, necessitating engine shut-down on one side. It soon became apparent that the aircraft could not maintain altitude on the remaining engine, and the pilots began to look for a place to make an emergency landing. Unfortunately, the land beneath was desert, without so much as a wet sponge available; consequently, they were obliged to land in a dry lake bed. Having suffered only superficial damage, the aircraft was mounted on beaching gear and flown out with little difficulty. This was an unusual first in flying boat history.

The PBM-5 was ordered into production on 3 January 1944, and the first of these were delivered in September of that year. This series used Pratt and

A PBM Mariner after an emergency waterless landing on a dry lake bed in Arizona, 1944. The aircraft was later flown off using beaching gear. (Martin Marietta)

Whitney R-2800-34 engines, which provided 2,100 horsepower for takeoff. The increased power output resulted in both greater speed and longer range, and permitted the installation of additional armament and protective armor similar to that on the PBM-3D. More sophisticated avionics equipment was later installed in some of these aircraft, resulting in the PBM-5E and -5S models. Several went to the U.S. Coast Guard as PBM-5Gs, and were used as air-sea rescue aircraft. Thirty-six amphibious PBM-5-As with retractable landing gear were built in the post-war period. In total, some 1,366 PBM-type aircraft were produced, and they served in many various roles until their retirement.

From August to October 1946, PBMs operating from the seaplane tender *Norton Sound* made flights over the Arctic ice cap, approaching within 450 miles of the North Pole. During that same summer, PBMs provided logistic services for Operation Crossroads, the first postwar testing of the atomic bomb. From December 1946 to March 1947, Mariners operating from tenders in the open sea around the Antarctic continent in Operation Highjump photographed the coastline and other unexplored areas of this great polar landmass. When the Korean War broke out in 1950, PBMs were the first patrol planes to operate in Korean airspace. Others, flying from Okinawa, Japan, and the Pescadores, patrolled the Formosa Strait in support of U.S. policy.

In 1956, Patrol Squadron Fifty returned to NAS Alameda from duty in the western Pacific, marking the end of the era of operational employment of the PBM. Their use in the Atlantic had already ended in 1949. The last of these big workhorses finished service as advanced trainers for prospective pilots of multi-engine aircraft at NAS Corpus Christi, Texas, in July 1958.

The Boeing XPBB-1 Sea Ranger was another fine flying boat which, like Consolidated's Model 31, never advanced to the production stage. It too was a twin-engine aircraft with a high aspect ratio wing, and a large deep hull. Although powered by the same Wright R-3350-8 Cyclone engines, the XPBB-1 was considerably larger than the Consolidated aircraft, with a wingspan of 139 feet 8 1/2 inches, and a height of 35 feet. This aircraft was specifically designed for war, although many of the ideas incorporated into the design were the result of Boeing's experience with the Model 314 Clippers. The XPBB-1 could carry a

The Martin PBM-5A amphibian. Thirty-six of these models having retractable landing gear were built following World War II. (U.S. Navy)

maximum fuel load of 9,575 gallons, and had a theoretical endurance of up to 72 hours. The gross weight was 101,129 pounds, and it was capable of carrying a bomb load of 20,000 pounds. Armament included twin 50-caliber machine guns in nose, dorsal, and tail power turrets, and single mounts in gun blisters on each side of the after part of the fuselage. The prototype was ordered on 29 June 1940, and was first test flown on 9 July 1942. Onlookers who watched the first takeoff run that day must have wondered whether two engines could really lift a machine of that size into the air. The XPBB-1 was the largest twin-engine flying boat produced during World War II.

The Wright R-3350 engines met the challenge well. Providing 2,300 horse-power each for takeoff, they powered the 50-ton boat to a maximum speed of 220 miles per hour and a cruising speed of 158. As always, range varied with weight; with no bomb load, maximum range was claimed to be in excess of 6,000 miles. This aircraft had great potential for long-range patrol operations. It would have been particularly useful for convoy protection over many vulnerable stretches of the Atlantic, which, because of the distances involved, had not been afforded adequate antisubmarine patrol coverage. Despite the impressive capabilities of the XPBB-1, however, its production program, like that of the Model 31, was discontinued to provide engines and plant facilities for the new B-29s. Only one Sea Ranger type was ever built, and it was promptly nicknamed the "Lone Ranger."

One very unusual flying boat type developed for World War II was the flying boat glider. Two basic designs were developed and flown, but did not go into production. The U.S. Marine Corps intended to use the gliders as assault aircraft for their island campaigns in the Pacific.

Two of the first design type, designated XLRQ-1, were constructed, with each capable of carrying two pilots and ten fully-equipped marines. Built by

The Boeing XPBB-1 Ranger was a one of a kind aircraft, dubbed the "Lone Ranger."
(Boeing Aircraft Co.)

the Bristol Aeronautical Corporation of New Haven, Connecticut, the first prototype was delivered to the U.S. Navy in October 1942, and test flown in January of the following year. The XLRQ-1 had a wingspan of 71 feet and an empty weight of 2,800 pounds. A second test model delivered in May 1943 was amphibious and featured tricycle landing gear. The Allied Aviation Corporation of Baltimore, Maryland, built two similar prototypes designated the XLRA-1 and -2. They had a wingspan of 70.5 feet and an empty weight of 2,800 pounds. The XLRA-1 had a double wheel mounted on the center-line, and wing-tip skids much like the traditional arrangement on sport sailplanes. The XLRA-2 had conventional landing gear, which could be jettisoned in flight.

The AGA Corporation of Willow Grove, Pennsylvania, formerly Pitcairn-Larsen Autogyro Company, was awarded a contract to build a 2/5–scale working prototype of a large twenty-four-place twin-hulled assault glider-boat, to be known as the XLRG-1. This was an odd-looking aircraft, with a wing spanning 109 feet mounted on top of the two hulls. Empty weight was 4,800 pounds. A short boom protruded from the aft end of each hull, and together they supported a tail assembly with twin vertical stabilizers and rudders. A cabin designed to carry two pilots and twelve marines was built over the wings, and ten additional men could ride in the two hulls, five on each side.

Test flights were conducted by the project officer, Captain Ralph S. Barnaby, following which AGA was given the go-ahead to construct a full-scale prototype. A second firm, Sead and Company, was also selected to build its version, to be designated the XLRH-1. Both contracts were cancelled, however, before either prototype was built.

During the years just prior to World War II, the PBY (Consolidated Model 28) was the mainstay of patrol aviation in the U.S. Navy. In June 1938, fifteen PBYs under the command of Lieutenant Commander S. L. LaHache cut the flight time from San Diego to Hawaii to 16 hours and 35 minutes, while in September a flight of seventeen of these aircraft, commanded by Lieutenant A. P. "Putt" Storrs, repeated the feat in 16 hours and 44 minutes.*

By this time, the reputation of the PBY flying boat for dependability had also attracted attention outside the U.S. Navy. The first aircraft of this type sold to a private operator, Model 28-1, was delivered to Dr. Richard Archbold for use in scientific expeditions in New Guinea. In June 1937 Archbold and Consolidated test pilot Bill Wheatley flew the aircraft, named *Guba*, nonstop from San Diego, California, to New York City in 17 hours and 3 minutes. Upon arrival at New York, *Guba* had enough fuel remaining to have continued on for another 1,200 miles or more. The transcontinental flight was a first in flying boat history. *Guba* never got to New Guinea, however, because that same year it was sold to the Soviet Union for use in an attempt to find and rescue Russian flyers who had become lost in the vicinity of the North Pole. *Guba* met its end in July 1942, when the German submarine *U-601* shelled and sank it off the Soviet island Novaya Zemlya in the Barents Sea. At the time they acquired *Guba*, the Russians also placed orders for three additional PBYs, delivered in 1938 as Model 28-2s. These and the original *Guba* were all essentially PBY-1s. Consolidated also agreed to certain licensing arrangements and provided some technical expertise as part of the sales agreement. The Russians used these aircraft as training models to begin their own PBY plant at Taganrog on the Sea of Azov. Instead of the customary Pratt and Whitney R-1830s, the three 28-2s were powered by Wright 1820-G3 Cyclone engines, which the Russians were licensed to build as M-62s for use in their production aircraft. Approximately 150 of these Russian PBYs, designated GSTs by the Soviets, were built at Taganrog before the German Army swept through the area in 1941.

In the meantime, Dr. Archbold had purchased a PBY-2 aircraft (Model 28-3), naming it *Guba II*. This flying boat was used extensively by the Archbold expedition in New Guinea during 1938 and 1939, and was flown home via the Indian Ocean, Africa, and the Atlantic, arriving in San Diego on 6 July 1939. *Guba II* was subsequently purchased by the British Overseas Airways Corporation (BOAC) and used as a transport between England and West Africa.

American Export Airlines ordered a PBY-4 aircraft in September 1938, to use in an attempt to establish a second U.S. transoceanic airline to compete with Pan American Airways. Designated Model 28-4, it was christened *Transatlantic* on 20 June 1939 by Mrs. John H. Towers, whose husband Rear Admiral Towers was then serving as Chief of the Bureau of Aeronautics. The *Transatlantic* was employed as a survey aircraft to establish a competitive route for the fledgling airline. This organization later became American Overseas Airlines, and was finally absorbed by Pan American in the late 1940s.

But the overwhelming majority of PBYs were built for war. One PBY-4 was sold to the British Air Ministry for test and evaluation as Model 28-5, and was flown to England in July 1939. It was the first military aircraft to be ferried

---

*Time for the Storrs flight is taken from the navigator's report, which was provided by RADM Storrs. It is at variance with the time reported in *Aviation Year Book, 1939*.

across the Atlantic. The British, impressed with the performance and dependability of this flying boat, ordered fifty PBY-5s equipped with R-1830-82 engines of 1,200 horsepower. They dubbed these airplanes Catalinas after Santa Catalina Island, California. The U.S. Navy liked the name, and adopted it officially in 1941.

Other countries had also been favorably impressed by the unique characteristics of this aircraft, and desired to adapt them to solve their own special problems. During the years just prior to the entry of the United States into World War II, eighteen were sold to Australia, and fifty to Canada; thirty were ordered by France, and forty-eight were earmarked for the Netherlands, for use throughout her island holdings in the East Indies. France fell before the German onslaught in June 1940 before any of her PBYs could be delivered, but thirty-six were ferried to the Dutch East Indies before the area was overrun by the Japanese in 1941.

During these years the U.S. Navy aviation arm continued to prepare for the coming conflict. By the latter part of 1937, all of an order of sixty-six PBY-3 aircraft with R-1830-66 Pratt and Whitney Wasp engines had been delivered to the Navy. Before the year was out, another order had been placed for thirty-three PBY-4s, powered by R-1830-72s. This series was the first to locate the single-mount 50-caliber machine guns in blisters on each side of the fuselage, instead of behind sliding hatches as in previous models.

In January 1939, forty-five PBYs of Patrol Wing One, led by Captain Marc Mitscher, conducted the largest long-distance mass flight ever made, transiting from San Diego to Coco Solo in the Panama Canal Zone, and thence on to the Caribbean to participate in fleet exercises there.

On 3 September 1939 England and France declared war on Germany, and shortly thereafter, President Franklin D. Roosevelt ordered the U.S. Navy to initiate a patrol "extending several hundred miles to sea" in the Atlantic. Both aircraft and ships were employed in this effort to secure the Atlantic approaches to the United States and the Caribbean Sea, and on 11 September PBYs of VP-33 were transferred from the Panama Canal Zone to Guantanamo Bay, Cuba. VP-51 Catalinas based at Norfolk, Virginia, were deployed to operate from San Juan, Puerto Rico, two days later.

More ships and planes were obviously needed to cover the U.S. Navy's rapidly expanding responsibilities. The number of available flying boats was not nearly adequate for the job, and more had to be acquired as quickly as possible. As discussed earlier, there were several promising possibilities in the development stage, some of which would prove their value later in the war. But Navy planners knew that time was running out, and chose the reliable PBY for the job. Other flying boats were bigger, faster, and more sophisticated, but size, speed, and complexity were not necessarily desirable for the task at hand. The PBYs were relatively uncomplicated to operate, easy to maintain, remarkably dependable, and available in large numbers in a reasonable time frame at an acceptable price. The Navy placed an order for 200 PBY-5s on 20 December 1939, the first of which was delivered on 18 September 1940. The PBY-5 burned 100-octane fuel in two R-1830-82 engines, each of which provided 1,200 horsepower for takeoff. The second PBY-5 to come off the production line went to the U.S. Coast Guard in October, but deliveries to the Navy resumed in November.

Meanwhile, on 19 June 1940, President Roosevelt had signed into law the "Two Ocean Navy Bill." Funding to implement this legislation was made available on 9 September, and the Navy was authorized to build 200 new ships and 2,400 additional aircraft. In October, Navy flying boat assets in the Atlantic were reorganized into patrol forces to better address the task of guarding vast ocean areas off the American continent. In keeping with this arrangement, the Aircraft Scouting Force commanded by Rear Admiral Arthur B. Cook became the Aircraft Patrol Force, U.S. Fleet.

In November, Patrol Squadron Fifty-four (VP-54), flying PBY-2s, began operating out of Bermuda, thereby extending antisubmarine coverage still further from the U.S. coast. Beginning in May 1941, VP-52, with their PBY-5s, conducted patrols using as a base the seaplane tender *Albemarle* located at Argentia, Newfoundland. Starting in August, VP-73 and 74, flying PBY-5s and PBM-1s respectively, made patrols over the Atlantic from Iceland.

It was about at this time that airborne radar, developed by the British, began to make its appearance on U.S. Navy flying boats. This was an important breakthrough, and as the crews became skilled in its use, the long-range detection capabilities of patrol aircraft were greatly enhanced. The so-called Magnetic Anomaly Detection (MAD) device followed a short time later, and gave the boats an additional advantage. This sensor detects changes in the earth's magnetic field caused by the presence of a large metallic object, even though it may lie submerged and unseen beneath the ocean's surface.*

On 4 September 1941 a U.S. warship, the destroyer *Greer*, was fired upon by a German submarine southwest of Iceland. The U-boat skipper no doubt felt he had good cause for his action, because the *Greer* had reported the submarine's position to a British patrol plane that was in the vicinity, which subsequently made an attack with depth bombs. After the initial attack, the U-boat and the *Greer* then engaged each other with torpedoes and depth charges. Neither was damaged, and the submarine finally dove deep and escaped, while *Greer* continued to her destination. One week later President Roosevelt announced,

> From now on, if German or Italian vessels of war enter the waters, the protection of which is necessary for American defense, they do so at their own peril.

The line between U.S. neutrality and belligerency was now thin indeed.

Ironically, unknown to the world, U.S. Navy aviators had already participated in an important battle with the naval forces of the Third Reich some months before. Seventeen PBY pilots, all volunteers, had been sent to England in early 1941, to instruct the British in the operation of their new PBY aircraft. Twenty-six year old Ensign Leonard B. Smith was assigned to 209 Squadron of the Coastal Command, based at Lough Erne in Northern Ireland. Because the British were short-handed, Smith became copilot of PBY aircraft Z, whose pilot was Flight Officer Dennis Briggs of the Royal Air Force.

On 24 May 1941 the 45,000-ton German battleship *Bismarck* had engaged British surface forces, and during the fray she had literally blown the battle cruiser *Hood* in two. Sometime later, the raider had slipped away from pursuing British vessels, and was again at large in the North Atlantic. The British were shocked by the loss of the *Hood*, and gravely concerned by the threat of what the *Bismarck* could do to any convoy she might encounter. She had to be found and destroyed.

At about 3:00 A.M. on 26 May, PBY Z from 209 Squadron (Z/209) took off from Lough Erne to join the hunt for the *Bismarck*. Out over the ocean, the steady drone of the Pratt and Whitney Wasp engines reinforced the familiar monotony of search operations, and by daylight the high point in the flight had been breakfast. The day dawned cloudy and gray, and a heavy sea only added to the problem of poor visibility. They flew along 500 feet over the water, which altitude had been chosen as best for the search, and the pilots alternated at the controls. Ensign Smith, who had just settled into the pilot's seat, looked down and was startled to see a large warship ahead. He alerted Briggs, and as they flew closer, they were almost positive they had located their illusive quarry. Smith had climbed to 2,000 feet, and Briggs had hurried aft to get out a mes-

*The first kill of a submerged submarine using MAD gear was made in 1944, when PBYs from VP-63 sank the U-761 in the Strait of Gibraltar.

sage, when the *Bismarck* opened fire. Smith jettisoned the depth charges and began to maneuver violently as deadly bursts of anti-aircraft fire shook the aircraft. Pieces of shrapnel pierced the hull in several places. There was no doubt about it now. They had found the *Bismarck*.

Two other Catalinas, *M/240* also from Lough Erne, and *O/210* from Oban, Scotland, with American pilots Lieutenant Jimmy Johnson and Ensign Carl Rinehart, respectively, helped to track the *Bismarck* before she met her end on the morning of 27 May 1941.

The Incomparable Catalina

WHEN WAR finally came to America, it was the foresight of those who had insisted upon preparedness that gave the United States a fighting chance. Still, despite these valiant efforts, the defense buildup had only just begun when Pearl Harbor became a household name. As a practical matter, this meant that those Navy patrol squadrons charged with maintaining operations until the full weight of American industry could be brought to bear, had to make do with what they had—the slow, docile PBY Catalinas, the only flying boats, and the only patrol planes then available or being produced in any sizable numbers. As combat aircraft, they did not look particularly impressive, to say the least. Yet, the inspiring exploits of these venerable warboats could fill several volumes. Almost overnight, the purring "Cats" became snarling tigers that would attack anything carrying the red ball insignia of Japan, including cruisers, destroyers, submarines, airfields and ground installations, and other aircraft. They became dive bombers and torpedo planes, and they took on all adversaries. More than 3,300 Catalinas were produced, the largest number of a single flying boat type ever built.*

In the months before the surprise attack on Pearl Harbor, Patrol Wings One and Two, based at Kaneohe and Ford Island respectively, had been busily engaged in training pilots and crew members to meet the rapidly expanding needs of naval aviation. As fast as they could be trained, these crews were sent elsewhere to become the nuclei of new PBY squadrons then being formed.

During this period, Commander "Soc" McGinnis commanded Patrol Wing One, made up of Patrol Squadrons 11, 12, and 14, while Rear Admiral "Pat" Bellinger was in charge of Patrol Wing Two, consisting of Patrol Squadrons 21 through 24. Bellinger also served as Commander, Task Force Nine, and in this capacity, exercised operational control over all U.S. Navy patrol aviation in the area, including the planes of McGinnis' squadrons. He shared responsibility for overall air defense of the islands with Brigadier General F. L. Martin of the U.S. Army Air Corps. Together they had surveyed their charge, and on 31 March 1941 had written a joint estimate of the situation. Their analysis proved to be only too accurate. "It appears," they said, "that the most likely and dangerous form of attack on Oahu would be an air attack. It is believed that at present such an attack would most likely be launched from one or more carriers, which would probably approach inside of 300 miles." Thus they had unknowingly predicted what would shortly become a grim reality. To guard against such an eventuality, they had discussed the desirability of ". . . daily patrols as far as possible to seaward through 360 degrees. . . ," but they also pointed out that such an ambitious patrol plan could ". . . only be effectively maintained with present personnel and material for a very short period and as a practical measure cannot, therefore, be undertaken unless other intelligence indicates that a surface raid is probable within narrow limits."†

*The exact number of these aircraft produced by the Soviets at Taganrog cannot be accurately determined.

†Hearings before the Joint Committee on the Investigation of the Pearl Harbor Attack, 79th Congress, Part 15, p. 1437f.

Pearl Harbor, Hawaii, as it looked from the air on 30 October 1941. (U.S. Navy)

During the intervening months before the attack on Pearl Harbor, there were several instances of such intelligence, but when responded to by a general alert, they always turned out to be false alarms. It was the old story of the boy who cried wolf too often. The alerts disrupted training schedules, and seemed to confirm the widely held belief that the Japanese would not be so foolish as to attack the fortress of Pearl Harbor, home port of the U.S. Pacific Fleet. The majority opinion was that if and when the Japanese attack did come, the initial thrust would be made against the Philippines. It was this mental attitude which prevailed on 27 November 1941 when the Chief of Naval Operations, Admiral Harold R. Stark, dispatched a message to Admiral Husband E. Kimmel, Commander in Chief, Pacific Fleet, warning him to expect "... an aggressive move by Japan within the next few days. ..." But not even Stark expected an attack on Pearl Harbor, and neither Kimmel nor the Army commander, General Short, felt it necessary to take extraordinary precautions. The attack was expected to take place somewhere else, if it came at all. Security was increased to guard against sabotage, but it was apparently not considered necessary to inform air defense commanders Bellinger and Martin of the warning.

So it was that on the Sunday morning of 7 December 1941, VP-24 at Ford Island had only four PBY aircraft airborne conducting routine exercises with U.S. submarines, while three other flying boats from VP-14 at Kaneohe flew the regular morning security patrol, armed with depth charges.

One of these latter three Catalinas was *14-P-1*, flown by Ensigns William Tanner and Clark Greevy. That morning *14-P-1* became the first U.S. Navy aircraft to engage the Japanese in World War II, for at 6:33 A.M. Tanner and Greevy sighted what appeared to be the periscope and part of the conning tower of a small submarine, about a mile or more off the entrance to Pearl Harbor. They marked the sub's position with smokelights, and minutes later the destroyer *Ward*, which was operating nearby, attacked the intruder with depth charges and gunfire. Tanner followed this up with a depth charge attack of his own, and then sent a coded message back to base reporting the action he had taken. It was about this time that he began to have second thoughts about what he had done. He reminded himself that he had acted in accordance with firm standing orders to attack any submarine found in this area. But suppose there had been a foul-up? Suppose he had helped to sink an American submarine?

Ashore, there were others who shared his doubts. Commander "Soc" Mc-Ginnis, who was in his headquarters that morning, began checking to see whether his three planes had been provided with the latest positions of all U.S. submarines in the vicinity.

At Ford Island, Admiral Bellinger's Operations Officer, Commander Logan Ramsey, had also received Tanner's disconcerting message at 7:37 A.M. He too was certain there had been some mistake, and told the wing duty officer to call the aircraft and ask for authentication. In the meantime, he picked up the telephone and called CINCPAC Headquarters, to learn that the duty officer there had just received a similarly puzzling report from the destroyer *Ward*. By 7:40 A.M., Admiral Kimmel himself had been notified.

In the interim, Ramsey had begun to draw up a search plan, just in case it might be needed. At 7:57 A.M. he was rudely interrupted by the sound of a plane which came diving out of the bright morning sky. Seconds later, the first bomb hit the ramp near the VP-22 hangar. In a matter of minutes, the entire aircraft parking area was transformed into a scene of burning aircraft and demolished hangars. The air was thick with smoke, and the ground was littered with debris. At 7:58 A.M. Ramsey got out the message which heralded U.S. entry into World War II: "Air raid Pearl Harbor—This is no drill."

Admiral Bellinger arrived at about this time, and took charge of the situation. Others, however, had already begun to respond on their own. Machine guns on several of the aircraft had been manned, and grim-faced sailors fired back at the diving Japanese planes as best they could.

When the first attack ended, Bellinger was soon informed that among the six PBY squadrons under his command at Hawaii, only three aircraft had survived the attack in flyable condition: two at Kaneohe, and one at Ford Island. This excluded, of course, the planes which were already airborne, and those of VP-21, which were deployed at Midway Island. The remaining three Catalinas were ordered into the air immediately to search for the Japanese fleet. But the single flyable PBY at Ford Island had difficulty getting to the ramp and into the water, because of all the burning aircraft and debris. As men attempted to clear a path through the wreckage, the second attack came in.

By this time, guns had been removed from burning aircraft and mounted elsewhere in a variety of ingenious ways. Workbench vises seemed to work best, and Bellinger later indicated in his official report that as nearly as could be determined, four Japanese planes were shot down by patrol squadron personnel on the ground.* But this was little consolation, in light of the destruction of more than half of the Hawaii-based Catalinas, and severe damage to most of

*Commander Task Force Nine (Commander Patrol Wing Two)—Report of Operations on 7 December 1941—(20 Dec 1941).

In a matter of minutes after the Japanese attack on 7 December, the entire aircraft parking area at NAS Pearl Harbor was transformed into a scene of burning aircraft. (U.S. Navy)

Squadron personnel at Kaneohe attempt to save part of a burning PBY. (U.S. Navy)

The PBY squadrons were virtually demolished after the Japanese attack. (U.S. Navy)

the others. After the second attack, the word was relayed that the two aircraft previously reported flyable at Kaneohe had also been hit and knocked out of commission.* At Ford Island, the one remaining flying boat which was still operable somehow survived the second attack, and was launched to search a sector to the northwest.

Meanwhile, Ensign Fred Meyer in *14-P-2* had been patrolling south of Oahu when the first attack commenced. He became aware of the situation when he received an emergency radio message from Kaneohe, telling him to conduct a search to the northwest. He had proceeded to execute his orders, when he spotted a flight of aircraft heading for Oahu. Thinking these might be enemy planes, he quickly descended and flew the Catalina a few feet off the surface of the water to avoid being fired upon from below. His caution was well advised, for a few minutes later *14-P-2* came under attack by the incoming Japanese. Meyer's gunners fought back, and sent one plane away trailing smoke. The Japanese did not press their advantage further, however, because of more important business at Pearl. Meyer reported the attack and resumed his patrol, but he did not make contact with the Japanese fleet. He returned to Kaneohe after dark to find the fires still burning.

Almost 5,000 miles to the west lay the Philippines, the next target on the Japanese timetable. Here too, the Catalinas found themselves in the thick of battle. Patrol Wing Ten, commanded by Captain F. D. Wagner, had twenty-eight PBYs to do the work of a hundred. Two squadrons, VP-101 and 102, operated from Manila Bay and Olongapo on Luzon, supported by the old *Langley* (then a seaplane tender) and the *Childs* (AVD-1). Three PBYs were also operating with the tender *William B. Preston* (AVD-7), anchored in Davao Gulf on the southeastern coast of Mindanao.

At about 3:00 A.M. Manila time on 8 December, word of the attack on Pearl Harbor reached Admiral Thomas C. Hart, Commander in Chief, U.S. Asiatic Fleet, who alerted his forces to the inevitable. The opening shots came at daylight, when fighters from the Japanese carrier *Ryujo* pounced on *William B. Preston* at Davao Gulf, and destroyed two of her PBYs on the water. The Japanese launched other attacks during the day, including one on Clark Army Airbase, which destroyed twelve B-17 Flying Fortresses, thirty P-40 fighters, and severely damaged several other aircraft. On 12 December seven Catalinas operating from Olongapo were caught at their moorings, having been followed home from a patrol by Japanese fighters. All seven aircraft were destroyed.

By this time the Japanese invasion was well underway, and the enemy had established overwhelming air superiority. It was clear that if the PBYs were to

*Commander Patrol Wing One—Report of Japanese Air Attack in Kaneoke Bay, T. H., December 7, 1941 (1 Jan 1942).

survive to fight again, their bases of operation would have to be moved south. Accordingly, PATWING Ten was ordered to depart the Philippines.

The tender *Childs* with the wing staff aboard left on the night of 14 December, while the PBYs flew south to Surabaja and Ambon. From these locations Captain Wagner hoped to inflict as much damage as possible on the Japanese as they continued their drive to the south.

On 27 December six Catalinas sortied from Ambon to attack the Japanese at Jolo in the Philippines, but were intercepted by enemy fighters which shot down four of them, one of which made a successful landing in the open sea. The aircraft had to be sunk, but the crew was rescued the following day. Surviving members of the other crews, led by Lieutenants E. L. Christman and Jack Dawley, were able to reach the shore, and were also eventually picked up.

Ambon began to come under heavy air attack, and on 16 January Patrol Squadron 101 was ordered to evacuate. By the twenty-eighth all Navy personnel had left the area. The Catalinas continued their operations from Surabaja and Australia in the face of increasing enemy strength. By 11 February PATWING Ten had only twelve remaining aircraft.* Six of these were at Surabaja, and six were operating from the tender *William B. Preston* at Darwin, Australia.

On 19 February the Japanese made an air attack on Darwin, sinking seventeen allied ships, damaging the *William B. Preston*, and destroying three PBYs. Lieutenant Thomas H. Moorer, later to become Chief of Naval Operations and eventually Chairman of the Joint Chiefs of Staff, was out on patrol during the attack. He was engaged by a swarm of incoming fighters, and his aircraft was shot down in a withering rain of enemy fire. Miraculously, he and his crew survived, and were plucked from the water a short time later by a freighter. This ship was itself attacked and sunk by the Japanese shortly thereafter, but Moorer and all but one of his crew reached an island and were eventually rescued by friendly forces.

By this time, Surabaja was under regular air attack. Japanese planes were operating from Bali only 150 miles away, and the PBYs were obliged to take off at dawn and return late in the day to avoid being caught on the ground. Java itself was soon to fall to the advancing enemy, and the PBYs at Surabaja moved on to Broome on the northwest coast of Australia. By this time PATWING Ten had only a few aircraft left in combat condition. Nevertheless, the Catalinas continued their operations against hopeless odds. On 29 April 1942 two PATWING Ten PBYs, commanded by Lieutenant Commander Edgar T. Neale and flown by Lieutenants j.g. Thomas F. Pollock and Leroy C. Deede, slipped into the Philippines for a daring night evacuation of some fifty staff officers and nurses from Corregidor. "Why we were not destroyed on the water during the transfer of cargo and passengers can only be answered by Divine Providence," Pollock later commented.† On the return flight, Pollock's boat was holed by a coral reef at Lake Lanao on Mindanao. The passengers stuffed blankets into the holes to keep the aircraft from sinking until Pollock could run it up onto the beach. With the Japanese not far away, crude repairs were made under extremely difficult conditions, and both planes made it back to Australia.

The tide of Japanese victory in the Pacific first began to turn in June 1942. The event was the Battle of Midway, and the PBYs were there to play a part.

Commander Joseph J. Roche Jr., chief of the intelligence center at Pearl Harbor, had managed to intercept enemy coded communications, and had learned that the Japanese were planning a big push into the central Pacific. The

*PATWING Ten started the war with twenty-eight PBYs, and had received twelve additional aircraft from VP-22 and five from the Dutch, for a total of forty-five.

†Operation Flight Gridiron 27 April–3 May 1942, as summarized by Capt. Thomas F. Pollock, USN.

Midway Island from the air in November 1941. It was a tiny island, hardly more than a sandbar. (U.S. Navy)

target was a tiny island, hardly more than a sandbar, named Midway, which the Japanese wanted because of its strategic location. Admiral Isoroku Yamamoto, Commander in Chief of the Combined Japanese Fleet, also hoped to draw out the remnants of the American Navy in order to completely destroy them. He had at his disposal almost 200 ships, including over 100 combatants. An occupation force of transports and their escorts approached Midway from the southwest, while a striking force of powerful combatants, including four aircraft carriers, made its thrust from the northwest. Admiral Yamamoto himself followed about 600 miles behind, with still another large force. To confuse the Americans, he had dispatched two more carriers and associated ships to attack Dutch Harbor in the Aleutians.

For their part, the Americans had only twenty-five combatant ships to throw into the fray at Midway. Three of these were carriers, but one, *Yorktown*, was still badly damaged from the Battle of the Coral Sea. The Americans, however, had the advantage of Roche's intelligence, and they were ready. Rear Admiral Pat Bellinger's PBYs, flying from Midway, ranged far to the west on fifteen-hour patrols, seeking the first signs of the enemy.

At about 9:20 A.M. on the morning of 3 June 1942, Ensign Jack Reid and crew in his Catalina were 700 miles from Midway, near the outer limit of their patrol sector, when he spotted the Japanese occupation force. He mistook the transports and their combatant escorts for the striking group, and radioed a contact report back to base indicating that this was the "main body." Reports from other PBYs began to come in, all testifying to the fact that a sizable Japanese naval force was rapidly approaching Midway from the southwest.

That same morning, a flight of four Catalinas had taken off from Pearl Harbor, and headed for Midway. These were some of the new PBY-5A amphibians which had replaced those destroyed on 7 December. Three were from VP-24, and one from VP-51:

Aircraft	Plane Commander
24-P-12	Lieutenant j.g. C. P. Hibberd*
24-P-7	Lieutenant j.g. D. C. Davis
24-P-11	Ensign G. D. Probst
51-P-5	Ensign A. Rothenberg

*Mission commander Lt. W. L. Richards flew in this aircraft.

The four aircraft made the flight south in just over nine hours, arriving at Midway about 5:00 P.M. There, the crews learned that they were to be launched four hours later in a daring attempt to locate and attack the Japanese force spotted earlier in the day, which was now steaming steadily toward them from the southwest. Ground crews began to load each "Cat" with a Mark XIII torpedo for the first airborne night torpedo attack ever attempted.*

At 9:15 P.M. the four PBYs took off to seek their prey. Lieutenant W. L. Richards of VP-44 had been assigned to direct the mission from Lieutenant Hibberd's plane, 24-P-12, as the flight commander. They flew west-south-west on a course of 261°, and all went well until midnight, when 51-P-5 lost sight of the formation. An hour later, 24-P-11 also became separated from the flight during passage through a cloud bank. Richards knew nothing of these events, because the three following aircraft had been flying without lights as instructed.

At 1:15 A.M. the radar operator in the lead aircraft picked up ten ships, and about five minutes later, the Japanese task force was sighted in the moonlight some seven miles ahead. The ships were steaming in two columns; it was easy to pick out the larger ships, although it was difficult to identify them by type from that distance. The pilot of the lead plane picked out what appeared to be the largest ship, hoping that it was a carrier, and began a glide toward it, with engines throttled back and lights out. At closer range, the target was clearly identified as a large troop transport or cargo ship, and the attack run was continued. The torpedo was released 100 feet off the water at 800 yards range, and the "Cat" went into a sharp climbing turn to the right, taking it over the stern of the Japanese vessel. There was no opposing fire, and the waist gunners reported a large explosion and heavy smoke. The enemy had not expected a night torpedo attack, and they were taken completely by surprise.

Davis in 24-P-7 chose his target and made the next run, but not being satisfied with his alignment, he broke off the attack before releasing his torpedo. A few minutes later he began his second approach, and did not release the torpedo until only about 200 yards from the target. As he made his pull-up, the port waist gunner raked the deck of the ship with 50-caliber gunfire. But this time the Japanese gunners were ready, and responded in kind. The Catalina was hit several times before drawing out of range. The torpedo failed to find its mark.

Ensign Probst, who had become separated from the flight earlier in 24-P-11, found the enemy ships on his own, and arrived just in time to make the third attack. He dropped his torpedo at about 800 yards, feinted to the right, and then went into a tight left turn. There was an explosive flash, and the enemy opened fire. As Probst withdrew, his aircraft was attacked by a float-plane fighter, but was able to evade it with the help of scattered cloud cover.

*VP-44, Lt. W. L. Richards' report of Night Torpedo Attack, 3–4 June (18 June 1942).

Rothenberg in *51-P-5* had also continued on in search of the Japanese formation, but was not as lucky as Probst. At about 2:00 A.M. with half of his fuel consumed, he headed for home. The other three aircraft proceeded toward Midway independently, when at 6:41 A.M. they picked up a broadcast, "Air raid Midway—Midway is now undergoing air raid." Richards, Davis, and Rothenberg diverted to Laysan, approximately 335 nautical miles east-southeast of Midway, arriving there safely with only a few gallons of fuel left in the tanks. Probst ran out of gas and landed in the open sea, where he and his crew floated for two days before they were rescued.

At about 5:40 A.M. on 4 June, a Catalina flown by Lieutenant William Chase had spotted planes from the Japanese striking force approaching from the northwest, and flashed out a message in plain language, "Many planes heading Midway." Meanwhile, Lieutenant Howard Ady of VP-23 had located the striking force itself. The carriers *Yorktown, Enterprise* and *Hornet* were ready, and the battle which would change the course of the Pacific war was joined. When it ended, the Americans had lost more than 300 men, 150 planes, a destroyer, and the aircraft carrier *Yorktown*. But the Japanese fleet was retreating toward Japan. Enemy losses included more than 2,500 men, 332 aircraft, a heavy cruiser, and four aircraft carriers. It was a staggering blow, and the beginning of the end for Japan.

In the aftermath of the battle, the Catalinas scoured the ocean for stragglers from the Japanese force. All they found was a boat from the sunken carrier *Hiryu* with a mast and a blanket sail rigged, trying to make it to Japanese-held Wake Island. Lieutenant Campbell in the PBY-5 from VP-11 radioed for a ship to pick them up, and continued on his way.

The Catalinas made numerous open sea landings, and rescued 27 Americans, including four crew members of a PBY which had been shot down by Japanese fighters. The sole survivor of Torpedo Squadron Eight, Ensign George Gay, had been in the water for about 30 hours before he was picked up on 5 June, and remembers his rescue vividly:

> I had a bullet hole in my left arm, a piece of shrapnel in my left hand, and my left leg was fairly badly burned. I lost somewhere in the neighborhood of a pound an hour while I was in the water, from dehydration, blood loss and high adrenalin flow.
>
> A PBY-5A came out looking for the remnants of the Japanese Fleet on the 5th. The pilot spotted me and flew on by. After he had completed his mission late that afternoon he came back to pick me up. He radioed to Midway for a PT boat to get me, but it would have taken about three days to reach me. The pilot, "Pappy" Cole, put it to his crew. He said, "I want to land and pick this guy up, but I want to put it to a vote." So they voted and all said yes. The first thing they yelled as they taxied up was "Have you seen any Zeros today?" I answered no. They said, "Good, let's get the hell out of here." I said, "Let's go," and they just jerked me out of that raft and went.
>
> If a Japanese aircraft had caught them on the water, it would have been all over.*

Far to the north in the Aleutians, the struggle had only begun. The Catalinas based there were to carry a full share of the combat burden, but many of the pilots considered the weather even more deadly than the enemy. The Aleuts had long referred to this 1,000-mile island chain as the place where storms are created, and there was more substance to this belief than superstition. It is here that the warm Japan Stream ocean current clashes with the icy waters of the Bering Sea, producing meteorological phenomena of great intensity, ranging from thick blankets of fog and freezing rain to violent winds called Williwaws which reach 100 knots or more. These sharp high velocity gusts can change direction suddenly, and their severe vertical currents

*Author's interview of George Gay, 8 April 1977.

can cause structural damage to an aircraft in flight, or dash it against the side of a mountain. The Aleutian winters bring sub-zero temperatures which cause oil to congeal, and often necessitate thawing engines with a blowtorch. Immersion of a human body in the frigid sea results in death from exposure in a matter of minutes.

Yamamoto had decided to attack and occupy the Aleutians for several reasons. First, he wished to divert U.S. attention and forces from his primary thrust at Midway. Secondly, he wanted to take and hold the islands at the end of the chain to prevent U.S. forces from using the Aleutians as a staging area to attack Japan. Finally, he hoped that by putting troops ashore and establishing bases on U.S. soil, he would lower American morale and bolster Japanese spirits.

The United States knew of the planned attack, but not the precise date and time. Twenty-three Catalinas of PATWING Four, under the command of Captain Leslie E. Gehres, were dispersed with four seaplane tenders among several small coves, to avoid mass destruction in the event of surprise. These planes flew patrols day and night, searching for the enemy fleet that they knew was on the way. On 1 and 2 June, the Aleutian weather machine generated gale force winds and driving rain, but the PBYs flew regardless. Visibility was so reduced that the Catalinas, only a few of which were equipped with primitive radar sets, could have flown directly over the Japanese force without seeing it.

The attack against Dutch Harbor came on the morning of 3 June. At 5:40 A.M. a warning was flashed by the seaplane tender *Gillis,* which picked up the incoming Japanese planes on radar. Ensign Jack F. Litsey, who was taxiing on the water, hurriedly swung his PBY into the wind and was on his takeoff run when the enemy arrived overhead. The plane was hit several times and disabled. Ensign James T. Hildebrand managed to get his PBY off the water and set out to look for the enemy fleet. About three hours later, the "Cat" engaged two Japanese reconnaissance aircraft and shot down one of them.

The enemy carriers still had to be located. Lieutenant j.g. Jean Cusick, searching to the southwest of Dutch Harbor, was suddenly attacked by numerous fighters from the carrier *Junyo* and overwhelmed. With one engine out of commission and the aircraft riddled with holes and burning, Cusick, though wounded, managed a successful landing in the open sea. The plane sank almost immediately, but five of its crew escaped in a rubber life raft. Cusick and another crewman died of their wounds a short time later. The copilot, Lieutenant j.g. Wylie M. Hunt, and the other two crew members on the raft, were subsequently picked up by a Japanese warship, more dead than alive from exposure.

Lieutenant Lucius D. Campbell and his crew were also searching for the carriers to the south. But the attack on Dutch Harbor had caused them to take off from their dispersal point on Umnak Island without a full load of fuel. After flying for several hours in and out of snow squalls and high gusty winds, Campbell had headed for home with just enough fuel to make the return flight, when they were suddenly pounced upon by Japanese float-planes. A few moments later, Campbell sighted the carrier task force itself, and was almost immediately attacked by a carrier-based Zero. The Catalina ducked into a snow storm, but not before one man was wounded, the rudder control cables were severed, and the fuel tanks were riddled. Although they had escaped from the Japanese aircraft, the fuel was rapidly running out. Then the inevitable happened, and there was a silence which was almost deafening. Campbell eased the PBY down and made a beautiful no-rudder dead stick landing in the open sea, in spite of snow, high winds, and rough water. The problem then became one of keeping the perforated flying boat afloat, which they did until they were picked up by a U.S. Coast Guard vessel about three hours later. Campbell's radioman had managed to transmit two reports on

A Catalina PBY-4 on patrol in the vicinity of the Aleutians. (General Dynamics)

A Catalina rearms amid snow-covered terrain in the Aleutians. (U.S. Navy)

the enemy's whereabouts and disposition, but they were so distorted by static that they were unreadable at Dutch Harbor.

Lieutenant Marshall C. Freerks found the Japanese force again in the early morning hours of 4 June. He shadowed the enemy for a while, but since his aircraft had been airborne all night, his fuel supply was dangerously low, and he was obliged to leave his quarry and head for home. He was soon relieved, however, by Lieutenant Charles E. Perkins, executive officer of VP-42. Perkins had armed his Catalina with a torpedo and two 500-pound bombs, hoping that the opportunity to use them might arise. After watching the Japanese for about two hours, he was advised by radio that Lieutenant j.g. Eugene W. Stockstill and crew were on the way to the scene. Perkins decided that this would be a good time to expend his ordnance before going home. Taking advantage of his altitude, he put the "Cat" into a dive to gain speed. Pulling out just above the waves, he began a torpedo run toward the carrier *Junyo*. The Japanese fired all available guns at him as he came boring in at deck level. About halfway to the drop point, the intense anti-aircraft fire hit his starboard engine, putting it out of commission. Forced to jettison his torpedo and the two bombs, Perkins turned into the bad weather for protection, and set a course for home. The Catalina made it all the way on one engine.

Stockstill never arrived on station, and it is probable that his airplane was ambushed by Japanese fighters. He and his crew simply disappeared without a trace.

B-26 and B-17 bombers of the Army Air Force also tried their luck against the Japanese on the 4th but scored no hits, and lost one B-17 and its crew in the attempt. That afternoon the enemy task force launched its second and final attack against Dutch Harbor. Damage included the destruction of a hangar, a warehouse, and some fuel storage facilities, but for the most part, Dutch Harbor weathered the attack well.

The Japanese task force then faded into the miserable Aleutian weather and steamed toward the islands of Kiska and Attu, hundreds of miles to the west. The Americans were unaware that the Japanese had departed the area and continued to search for several days, but by the time they began to suspect the enemy intentions, the Japanese had put their invasion forces ashore on the two islands. During this period, twelve PBYs of VP-43, commanded by Lieutenant Commander Carrol B. "Doc" Jones, arrived to reinforce the other two squadrons of PATWING Four, whose crews and planes had been depleted during the fighting.

A Catalina flown by Lieutenant j.g. Milton R. Dahl found the Japanese entrenched on Kiska and Attu on 10 June, and later that same day, Lieutenant j.g. William J. Bowers and his crew brought back further intelligence information on the enemy disposition.

Army bombers and Navy Catalinas hit Kiska on the eleventh. Bombing from an altitude of about 3,000 feet, the Army's level bombing runs proved ineffective against this type target. To make matters worse, the Army planes were obliged to fly some 600 miles each way to and from their base at Umnak, which limited their strikes to one or two per day. On the other hand, the special characteristics of the flying boat were used to great advantage by the Navy pilots. Operating from *Gillis,* which had been moved forward to Nazan Bay at Atka Island, the "Cats" hit Kiska almost every hour, night and day, for forty-eight hours, stopping only when munitions supplies ran out. It was truly a PBY blitz.

The weather in the target area was generally overcast with breaks in the cloud cover over Kiska Harbor. The PBYs came in above the overcast, and made their attacks individually from a position almost directly over the objective. The pilot pushed the nose of his plane over into a steep dive and descended through a hole, if one was available, at about 200 knots, dropping his bombs on enemy installations or ships in the harbor. The gunners came into action also, strafing the target as the plane flashed by. Pullouts were sometimes begun as low as 500 feet, which put the Catalinas a few feet off the water at the bottom of the recovery arc. But the PBY pilots knew better than to linger there, and used the speed gained in the dive to climb quickly into the clouds for cover.

One PBY attacking a light cruiser was almost flipped on its back from the force of a direct hit on the unfortunate Japanese vessel. Another, flown by Warrant Officer Leland L. Davis of VP-43, was so riddled with holes that upon returning to base it could not be kept afloat, and sank alongside the tender. "Doc" Jones described the situation in a report of the action as follows:

One plane returned to the base with about 200 holes, one engine shot out, and one aileron gone. Enemy light anti-aircraft was very accurate at low altitudes. Heavy anti-aircraft was not troublesome, unless course and speed were maintained for about one minute.*

The blitz ended on the morning of 13 June. Although the "Cats" had failed to dislodge the enemy, they had inflicted substantial damage on the shore installations, scored hits on several warships, and destroyed four enemy flying boats.

After the blitz, strikes against Kiska continued at a more moderate pace. The Japanese employed Nakijima Rufe-type float fighters against the Catalinas, but the flying boats put up a credible defense. "Doc" Jones reported that on an 8 August mission against Kiska, four of these single-float fighters attacked the PBYs using quarter and beam approaches, the latter in an attempt to use the PBY's own wing for protection from the waist gunner as they came in. The "Cats," however, had some tricks of their own.

One gunner, Battuello AMM 2/C, caused one fighter to close range by pretending his gun was out of action by slumping over and pointing gun in air. Jap closed rapidly to about 100 yds. without firing, and Battuello re-manned gun and emptied 50 cal. can into him. Tracers indicated many hits. Jap executed wing over and dove straight down into fog.†

The Catalinas continued to be active participants throughout the Aleutians campaign. In addition to their functions as torpedo planes and dive bombers, they performed rescue missions and engaged in antisubmarine warfare with considerable success. When the Japanese finally evacuated the last of their battered forces from the Aleutians in July 1943, the Catalinas could justly claim a substantial contribution to the final outcome.

In the southwest Pacific the allies had stemmed the Japanese tide, and had begun to fight their way back via island stepping stones toward the Philippines, with the ultimate target being the home islands of Japan itself. The initial assaults were made in the Solomons, where the Japanese held Guadalcanal as well as other islands along the chain stretching to the northwest.

The PBYs were employed in the area at an early stage, to search for any Japanese naval forces coming down from the north to oppose the landings. As early as 5 August 1942, they were operating out of the Santa Cruz Islands from the seaplane tender *McFarland*. While the marines landed on Guadalcanal on 7 August, the tender *Mackinac* anchored off adjacent Malaita Island to provide a floating base for nine more Catalinas.

The landing on Guadalcanal went well, but it was to be followed by six months of stubborn Japanese resistance ashore, and by hard-fought naval engagements at sea, including the stinging defeat of U.S. surface forces in the battle of Savo Island in the early morning hours of 9 August.

In October, the enemy made a concerted effort to overpower the marines on Gaudalcanal. During daylight hours on the thirteenth and fourteenth, Henderson Field was attacked several times by Japanese bombers, but the real devastation was inflicted at night by heavy naval bombardment from enemy battleships and cruisers. Then on the fifteenth, with the field in ruins and most of its aircraft destroyed or disabled, a Japanese invasion force that included six transports began to put troop reinforcements ashore about ten miles away. Still, the Marine mechanics, with great effort and resourcefulness, were able to put a few SBD aircraft into flyable condition to mount a modest attack on the enemy. Major Jack Cram, pilot of General Geiger's personal aircraft the *Blue Goose*, was not to be left out of the action. He took off in the *Blue Goose* with a torpedo mounted under each wing, and flew to the assault area to attack the shipping in company with the resurrected SBD dive bombers. When they

*VP-43 Report of Action 10–20 June 1942.
†VP-43 Report of Action 8 August 1942.

arrived, the sky was full of Zeros providing air cover for the transports, as they disgorged troops and material. As the SBDs began their bombing runs from the west, Cram commenced an attack from the opposite direction, plunging his Catalina earthward at a speed well in excess of 200 knots. The SBDs released their bombs and pulled out in the customary fashion, but Cram kept going, leveling off just over the water to rush headlong at a big transport. As he closed to within a few hundred yards, he released his two torpedoes in quick succession. One of the torpedoes found its way to the target, and the ship shuddered from the explosion. As Cram headed triumphantly home, he was attacked from all directions by Zeros whose angry pilots shot the Catalina full of holes. By some miracle he made it all the way back to Henderson Field, where friendly anti-aircraft gunners shot down two of his pursuers, and a Grumman Wildcat fighter finished off a third.

The Catalinas were forever being called upon to perform unusual tasks. One of their many functions in the southwest Pacific was to support the Australian coastwatchers, who provided the allies with the best and latest intelligence information on approaching enemy forces. The "Cats" supplied the coastwatchers by air drops, and sometimes went in to rescue these gutsy Australians from enemy-held areas when the Japanese were about to capture them. In mid-November 1942, Paul Mason, who was providing vital information on Japanese fleet and aircraft movements from Bougainville Island, was in trouble. The Japanese were well aware of Mason's timely alerting of allied forces to the south, and decided to eliminate him. Because he was so adept at using the jungle to conceal himself, eluding all previous efforts to capture him, the Japanese imported a number of hunting dogs to track him down. Mason's native cohorts lost no time reporting this development to him, and he immediately requested air support. A Catalina was dispatched to the scene and bombed the kennel, the exact location of which Mason pinpointed from the ground. The crafty coastwatcher observed the action from a nearby hill, and afterward confirmed the complete annihilation of the unfortunate canine pack.

By 8 February 1943, after long months of bloody fighting, the Japanese had evacuated their troops from Guadalcanal. On the twentieth of that month the Marines made an unopposed landing in the Russel Islands, and on 30 June they assaulted the larger island of New Georgia. The Japanese tenaciously defended every inch of ground, and it took until 5 August to capture the enemy airfield at Munda. On 11 July three PBY-5s of VP-24 were caught on the water at Enogai Inlet on the western side of New Georgia by two Japanese Pete float-planes, as they were attempting to evacuate wounded marines. The boats fought back, and one was hit by machine gun fire and fragments from a near bomb miss. Another Catalina from the same squadron with a load of wounded aboard was jumped at Enogai by two strafing Zeros on 21 July, and was hit several times before F4U Corsairs arrived on the scene and drove the attackers off. The pilot, Lieutenant j.g. Ariel L. Lane, had managed to start the engines and get the aircraft on the step for takeoff, when the Zeros made their third and final run. The port engine was hit, and Lane was obliged to settle back down onto the water again to check the damage. There, with both engines shut down, the Catalina drifted onto a reef and sank in three feet of water. The evacuees were hurriedly unloaded into boats, while a bailing-party managed to float the aircraft and make temporary repairs. The following day it took off on one engine and returned to base for repairs.

The island of Kolombangara, with a strong Japanese garrison, was bypassed by the Americans in favor of a landing on Vella Lavella, where they constructed an airfield from which to project air power against the Japanese at Bougainville to the north, and Kolombangara just to the south.

The Americans made concerted efforts to cut the enemy supply lines to Kolombangara, but warships and cargo vessels of the "Tokyo Express" continued to support Japanese troops as they had done at New Georgia and Guadal-

The Black Cats searched untiringly for the Tokyo Express in the Solomons. (U.S. Navy)

canal. One of the more colorful chapters in the history of naval aviation during this phase of the Pacific War deals with the exploits of the legendary "Black Cats," PBYs painted flat black and deployed at night to wreak havoc on the Japanese. VP-12, whose planes began operating out of Nandi Bay in the Fijis in November 1942, was the original "Black Cat" squadron. Shortly thereafter, the "Cats" moved north to Espiritu Santo Island in the New Hebrides, and in December, five "Cats" under the command of Commander Clarence O. Taff were operating on a full schedule from Guadalcanal. In March 1943, VP-12 was relieved by VP-54 under Commander Carl Schoenweiss. The newcomers adapted quickly to the nocturnal environment, and almost immediately took up the task of night bombing raids against the Munda airfield on New Georgia. Their most dramatic mission, however, was seeking out and attacking enemy warships and logistics vessels making their way down "The Slot" in the Solomon Islands.

While the slow-moving Catalinas were vulnerable to anti-aircraft fire and fighter attack during the day, they were stealthy and aggressive hunters at night. The Japanese, who did not have radar, were at a decided disadvantage, and were often unaware of the approach of the "Cats" until it was too late. The PBYs searched relentlessly both visually and with radar for the pertinacious "Tokyo Express," which continued to challenge American naval forces in the area, and provide gunfire and logistics support for their compatriots ashore. Sometimes the "Cats" teamed up with surface combatants, especially the PT boats. Just as often, however, they engaged the enemy by themselves.

A VP-54 report of a combined action with the enemy off Kolombangara in mid-July provides a vivid description of "Black Cat" operations.

The "Cat" involved in this particular incident was a PBY-5A flown by Lieutenants j.g. William E. Carter and Harry G. Charp Jr. They took off from Henderson Field at 6:28 P.M. and began searching "The Slot" between New Georgia and the Shortland Islands for the "Tokyo Express." Shortly after midnight, they discovered a Japanese force of four destroyers and one light cruiser about fifteen miles north of Kolombangara. Contact and amplifying reports were made, and voice communications were established with an allied naval task force nearby, which closed the enemy and opened fire. The Japanese cruiser was hit and lost all headway. A destroyer which had been the lead ship in the column also appeared to have been hit, but the four remaining destroyers turned north into a rain squall. The "Cat" lost radar contact on these, but two of them

The Black Cats' search area in the Solomons, 1942–43.

were detected again as they headed up "The Slot" toward Bougainville. Since there were no other American forces in the immediate vicinity, Carter decided to make an attack himself. On his first run he dropped two 500-pound bombs, which fell wide of the target. He tried again, this time under heavy anti-aircraft fire which repeatedly hit the PBY. Low on fuel, Carter was obliged to head for home. Upon landing at Henderson Field and inspecting the aircraft for damage, Carter found "large holes about 3 feet in diameter in the trailing edge of the starboard wing," and several holes in the port wing.*

In September 1943, Fleet Air Wing Seventeen was formed, comprised of Patrol Squadrons 11, 52 and 101. There was plenty for them to do. During the month of October, VP-11 aircraft, operating from a tender on the eastern tip of New Guinea, made bombing and strafing attacks on enemy installations on New Britain and other islands in the Bismarck Archipelago. They resupplied coastwatchers on New Britain and New Ireland, and ranged as far east as Buka Island in the Solomons. They stalked Japanese convoys, and made numerous night attacks on merchant ships, submarines, and surface combatants, leaving two destroyers engulfed in flame, and sinking or damaging several other vessels. The "Cats" suffered many hits themselves from intense anti-aircraft fire, but

*Although the date appearing in the report of combined action is 15 July, the events can be clearly identified with the Battle of Kolombangara of 13 July 1943, in which the Japanese cruiser *Jintsu* was sunk with heavy loss of life. Samuel Eliot Morison in his *History of U.S. Naval Operations in World War II* credits a spotter, Lt. Marvin E. Barnett, in a "Black Cat," probably this one, with directing allied naval gunfire onto the *Jintsu* in this action.

An aerial view of a typical Black Cat island base in the South Pacific during World War II. (U.S. Navy)

the rugged old flying boats gave ample evidence that they could take punishment, as well as dish it out.*

Just before midnight on 11 October, Lieutenant j.g. T. L. Hine surprised an enemy submarine on the surface and attacked. To increase the odds of sinking the submarine, he dropped his depth charges at an altitude of 200 feet. One of the two charges detonated prematurely, and the shock of the explosion nearly blew the tail off the Catalina, and seriously holed the hull. The horizontal stabilizer was badly twisted, but Hine managed to keep the aircraft under control until he could ease it down for an open sea landing. After coming to rest on the water, the aircraft with its damaged hull sank almost immediately, but not before the crew launched two rubber life rafts and scrambled aboard them. Although they were only a short distance from New Britain, Hine had no intention of subjecting his crew or himself to capture by the Japanese, so he set a course for Kiriwina Island, 150 miles to the south. They rowed steadily for 65 hours before being spotted by an Australian aircraft. When they were rescued a short time later by an Army OA-10 (USAAF version of a PBY-5), they were only 60 miles from Kiriwina. Had they not been picked up, they would have reached their destination under their own power in another day or two.

The hunting in November turned out to be good for the "Black Cats." At 2:00 A.M. on 14 November, Lieutenant W. E. Shinn of VP-11 found and attacked an enemy light cruiser and two merchant ships in the Bismarck Sea heading for Rabaul. On his first pass he missed the larger of the two merchants, but on

*During a twenty-month period in the vicinity of New Guinea and the Philippines, VP-11 sank 75,000 tons of Japanese shipping, rescued 15 aviators in open sea landings, and evacuated 219 Australians and their equipment, landing on the narrow Sepic River near Wewak in northeast New Guinea very close to the Japanese positions.

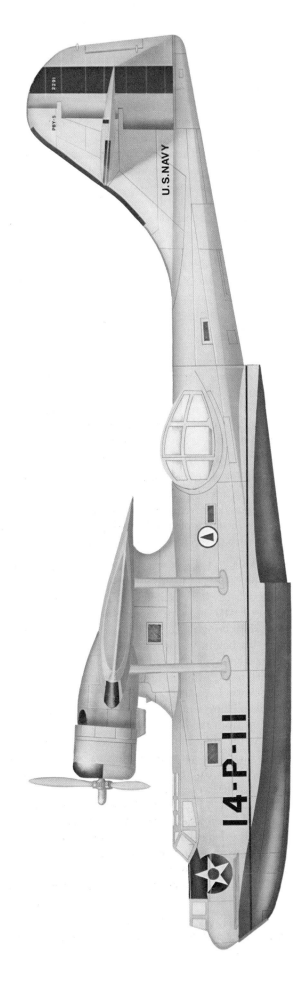

The uses to which the PBY Catalina, like this PBY-5 of VP-14, were put in World War II were many and varied. Their duties included reconnaissance, search and rescue, submarine patrol, torpedo and dive bombing, and support of ground combat operations. (John Ficklen)

his second attack he made a direct hit on the cruiser with a 1,000-pound bomb, which exploded below decks. A few minutes prior to this, Lieutenant J. R. Penfold had attacked a small convoy off the coast of New Ireland, and inflicted heavy damage to a large merchant vessel.

On the sixteenth Lieutenant j.g. Haas spotted an enemy convoy, which he unsuccessfully attacked with two 1,000-pound bombs. Lieutenant J. D. Cruze heard his contact report, however, and proceeded to the scene to participate in the action. He succeeded in dropping one 250-pound and one 1,000-pound bomb on a large merchant ship, damaging the ship so severely that it is doubtful that she ever made port. Lieutenant G. R. Taylor found the same ships, and made an unsuccessful torpedo run. During the attack his port engine was put out of commission by anti-aircraft fire, but he made it without much difficulty to Kiriwina for repairs.

VP-52, under Lieutenant Commander Harold Summer, was no less active. Operating from New Guinea, his boats performed "Black Cat" missions, and provided air support for an amphibious landing on New Britain. On 13 November despite heavy anti-aircraft fire from the ship and the shore, Lieutenant j.g. Lloyd got two direct hits on a cruiser anchored in the Steffen Strait, and Lieutenant William Lahodney's bombs heavily damaged another near Rabaul on 24 November. To add to the score, the "Cats" of VP-52 mauled two submarines, three destroyers, and sank several thousand tons of merchant shipping during November and December.

VP-34 began "Black Cat" operations from Samarai, New Guinea, on 31 December 1943, and continued until 16 February 1944. During the seven-week period of "Black Cat" operations, VP-34 aircraft made fifty-one attacks, thirty-four of which were successful. The squadron was officially credited with:

—three destroyers and one escort vessel damaged by 500 and 1,000-pound bombs;
—one destroyer damaged by strafing;
—70,000 tons of merchant shipping sunk or destroyed;
—fifty to seventy-five barges destroyed or damaged.

Other squadrons were also employed as "Black Cats" and served with distinction. The daring adventures of the pilots and crews could themselves comprise a book. The excitement of Lieutenant j.g. R. W. Schultz of VP-33 can almost be felt as, with one engine shot out, he continued an attack on a Japanese ship, bringing his "Cat" down to seventy-five feet of altitude before dropping his bombs.* Nor is it difficult to imagine the frustration of still another pilot, who, after repeated attacks on a large merchant vessel with no apparent results, made a final run so low that the starboard wing struck one of the ship's king-posts. Even so, this PBY was able to return to its base, with a sizable chunk missing from the wing's leading edge, and pieces of the king-post protruding from the damaged area.

As the allies moved slowly toward the Philippines, the Catalinas advanced with them. VP-34, then serving as an air-sea rescue squadron, moved from eastern New Guinea to the Admiralty Islands in April 1944, and then some 750 miles farther west to Biak Island in mid-July. During a five-month period, the Catalinas of VP-34 rescued seventy-seven men in open sea landings, mostly made in enemy-held areas. One of the squadron's more spectacular rescues occurred off the Japanese stronghold of Kavieng on the northwest tip of New Ireland. A major low-level attack by A-20s and B-25s of the Fifth Air Force was launched against Kavieng on 15 February 1944. Navy Lieutenant Nathan G. Gordon and his Catalina orbited a few miles offshore, ready to rescue crewmen

*The navigator was fatally wounded in this attack, and the starboard engine was virtually demolished, but the PBY severely damaged the target and returned safely to base on one engine.

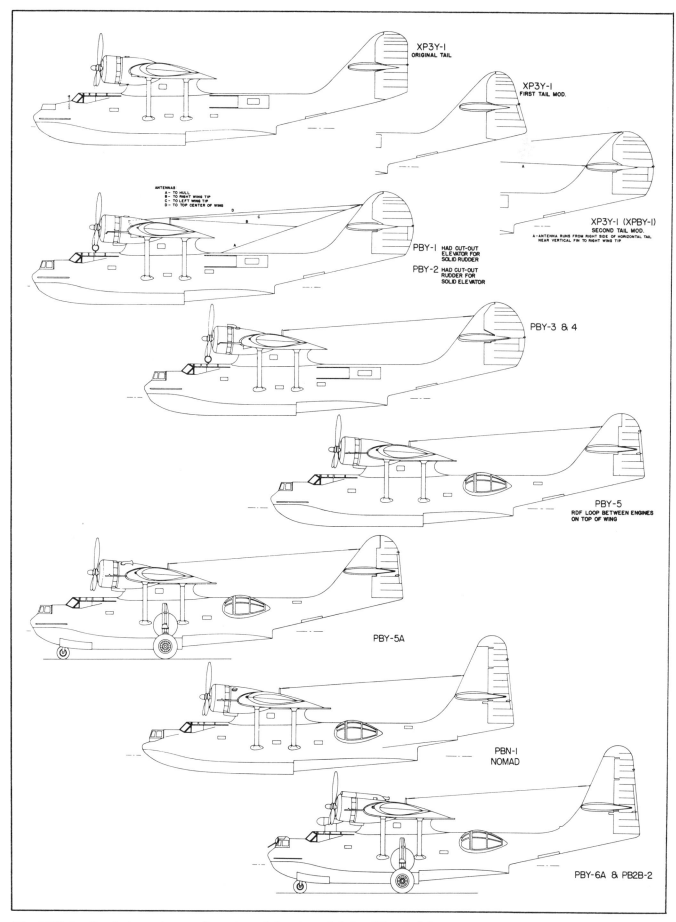

The PBY Catalina in its various configurations. (*American Aviation Historical Society Journal*)

The crew of the Black Cat *Pugnacious Puss* during a rare moment of relaxation in October 1943. (U.S. Navy)

from the Army bombers who might fall victim to the intense antiaircraft defense. The sea was rough that day, with long swells, which made open sea landings particularly hazardous.

After the B-25 attacks began, Gordon moved in close to shore, and immediately spotted a drifting life raft. No one was inside it, but in the rough water it was difficult to determine whether someone might be clinging to the raft, hiding beneath it, or swimming in the water nearby. Gordon elected to land for a closer look, and in a jolting touchdown opened up seams in the hull. Satisfying himself that there were no survivors in the vicinity of the raft, he got the badly-leaking aircraft airborne again, when another two rafts fastened together were sighted closer to shore, with six people aboard. As the PBY approached the downed flyers, the Japanese commenced firing anti-aircraft batteries. Another landing was made, and although it apparently caused no further damage to the plane, water continued to flow into the hull through the seams which had been previously sprung. Despite frenzied Japanese efforts to drive the Catalina off, Gordon taxied to the rafts and stopped the engines. Now the PBY was an easy target, but there was no other way to get the men, some of whom were wounded, aboard. Then they took off, only to be summoned a few minutes later to make another pickup. Again the PBY landed and stopped its engines, while more survivors climbed aboard in a hail of enemy gunfire. Groaning with a load of nineteen men and a bilge full of seawater, the "Cat" lumbered into the air and headed for home. Twenty miles from Kavieng, Gordon received still another urgent call from a B-25 circling overhead. The Army bomber had spotted a life raft with six men aboard only a few hundred yards offshore. Gordon and company returned to the scene, landed in the sea just off the beach, stopped the engines, and pulled six grateful men aboard with the Japanese firing at them all the time. After an unusually long takeoff run, the "Cat" lifted off the water again, and this time made for home in earnest with twenty-five rescued airmen aboard. Gordon was later awarded the Congressional Medal of Honor for his heroism that day.

Another particularly spectacular rescue took place on 4 December 1944. The destroyer USS *Cooper* had been sunk at Ormoc Bay in the Philippines the day before, leaving a large number of the American crew floating helplessly in the water off Japanese-held Leyte. Five "Cats" from VP-34 and an Army Air Force PBY-5A (OA-10-A) were dispatched to the scene, where they landed and began hauling survivors aboard as fast as they could. Lieutenant Joe F. Ball landed about a half-mile from shore, and began picking up survivors without taking time to count them. The jungle here was very thick, and came right down to the water. As Ball taxied along not far from the wall of trees and tropical growth, he suddenly became aware of two Japanese destroyer escorts expertly camouflaged to blend with the foliage. They did not open fire upon the PBY, however, apparently for fear of giving away their position. Ball wisely pretended not to notice their presence as he taxied about, plucking waterlogged sailors from Ormoc Bay. Finally, when at least fifty-six survivors plus a crew of seven had been crowded aboard, the overloaded aircraft staggered off the water and flew its precious cargo safely to the tender. Lieutenant Essary and his crew in another VP-34 aircraft did almost as well, rescuing forty-six; Lieutenant Day picked up twenty-five, while the other two VP-34 aircraft and the Army OA-10-A together accounted for at least thirty-seven more.*

The phenomenal exploits of the PBY in World War II are legion. No one will seriously dispute, however, that the PBY was painfully slow, aesthetically unattractive, and technologically obsolescent. Yet it was the deliberateness of movement that gave this aircraft an aura of dignity by day, and the sure-footedness of a cat by night. Its ungainly profile bespoke character and uniqueness, and if the Catalina was not pleasing to the eye, it was much respected by the men who flew it, to say nothing of the countless numbers of survivors snatched from watery peril. Simplicity of design imbued the PBY with reliability, and pilots and crewmen alike routinely trusted it with their lives in weather and combat conditions which would have tested the faith of the saints. A thousand incidents stand as mute testimony to a well-earned reputation. The dependable old flying boat could, and often did, bring its crew safely home with one engine hanging limp in its mounts, or with holes as big as stop signs in the wings.

Following World War II, the PBYs continued to serve in many countries as patrol and rescue aircraft. Several were converted to commercial use as passenger and cargo carriers. The International Ice Patrol was inaugurated by a U.S. Coast Guard PBY-5A on 6 February 1946. Others were configured as water bombers, and used to fight forest fires in the United States and Canada.

Despite the large number built, only a few examples of the PBY Catalina remain in flyable condition today, but its place in history remains secure.

*These data represent numbers of survivors which the aircraft commanders reported they had rescued. A later count revealed more survivors brought in by the Catalinas than the total claimed.

CHAPTER TEN

The Leviathans

IN LARGE MEASURE, the aura surrounding the flying boats is a consequence of their size. The big aircraft have long been prominent among the world's aerial giants, and were for many years in the forefront of large aircraft development. Perhaps the most successful of the flying leviathans was the Martin Mars. Six of these great boats were built, and two of them remain in an operational status even today.

The Mars was a product of the imagination and energy of Glenn L. Martin, aviation pioneer, longtime proponent of seaplanes, and manufacturer of fine flying boats. In the late 1930s, he, like many others in the industry, believed that the age of the flying boat had just begun, and saw the Mars as a major step toward mammoth seaplane transports of the future, which would have gross weights of a half million pounds or more.

Originally conceived as a patrol bomber, the prototype Mars XPB2M-1 was ordered by the Navy on 23 August 1938. It took over three years to complete, consuming sixty thousand pounds of aluminum alloy, three million rivets, and three hundred gallons of paint in the process. Its systems were linked with almost two miles of conduit and piping, and seven and a half miles of wiring.

The XPB2M-1 was launched into the Patapsco River from the Glenn L. Martin plant at Little River, Maryland, on 5 November 1941. Four Wright Cyclone R-3350-18 engines each delivered 2,200 horsepower for takeoff, and could be serviced in flight through passageways in the wings. But in December, before the prototype could actually be flown, an accident put it out of commission for several months. While the aircraft was securely moored in the river for engine run-in, the number three engine threw a propeller blade, and the engine caught fire. Unable to extinguish it, the crew cut the mooring lines and taxied the plane into shallow water close to shore. There the fire was put out, but not before the number three engine had burned completely out of its mounts. Considerable damage had been done to the wing and engine nacelle, and the errant propeller blade had left a large jagged gash in the upper part of the hull just forward of the wing root.

While extensive repairs were being made, the decision was made to reconfigure the aircraft as a transport, and with a new designation, XPB2M-1R, it made its first flight on 23 June 1942. Power gun turrets in the nose and tail were later removed, to make the transformation to passenger and cargo configuration complete.

In many respects, the XPB2M-1R was a one of a kind aircraft. Because of the originally intended application, the hull was divided into several sections, and the overall dimensions were somewhat smaller than the Mars aircraft subsequently delivered. Externally, the major distinguishing features were ovalshaped twin vertical fins, which were canted inward at the top as a result of a high dihedral on the horizontal stabilizer. Otherwise, the XPB2M-1R was outwardly little different from later Mars flying boats.

The Mars prototype remained with the Martin Company for a year and a half after completion, and was affectionately dubbed the "Old Lady." But the aircraft's performance belied that nickname. It could carry record payloads over

The Old Lady broke the international seaplane endurance record in 1942, flying 4,600 miles and remaining aloft 32 hours and 17 minutes. (Martin Marietta)

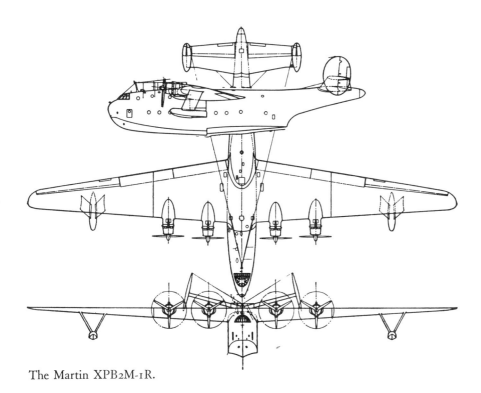

The Martin XPB2M-1R.

great distances, and could climb at the rate of 300 feet per minute with two engines shut down. On 4 and 5 October 1942, it broke the international seaplane endurance record by flying 4,600 miles over a closed course, remaining aloft almost a day and a half.*

The PB2M-1R was delivered to Naval Air Transport Squadron Eight (VR-8) at Patuxent River, Maryland, on 27 November 1943 on temporary assignment. That same month it made another record-breaking flight from NAS Patuxent River to Natal, Brazil, a distance of 4,375 miles, with a payload of 13,000 pounds.† In order to carry both the cargo and the fuel required to fly

*The official time for the flight was 32 hours and 17 minutes.
†The pilot on this flight was Lieutenant Commander W. E. Coney. The Naval Air Transport Service (NATS), of which VR-2 was a part, used a large number of flying boats for its passenger/cargo mission. On 1 October 1944 NATS had over 120 flying boats in worldwide service.

that far, it took off with a record gross weight of 148,500 pounds, 8,500 pounds overweight, and did so with ease. The return flight was made in four legs, with the aircraft setting still another record on one of them, carrying a 34,811-pound payload between Belem, Brazil, and Trinidad in the British West Indies.

In January 1944, the "Old Lady" was flown to the west coast of the United States and delivered to VR-2, which operated out of NAS Alameda, California. The following month it made a 2,400-mile flight from Alameda to Hawaii with over 20,000 pounds of cargo. The Mars was used extensively on this run, which was then the longest overwater air route in the world. By this time the Japanese had been placed on the defensive, reeling from the allies' island-hopping campaign, and VR-2 was operating full time, delivering priority cargo to forward areas. The Mars aircraft was a particularly useful asset, because of its substantial weight-carrying capability. It flew tons of plasma across the Pacific during the Iwo Jima campaign, carrying 14,000 pounds of the life-saving fluid from San Francisco to Honolulu on one flight. By the time it was retired from service in March 1945, it had delivered some three million pounds of cargo to various Pacific locations in support of allied forces.

The "Old Lady" had performed so well that in January 1945 the Navy contracted for the construction of twenty greatly improved JRM-1 models of the Mars type; ultimately, only five JRM-1s and one follow-on JRM-2 model were built under this contract, because of postwar cutbacks. All six were designed and built as cargo and transport aircraft from the start. Like the prototype, the JRM-1 had two levels, but frames were substituted for bulkheads, cargo hatches were greatly enlarged, and decking was reinforced to accommodate motor vehicles, field pieces, and other heavy equipment. An electric 5,000-pound capacity cargo hoist was mounted on an overhead track extending across the aircraft under the wing and out an oversized cargo hatch on the port side.

The external appearance of the JRM-1 was somewhat different from the prototype. The twin tail fins were replaced by a single vertical stabilizer and rudder, which added 10 feet to the height of the aircraft and improved directional control. The rear step was moved aft to provide additional cargo space, and the hull was lengthened by 3 feet. Larger fuel tanks in the hull extended the range to almost 5,000 miles, while the R-3350-8 engine provided 2,300 horsepower for takeoff and allowed the gross weight to be increased to 155,000 pounds.

The first JRM-1 was flown on 21 July 1945. Unfortunately, its career was cut short by a landing mishap which occurred on 5 August and caused it to sink in Chesapeake Bay. The cost of rebuilding and refurbishing the aircraft was considered prohibitive, and it eventually was disposed of for scrap.

The second JRM-1, named the *Marshall Mars*, was completed a short time after the August accident, and began service with VR-2 in February 1946. On its second run to Hawaii, it broke the record set by the "Old Lady" in 1944, with a cargo load of 27,427 pounds.

Original plans to assign some of the Mars boats to VR-1 at NAS Norfolk, Virginia, for use on transatlantic runs, were shelved when the Navy cut the contract for twenty Mars aircraft to six, as mentioned above. With the loss of the first production model, the remaining four JRM-1s and the JRM-2 were all assigned to NAS Alameda, to optimize material, maintenance, and operational efficiency. The *Marshall Mars* was followed by the *Marianas*, the *Philippine* and the *Hawaii Mars*, and by July 1946, all four JRM-1s were making scheduled runs in the Pacific area.

The Martin company had hoped that the Navy Mars boats would be the forerunners of an extensive series of commercial flying boats to be known as the Martin 170. But after the war, the airline companies began looking to large four-engine land-based planes as the overseas commercial aircraft of the future. Even Pan American had decided that its new postwar clippers would be land-based planes. During the war, large airfields had been built all over the world,

The *Philippine Mars* taking off from NAS Alameda. By July 1946 four of these giants were plying the Pacific airways. (U.S. Navy)

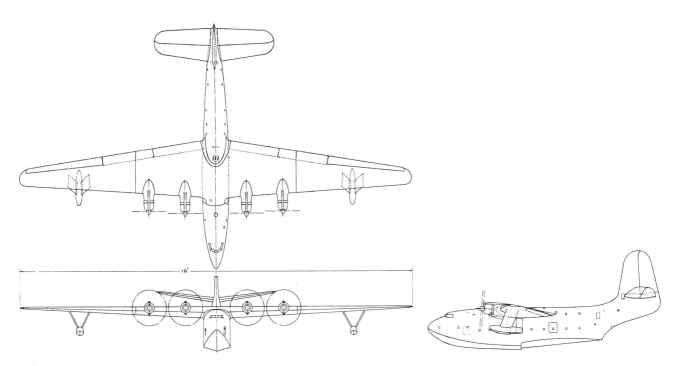

The Martin JRM-1.

together with modern airport facilities. Many of these were now adapted to peaceful purposes. They provided new passenger conveniences, and offered enhanced air carrier flexibility. Great cities with no convenient or suitable bodies of water could now become linked by transoceanic air travel. In fact, if such cities were without modern airports at the end of the war, they hastened to construct them. The proliferation of airfields worldwide meant that the design of transoceanic aircraft was no longer constrained by the necessity to provide large, seaworthy hulls with hydrodynamic characteristics not necessarily conforming to aerodynamic principles. The use of land-based planes greatly reduced transit time, and transoceanic travelers no longer needed the sleeping accommodations unique to the commercial flying boat. With coach-type seating arrangements, many more passengers could be carried at a lower fare, and this in itself stimulated greater use of air travel. Passengers no longer had to be shuttled to and from their aircraft by boat, or wait for the aircraft to dock or

The *Caroline Mars* was the last Mars boat, and the only JRM-2 built. (Martin Marietta.

to be pulled up a seaplane ramp. Pilots no longer had to worry about the effects of high winds and currents while maneuvering on the water, or the ever-present danger of striking a log or other partially submerged object while landing or taking off. Corrosion problems were virtually eliminated, and ground crews were spared the discomfort in winter of wading into icy waters to attach beaching gear and prepare the aircraft to be hauled up the ramp. Aircraft had become more reliable, resulting in transoceanic passengers having considerably less fear of being forced down on the ocean. The twilight of the flying boat as a commercial passenger airliner was at hand.

The JRM-2, the last plane of the Mars series constructed, had few structural changes, but it was powered by four new Pratt and Whitney R-4360 Wasp Major engines. These unique reciprocating engines had four rows of seven cylinders, and each developed 3,000 horsepower for takeoff. They enabled the gross weight to be increased again to 165,000 pounds, and cruising speed to be boosted to 173 miles per hour.

The JRM-2 was delivered to VR-2 in May 1948, and was later christened the *Caroline Mars*. Payloads between Alameda and Honolulu were increased to as much as 38,000 pounds on some flights, and in August of that year, it flew 4,738 statute miles nonstop from Honolulu to Chicago. In September it flew with a 68,327-pound cargo load from NAS Patuxent River, Maryland, to Cleveland, Ohio, setting still another impressive record.

The *Marshall Mars* with its Wright R-3350 engines was not to be outdone. On 19 May 1949, 301 men of a carrier air group embarked with the crew of 7 on a flight down the west coast of the United States from Alameda to San Diego, California. It was another world record for the Mars type.

The five giant aircraft established an enviable reputation for excellence, and in spite of a normal share of incidents, their passenger-carrying record remained unblemished. The complex Curtiss electric pitch-controlled propellers occasionally malfunctioned, and on one flight home across the Pacific, two engines had to be shut down, with a third beginning to run rough. Nevertheless, the aircraft safely reached Alameda, with "two out, one running, and one walking," according to the pilot.*

*See "Mars, No Bettah Da Kine" by Lieutenant Commander Andrew Serrell, in the August 1957 issue of the U.S. Naval Institute *Proceedings*.

The *Marshall Mars* came to an untimely end when it caught fire during a test flight off Hawaii in April 1950. After an emergency landing, it was abandoned and sank shortly thereafter. (U.S. Navy)

But perfection was too much to expect, and in April 1950, the record-breaking *Marshall Mars* caught fire during a test flight. Although the pilot was able to make a successful open sea landing, the crew was forced to abandon the aircraft, and it was consumed by flames. There were no passengers aboard, and none of the crew members were injured.

The remaining four Mars flying boats continued to serve with distinction for another six years. Servicemen and their dependents fortunate enough to have been carried by one of the big aircraft, still recall the experience with a degree of awe. During their fifteen years of U.S. Navy service, Mars aircraft logged more than eighty-seven thousand accident-free flight hours, while flying over two hundred thousand passengers a total of almost twelve million miles. The *Marianas Mars* was the last of the four to be used in Navy service, and made its final flight home to Alameda on 22 August 1956. All four of the boats were then temporarily stored pending permanent disposition. There was no longer any apparent use for them, and, were it not for their unique capabilities, they probably would have been scrapped.

Fortunately, however, the Mars flying boats were saved from oblivion by a consortium of major Canadian logging companies, which had joined together to combat their most difficult common problem—forest fires. They formed an organization called Forest Industries Flying Tankers Limited (FIFT), the mission of which was, and still is today, the "bombing" of forest fires with water. The founders of FIFT concluded that land-based planes were not very useful for the fire-fighting application, because the timber ranges to be serviced were often located in wilderness areas far from airstrips which could accommodate large, heavily laden, multi-engined tanker aircraft. But in Canada, where large lakes and quiet bays are numerous, the powerful Mars aircraft were well suited to the task.

In 1959, the four remaining Mars flying boats were purchased by FIFT, together with a large supply of spare parts and additional engines. The aircraft were ferried to Vancouver Island, where the *Marianas Mars* was reconfigured as a so-called "water-bomber" tanker aircraft, by Fairey Aviation of Canada Limited. The modifications consisted of the installation of a 6,000-gallon plywood water tank, release doors in the sides of the hull, and retractable probes designed to scoop up water from a lake or bay while the aircraft was in flight. Following the adaptation to its new mission, the *Marianas Mars* received the new Canadian registry designation C-FLYJ, and began its service as a water-bomber in mid-1960.

The technique for extinguishing fires still in use by FIFT today is simple yet effective. A Grumman Goose amphibian aircraft is dispatched to the scene of a fire to survey it, and establish communications with fire-fighters on the ground. When the Mars tanker arrives over the area, the amphibian provides a situation report, and leads the Mars into position over the site to be "bombed." Water is released in the form of a large cloud of gelled droplets from an altitude of about 250 feet, in order to inundate an area approximately 600 feet long by 200 feet wide. The tanker is then flown to a nearby body of water to replenish its water load. The pilot makes a normal touchdown at about eighty miles per hour, maintaining enough power to keep the big flying boat skimming over the surface. The two retractable probes are extended downward from the hull to scoop aboard a full load of 6,000 gallons of water, a process which normally takes about twenty-five seconds to complete. The elapsed time between the end of one drop and the beginning of another is rarely more than fifteen minutes; under ideal conditions, a single Mars tanker can drop about 50,000 gallons of water on a fire in a one-hour period. The aircraft is usually fueled for a flight duration of from five to six hours.

As the Mars boat picks up water, a powder called Gelgard is injected into the tank by compressed air. This causes the water to jell slightly, so that the falling mass stays together until it reaches the target. Enough Gelgard is carried to last for twenty to thirty drops.

The C-FLYJ *Marianas Mars* was an immediate success, and its performance during the last half of 1960 and the early months of 1961 amply demonstrated the soundness of the concept. Unfortunately, on 23 June 1961, the C-FLYJ struck some trees following a drop and crashed, killing her crew of four. There was no evidence of any mechanical malfunction, and the accident serves as mute testimony to the hazards of flying at virtually tree-top level over smoke-obscured, uneven terrain, which can suddenly seem to reach up and smite an aircraft to the ground. The C-FLYK *Philippine Mars* was tanker-configured in 1962, and *Hawaii Mars*, C-FLYL, underwent conversion during the summer of 1964. *Caroline Mars*, C-FLYM, the record-breaker of 1948, was lost on 12 October 1962 during a hurricane. It was on beaching gear and tied down at Victoria Airport when the storm hit, with winds gusting to 75 miles per hour. The tie-down lines parted, the beaching gear collapsed, and the huge aircraft was blown sideways across an apron for some distance. The hull and one wing were twisted beyond economical repair, and the once-proud *Caroline Mars* was scrapped.

The *Philippine Mars* and *Hawaii Mars* continue in service today, the last survivors of the distinguished Mars family. They are based at the headquarters of Forest Industries Flying Tankers Limited, located at Sproat Lake on Vancouver Island, British Columbia. The facility is comprised of a ramp, hangar, maintenance shops, fuel storage tanks, and administrative offices. The man who directs the operation and keeps it functioning is W. F. (Bill) Waddington, who serves as Manager and Chief Pilot. An experienced flying boat pilot himself, Waddington is meticulous in his choice of the pilots who fly the only two Mars boats still in existence. As a minimum qualification, 5,000 hours of seaplane experience is required. After being hired, it usually takes about three years for even such a well-seasoned pilot as this to become a captain of a Mars tanker.

The cost of the Mars water-bombing operation is high, but the cost of fighting forest fires without it would be much higher. It has been estimated that a hypothetical fire requiring a 100-man ground crew to fight would take at least

A Mars "Water Bomber" makes a test drop on a Canadian lake. (Forest Industries Flying Tankers Limited)

A dynamic duo, *Philippine Mars* and *Hawaii Mars* are still flying, and performing their assigned mission. To this day, they remain the largest operational flying boats ever built. (Forest Industries Flying Tankers Limited)

an additional five days to quell, if the Mars aircraft were not used. Although a less expensive conventional effort might ultimately extinguish the blaze, the real loss in this case would be an approximate two hundred seventy-five thousand additional cubic feet of logs, mature trees which would take many years to be regrown.

And so the great Mars boats are still flying, still performing their assigned mission better than any other aircraft. To this day, over thirty years since they first entered service, they remain the largest operational flying boats ever built. If these aircraft are ever lost, the cost of duplicating them today would be many millions of dollars each.

During the era of the Mars aircraft, other flying boats were proposed as successors or replacements. One contender was a Consolidated design which was to be known as the XPB3Y-1. This aircraft was somewhat smaller than the Mars, with a wingspan of 169 feet, but was still large enough to be classified as a giant flying boat. It was to be powered by four Pratt and Whitney R-2800-18 engines designed to provide the aircraft with a top speed of 241 miles per hour. But again wartime necessity dictated concentration on proven types, and a Navy order for a prototype placed in April of 1942 was canceled later that year.

In November 1941, Reuben Fleet arranged to sell his portion of Consolidated Aircraft Corporation, which he had formed in 1923 and guided to prominence. The resulting merger was formalized in March 1943, and the new company became Consolidated-Vultee, better known as Convair. Shortly thereafter, the Navy became interested in procuring a long-range flying boat patrol aircraft which could survive in an environment of active enemy air opposition, and operate from bases in forward areas. It had to be suitable for antisubmarine warfare, capable of mine-laying, and able to engage in night attacks on shipping, in the tradition of the Catalinas. Consolidated-Vultee's design concept for the U.S. Navy's first turboprop flying boat was selected, and on 27 May 1946 the Navy issued a procurement contract for two prototypes, which were later designated XP5Y-1s.

The first of these was originally scheduled for flight-testing in December 1948, but the aircraft was not completed until 1949, and first flew on 18 April 1950. The hull, which was 142 feet 6 inches in length, was the result of extensive hydrodynamic studies that indicated the practicability of the unusually high length-to-beam ratio of ten to one. This design provided improved performance on the water, and a radio-controlled flying model was used to determine that the long, narrow hull shape was also aerodynamically sound.

A cantilever wing with a 145-foot span was mounted almost halfway back on the hull, giving the aircraft an added appearance of speed. The tail assembly was characterized by a noticeable amount of dihedral in the horizontal plane, and a high single vertical fin which gave the aircraft a height of 51 feet 5 inches when resting on its beaching cradle.

True to the Navy's requirements, the XP5Y-1 was indeed a versatile combat aircraft capable of carrying heavy loads of bombs, torpedoes, mines, and rockets. It had five machine gun positions, of which two were located on each side of the hull fore and aft, and one accommodated a 20-millimeter cannon in the tail. Since the primary mission of this aircraft was to be antisubmarine warfare, it was to be equipped with the latest in radar, magnetic anomaly detection (MAD), and electronic countermeasures (ECM) devices. Aerial mining was a secondary mission, and although its faster speed was a distinct advantage, the survivability of an aircraft of this size engaged in laying mines in heavily defended harbor entrances or estuarine areas was somewhat questionable.

The XP5Y-1 was powered by four Allison T40A-4 gas turbine engines, which delivered 5,500 equivalent horsepower each. At that time the turboprop aircraft engine was in the early stages of development, and only three suitable

The Consolidated XP5Y-1 took off on its maiden flight from San Diego on 18 April 1950. (U.S. Navy)

models were available from American manufacturers.* The Allison model represented a completely new design concept, incorporating two contra-rotating propellers driven through a common gearbox. Although it never proved to be an entirely satisfactory arrangement, the new engine provided considerable engineering knowledge and experience, which was later applied to other more successful turboprop projects.

The two prototype patrol aircraft never were placed on active naval service, but were used by Convair in the early 1950s primarily for developmental testing of the new engine-propeller combination. For a flying boat, the XP5Y-1 was a fast aircraft. Its maximum speed exceeded 350 miles per hour, and the total of 22,000 equivalent horsepower permitted a maximum gross weight of more than 160,000 pounds. During the first part of August 1950, the XP5Y-1 established an endurance record for turboprop aircraft in a flight of 8 hours and 6 minutes. That same month the Navy made known its decision to discontinue the aircraft as a patrol bomber, and pursue its development as a passenger and cargo plane, to replace the Mars type. On 15 July 1953 one of the original two patrol prototypes experienced a loss of longitudinal stability control during high speed tests at 10,000 feet, and crashed into the sea off San Diego. The crew parachuted to safety, and no one was injured. Despite this unfavorable incident, development of the transport version was continued.

This model was designated the R3Y, and became known as the Tradewind. Two configurations, the R3Y-1 and the R3Y-2, were built. The basic dimensions of both were almost identical to those of the patrol prototype. Externally, the noticeable differences included elimination of the gun positions, slightly redesigned engine nacelles housing the newer T40A-10 engines, elimination of the dihedral in the horizontal tail plane, and the addition of a ten-foot-wide cargo loading hatch just aft of the wing on the port side. The aircraft featured a pressurized, air conditioned, and sound attenuated cabin for up to 103 passengers in seats facing aft. Some or all of these seats could be removed to transform the Tradewind into a cargo carrier, or it could be configured as a medical evacuation (medivac) aircraft accommodating 92 stretcher cases and 12 medical attendants.

*The other two competing designs in addition to the Allison T40A were the Westinghouse T-30 and the Pratt and Whitney T-34.

The Convair R3Y-2 Assault Transport could taxi up to an enemy beach and land a special mission force in minutes. (General Dynamics)

The R3Y-2 was classified an assault transport aircraft. It was designed to taxi up to the beach to land a special mission force of Marines on enemy territory, perhaps to secure a strategic position in advance of a full-scale landing, before the enemy had time to react. After having discharged his troops, the pilot could then reverse engines, back away from the beach, and take off again in a matter of minutes. For quick loading and unloading, the nose section of the aircraft was hinged at the top to form a large upward-swinging door, 6 feet 8 inches high and 8 feet 4 inches wide. A heavy-duty ramp folded onto the beach, to facilitate rapid movement of personnel and equipment. To provide clearance through this opening, the flight deck was built higher than on previous versions. Otherwise, the assault model was much like the R3Y-1.

Both the R3Y-1 and the R3Y-2 were first flown at San Diego in 1954 on 25 February and 22 October, respectively. The R3Y-1 was flown cross-country to the Naval Air Test Center, Patuxent River, Maryland, on 24 February 1955, averaging 403 miles per hour, in a record elapsed time of 6 hours.

Ultimately, five R3Y-1s and six R3Y-2s were built. A combined total of seven of these aircraft were placed into service with VR-2 at Alameda in 1956, the first plane being delivered on 31 March, and the last on 28 November of that year. In September 1956 an R3Y-2 configured as a tanker made history when it refueled four Grumman F9F-8 Cougars simultaneously in flight. On 18 October an R3Y-1 made a record transit from Honolulu to Alameda, averaging 360 miles per hour for the 6 hour and 45-minute flight, 3 hours and 49 minutes faster than the previous record set by one of the Mars aircraft in 1948.

Problems which were primarily associated with the engine and propeller combination continued to plague the R3Y project. On 10 May 1957 an R3Y-1 operating in the Alameda area lost both propellers on its number 3 engine, and suffered considerable hull damage in the resulting emergency landing. Partly

A Convair R3Y-2 Tradewind refueled four Grumman F9F-8 Cougars simultaneously in flight in 1956. (General Dynamics)

as a result of this incident, and partly because of substantial cutbacks in many Navy programs during this period, the inventory of operational R3Ys was reduced from seven to four aircraft, two R3Y-1s and two R3Y-2s.

On 2 January 1958 an R3Y-1 experienced a similar problem with the engine and propeller combination while 400 miles west of Alameda. Although the aircraft was able to return to base for a safe landing, the pilot had difficulty controlling it on the water, and the episode ended in a collision with the seawall. Both accidents were determined to have occurred as a result of the propellers and gearboxes separating from the aircraft in flight. The solution to the problem was not immediately apparent, and further development of the system at considerable additional cost was prohibitive in the austere fiscal climate. On 16 April 1958 the Chief of Naval Operations directed that all R3Y aircraft be placed in an inactive status, and ordered that VR-2 be decommissioned.

In any discussion of mammoth flying boats, there is one which because of its sheer awesomeness must be saved until last. Although it has been derided by scoffers and humorously referred to as the "Spruce Goose," it is nonetheless the largest flying machine in terms of wingspan that man has ever built. Today the Hughes H-4 *Hercules* occupies a large portion of high-priced land on Terminal Island, California, existing as if in a great cocoon, waiting to burst forth at the right moment after years of dormancy. It has been there since 1947, nestled in a dry dock and covered by a specially designed hangar, provided with both temperature and humidity control systems.

The wingspan of this monster is 320 feet, 125 feet more than that of a modern Boeing 747. The horizontal tail plane is larger in both area and span than the wings of a Boeing 727. A tall man can walk upright inside the wing, and at its thickest point, he will still have several feet of clearance. The vertical tail fin is almost ten stories high, and the interior of the cavernous hull gives one an idea of what the biblical Jonah might have experienced in the belly of the whale. What makes the H-4 even more unique is that the entire aircraft—hull, wings and tail assembly—is constructed of laminated wood. Only the hardware, the engines, and the engine mounts are metal.

The engines, which were not installed until 1947, were Pratt and Whitney R-4360s, the largest radial reciprocating engines ever built. There were eight of them in all, providing a total of 16,000 horsepower for takeoff. Each engine drove a four-bladed Hamilton Standard propeller with a diameter of 17 feet 2 inches, and the four inboard propellers had a reverse pitch capability. The

The vertical tail fin of the Hercules is almost ten stories tall. (Hughes Aircraft Corp.)

engines received fuel from two service tanks in the wings, which in turn were fed from fourteen hull tanks, each with a 1,000-gallon capacity.

This immense airplane was conceived in 1942 by Henry J. Kaiser, industrialist and well-known fabricator of Liberty Ships. He put forth the idea of building a fleet of giant flying boats, capable of airlifting huge quantities of men and material over the Atlantic, thus avoiding the ravenous German submarine wolf-packs, so effective at that time against allied shipping. Moreover, he proposed to accomplish the task without depleting supplies of aluminum and other scarce materials. The aircraft industry was highly skeptical of the Kaiser proposal, and doubted his ability to bring the project to fruition. The October 1942 issue of *Air News* asked a question typical of many in an article entitled "Is Kaiser Crazy?" It seemed to conclude, however, as many did, that a man who could organize the American shipping industry to produce 10,000-ton Liberty ships every forty-six days, should at least be given a chance to prove his claim. Donald Nelson, who headed the War Production Board, apparently thought so as well, and authorized Kaiser to proceed.

But the problems inherent in the design and construction of ships are not identical to those associated with airplanes, and Henry J. Kaiser knew very little about the latter. To compensate for his lack of aeronautical experience, Kaiser joined forces with a talented young entrepreneur who possessed the necessary expertise. His name was Howard Hughes.

Kaiser and Hughes were an unlikely duo who did not get along well with each other. Nonetheless, they formed the Kaiser-Hughes Corporation, and on 16 November 1942, contracted with the United States government to build three massive flying boats, to be called the HK-1s (Hughes-Kaiser, 1st aircraft). The sum of eighteen million dollars was made available to finance the project through the Defense Plant Corporation, a government entity created under provisions of the amended Reconstruction Finance Corporation Act. The contract stipulated that the three aircraft were to be constructed of materials non-critical to the war effort, with Howard Hughes responsible for directing the engineering and construction of the aircraft.

While the eccentric Hughes was a fortunate choice for the project, it soon became apparent that Kaiser had overextended himself, and could not possibly deliver these aircraft in either the quantity or the time frame envisioned. Kaiser's existing plants were either unsuitable or unavailable for construction of the big flying boats, and Hughes finally took it upon himself to finance and build the necessary facilities at Culver City, California. From that time forward, Kaiser left it almost entirely to Hughes to complete the extravagant project; by the end of the war, Kaiser had extricated himself completely from the enterprise. Subsequently, the aircraft was redesignated the H-4, to leave no doubt that it had become strictly a Hughes endeavor.

From the beginning Hughes plunged into the project with characteristic energy and attention to detail. He studied the problem thoroughly, and conducted numerous aero- and hydrodynamic experiments with shapes and models. Problems of weight and balance were researched using a Sikorsky S-43 amphibian flying boat which Hughes had acquired in 1937. Unfortunately, this modified aircraft crashed on a landing in Lake Mead, Nevada, injuring Hughes and killing both a mechanic and a representative of the Civil Aeronautics Administration. Undeterred, Hughes pushed on with the work.

Because of the restrictions imposed on the use of critical war materials, the *Hercules* was constructed of laminated wood, thus providing the basis for the uncomplimentary nicknames of "Flying Lumberyard" and "Spruce Goose." Actually, the material used was birch, chosen for its strength and relatively light weight. The laminating process known as "Duramold" was acquired on license from the Fairchild Corporation, which had developed the technique to a high state of dependability. Much of the aircraft was fastened together with special glues, with the materials being held in place by clamps and millions of small nails until the glue dried.

Despite the efforts of Hughes and others, the *Hercules* project was plagued with engineering problems, material shortages, and a dearth of skilled labor. A host of critics maligned the project, and there was an everpresent threat of government cancellation—with good reason. By February 1944, the first aircraft still had not been completed, much of the original eighteen million dollars had been spent, and the War Production Board had decided to cut its losses and terminate the project. At the last moment, however, President Roosevelt, who felt the undertaking had much merit, expressed his desire to complete at least one of the great flying boats. A new agreement was drawn up with Hughes which provided for the completion of only one aircraft on a cost basis.

The war in Europe ended in May 1945, with *Hercules* still far from finished, Kaiser gone, and Hughes close to a nervous breakdown. Advised to take an extended rest or suffer the consequences, he slipped away to Mexico to recuperate. Meanwhile, work on the big boat progressed, and in seven months Hughes was back at work on it.

One of the more critical problems which had to be resolved was that of perfecting the hydraulic power boost system, which would make it possible for a human to move the control surfaces of the big flying boat. The boost mechanism originally conceived for this aircraft turned out to be inadequate for the task, and Hughes contrived a new, more effective scheme consisting of two redundant boost systems.

Meanwhile, a waterfront assembly site had been leased on Terminal Island, and a concrete dry dock of the type used for ship overhauls was constructed to receive the huge hull. Star House Movers Incorporated, of Long Beach, California, was engaged to transport *Hercules* the twenty-eight miles from the Hughes Plant at Culver City to the assembly site on Terminal Island.

The cost of the move was $55,000, and involved a small army of people, including professional house movers, police from several jurisdictions, Park Department employees who trimmed back tree branches along the route, power and telephone company linemen, and others. The huge components of the great plane were moved separately, with the long 220-foot hull being the most difficult section to move. Each wing was transported on its own dolly, proceeding root end first. Even so, the wings overlapped road shoulders, and great care had to be taken not to hit telephone poles and other roadside obstructions along the way. It was slow going, and the trip took two days to complete. Thousands of people lined the route to watch the spectacle, and schools were recessed so children could get a first hand look at the world's largest aircraft. The operation was conducted in mid-June without mishap, and assembly began almost immediately.

Before the H-4 was completed, one serious incident occurred which almost ended Hughes' life, and threatened the project as well. Along with the giant flying boat, Hughes was concurrently developing a high-speed photographic reconnaissance plane for the Army, known as the FX-11. This was an unusual twin-boom twin-engine aircraft, similar in appearance to the Lockheed P-38, but featuring R-4360 engines with contra-rotating propellers. Hughes always insisted that he alone was responsible for the initial flight-testing of aircraft which he had personally designed, and the FX-11 was no exception. In the late afternoon of 7 July 1946, Hughes took off in this plane from the Culver City airstrip, and almost immediately experienced difficulty with retraction of the landing gear. A short time later, while trying to remedy the landing gear problem, the aircraft began to pull to the right and lose altitude. Hughes fought to control the aircraft all the way down, but in the end it plowed into a group of houses, damaging two and demolishing a third. Hughes was pulled from the burning wreckage critically injured. He was rushed to the hospital, where he began hemorrhaging the next morning and was not expected to live. But survive he did, to build another improved version of the FX-11 which he tested successfully in early 1947.

In July of that same year, a Senate subcommittee began hearings to determine whether Hughes had improperly influenced U.S. government officials regarding the award of certain war contracts. In a rare public appearance, Hughes confronted his inquisitors, and had the best of the exchange. Because the dashing and mysterious Howard Hughes was involved, and because some

The Hercules "Spruce Goose" was assembled at Terminal Island. The great aircraft is there today in a specially constructed temperature- and humidity-controlled hangar. (Hughes Aircraft Corp.)

members of the subcommittee had chosen to make the hearings a cause célèbre, the dispute received extensive coverage in the press, where charges and counter-charges were aired. Chief among Hughes' antagonists was Senator Owen Brewster, who referred to the H-4 as a "flying lumberyard," and asserted that the machine would never fly. The clear implication was that Hughes had deliberately bilked the U.S. government into spending millions of dollars on development of an airplane that could not even get off the water. Hughes was chagrined by the allegation, and stated emphatically that if his flying boat failed to fly, he would leave the country.

The hearings ended temporarily in August, and were scheduled to be re-convened in November. Howard Hughes used the intervening period to ready the great flying boat for a flight that would confirm his integrity and redeem his reputation as an aircraft designer.

By the first of November the aircraft was ready for its first test. Invitations to attend the special occasion and witness the event had gone out to the press, the entire Senate investigating committee, and several other dignitaries.

On 2 November a tug towed the H-4 out into open water, where the en-gines were started. Members of the press corps had been invited aboard for the ride, since only taxi tests were scheduled that day. Howard Hughes, in the pilot's seat, taxied the H-4 for some distance, to give the reporters a good feel for its handling qualities on the water. Then he returned to the starting point, where he had the press disembark into a waiting boat which took them ashore. This accomplished, he moved the aircraft into position and executed a high-speed taxi run, at about ninety miles per hour. Everything was operating smoothly and in accordance with expectations. The next test was also scheduled to be a high-speed taxi run, but as the big boat reached ninety miles per hour, it con-tinued to accelerate, and, to the surprise of the observers on shore, lifted into the air. After reaching an altitude of about seventy feet, it flew a distance of approximately a mile, before touching down again in the harbor. Hughes brought the plane back to its moorings and came ashore, where he was met by

The Hughes Hercules takes to the air on 2 November 1947 for its first and only flight. (Hughes Aircraft Corp.)

Howard Hughes at the controls of the Hercules. (Hughes Aircraft Corp.)

a throng of well-wishers. He was clearly pleased with his accomplishment. In a subsequent press conference, he is reported to have said, "It felt so buoyant and good, I just pulled it up."*

Hughes returned to the Senate hearings with his former assertions now validated, and his testimony was soon completed. *Hercules* was returned to the dry dock, where it has remained ever since. In 1953, the dock was accidentally flooded, floating the aircraft until it made contact with the top of the hangar, causing some damage. Hughes had a larger, higher hangar constructed to prevent a recurrence of the incident. And there the H-4 has spent the years. Much later, a proposal to cut the aircraft into sections and distribute it among museums met with considerable protest, and the H-4 was thereby saved from dismemberment, at least for the time being.

Early in 1976, the Summa Corporation offered the aircraft to the U.S. Navy as a test vehicle for wing-in-ground-effect experiments, but the Navy apparently declined this offer. At the time of this writing, the H-4 lies snugly in its great wooden cocoon, seemingly oblivious to the fact that technology has long since passed it by. But questions remain.

*John Keats, *Howard Hughes* (New York: Random House, 1966), p. 221.

Had Hughes really intended to fly the H-4 that November day in 1947? He had clearly put his reputation on the line, a self-imposed challenge from which a man like Hughes could never retreat. It seems likely that he had made the decision well in advance to fly that day, if everything checked out well, and he had made certain that the aviation world which had chided him so was watching. The theory is advanced by some that the big flying boat simply escaped his control and took to the air, but that is not very convincing. Large flying boats, by virtue of their size and weight, are not inclined toward such behavior in the hands of an experienced seaplane pilot. And if Hughes was nothing else, he was a highly skilled aviator who well knew the idiosyncrasies of flying boats.

But why was the H-4 never flown again? A few people suspect that during the brief flight, Hughes found the H-4 to be inherently unsafe, and unalterably flawed. Since he had already proven his case, the theory goes, he decided to quit at that point. Applied to some men, this might be a valid supposition, but it would have been unlike Hughes to have acted in this manner. A careful consideration of his modus operandi suggests that he would have been unable to live with the stain of imperfection and would probably have set to work furiously modifying the great boat to resolve any problems, much as he had done with the FX-11. While the H-4 undoubtedly had flaws, as does every new aircraft, Hughes must have believed that they could all have been overcome by further refinement. The most plausible explanation of his behavior is that after he had proven the aircraft would fly, he simply lost interest in it; strange as it may seem, this is entirely consistent with Hughes' previous and subsequent behavioral pattern. In any event, time had overtaken the project, and there was no longer a need for giant flying boats, especially this one made of wood at an astronomical cost. He apparently remained convinced, however, that the design and construction of the H-4 constituted a worthy accomplishment and one which deserved preservation, if only for his own satisfaction.

Finally, there is the question of what led Hughes to undertake this project in the first place. He was certainly aware of the skepticism of the aircraft industry and the complexity of the engineering problems involved, if not the extent of bureaucratic red tape and other interminable obstacles he would encounter. The probable answer to this question is also rooted in his character. Howard Hughes was not an ordinary man, and he accepted only extraordinary challenges. Moreover, he was obsessed with the idea that whatever he undertook must approach perfection, and be better than anyone had ever done before. When the flying boat idea was proposed by Kaiser, Hughes was drawn to it like a magnet. Flying boats had intrigued him since childhood, and he was convinced that their size and payload capacity would make them indispensable to any long-distance commercial airline operation in the foreseeable future. It is likely that the clamor of the experts proclaiming the folly of his involvement in Kaiser's super-boat project only made the prospect more enticing, and led directly to his decision to design and build the world's largest aircraft. He did, and it was and still is, a leviathan in every sense of the word.

The Versatile Amphibians

THE AMPHIBIAN FLYING BOAT is a unique breed, with its own distinctive personality and idiosyncrasies. It is and always has been a distinct engineering challenge to marry the land-based plane to the seaplane, and still produce an aircraft which performs as smoothly operating from dry land as it does from water. At the same time, it must be capable of a respectable speed, load-carrying capacity, and range, and have good maneuverability. There have been many variations of the amphibian flying boat, from the giant Sikorsky Clippers, to tiny private sportplanes. The Sikorsky S-40 amphibian eventually shed its retractable landing gear, and enjoyed a distinguished career operating strictly as a seaplane. Others, like the Consolidated PBY and Martin PBM, only became successful amphibians in later service. It is those aircraft which were designed as amphibians at the drawing board, and operated as such until their retirement, which are the subject of this chapter.

Glenn Curtiss produced the first practical powered amphibian aircraft, which he called the *Triad* because it was capable of operating from the land, the sea, and in the air. But the *Triad* was a float-plane, not a flying boat. Curtiss later experimented briefly with an amphibian version of the F-Boat, and was certainly one of the first to apply this concept to hulled aircraft. Indeed, one of the earliest Curtiss machines and the first amphibian flying boat built under U.S. Navy contract was an aircraft called the *OWL,* an acronym for "Over Water and Land." Completing its initial tests at Hammondsport, New York, in October 1913, it is considered to be the first U.S. Marine Corps aircraft. The *OWL'*s performance was not spectacular, but it was a beginning.

Other early aircraft designers, sensing the potential of such a flying machine, also experimented with the idea, but the primitive aircraft motors then available had all they could do to lift the planked wooden-hulled machines into the air. Wheels, plus the simple mechanisms then used to retract and extend them, only added extra weight, which might have meant the difference between getting airborne or not on any given day.

In 1919, Lawrence Sperry produced an amphibian flying boat patrol bomber for the Navy, powered by the new twelve-cylinder Liberty engine developed during the war. It was a triplane, an ungainly aircraft resembling a flying bathtub, with its wide hull and a blunt bow. Each of the three wings was 48 feet long, and each was set twelve inches aft of the one directly above, to provide a step-like stagger. The single 360-horsepower Liberty engine was mounted high between the two upper wings and drove a four-bladed pusher propeller. Sperry, a graduate of the Curtiss Flying School, had worked closely with the aviation pioneer on projects involving gyro-stabilized flight. He may have been influenced in the design of the tail assembly of his amphibian by the Curtiss NC boats, which set out on their historic flight in May of that year. The Sperry amphibian had a horizontal tail plane which spanned 22 feet, 4 1/2 inches, and a vertical stabilizer and rudder 8 feet high. These control members were supported by an assortment of booms, struts, and wires, very much like the tail of the Navy-Curtiss seaplane. The wheels were designed to swing in an arc up and away from the hull to their retracted position, almost

The Sperry amphibian resembled a flying bathtub, but was stable in flight and performed well. (Sperry Div. of Sperry Rand Corp.)

parallel to the lower wing. The pilot, copilot, and mechanic sat together in a single large cockpit, providing a somewhat comical "three men in a tub" appearance. Yet this airplane was stable in flight, and had a maximum speed of 90 miles per hour, with a cruising speed of approximately 85. Its gross weight was a respectable 6,000 pounds, and it was designed to carry a war load of four 250-pound bombs, two under each wing.

The Navy conducted extensive trials with the Sperry amphibian, but declined to place a production order for it. The prototype was therefore the lone model built.

The popularization of the amphibian flying boat was left to one Grover Cleveland Loening, a remarkable man whose contributions to aviation have been considerable.

While attending Columbia University as that institution's first student specializing in aeronautical engineering, Loening developed what was to become a lifelong interest in flying boats. He and several other students constructed a water-based glider, which they planned to launch by towing behind a fast motorboat. The hull was actually a small lightweight racing shell, which seemed ideal to the fledgling engineers. But when the concept was put to the test, the craft would not rise from the water. Loening had encountered the same perplexing suction problem that plagued Curtiss and other early seaplane experimenters.

Loening went on to complete a master's degree at Columbia, expanding his thesis into a book entitled *Monoplanes and Biplanes*. He then took a position with the Queen Aeroplane Company, where he designed a promising monoplane flying boat, which, unfortunately, was wrecked by a storm before being fully tested. Next he went to work for Orville Wright, who taught him to fly and added much to his rapidly increasing store of aeronautical knowledge. He served for a short time as the first aeronautical engineer ever employed by the U. S. Army Signal Corps, and afterward as general manager of the Sturtevant Aeroplane Company. In 1917, he formed his own organization, the Loening Aeronautical Engineering Corporation, and located his small plant in New York City, on the East River waterfront at the foot of Thirty-First Street.*

*Because of his company's location in downtown New York, Loening was sometimes referred to as the "Broadway Engineer."

There he worked on a Navy concept for a small plane which could be launched from destroyers, but this contract was cancelled at the end of World War I. He also built several M-8 pursuit planes, incorporating heavy rigid strut bracing which he had developed.

But by 1921, Loening was back pursuing his primary interest, the flying boat. It was in that year that he produced the five-place monoplane Air Yacht, a flying boat which he used in his short-lived New York—Newport Air Service, and which won for him the prestigious Collier Trophy.

The Air Yacht was a strut-braced monoplane, and in the early 1920s, people were not convinced that such an arrangement was entirely safe. Wings, after all, were what held an airplane aloft, and it seemed only reasonable to conclude that two sets could do the job twice as well as one.

Despite apprehension about the reliability of this new type of aircraft, the Air Yacht attracted several buyers. Wealthy sportsmen and businessmen accounted for some sales, and the Army bought nine for use as rescue aircraft.

As sales momentum in the U.S. aircraft industry decreased in the postwar years, Loening decided that to remain in business he would have to come up with an aircraft that was versatile, practical, and original, to spark buyer interest. The result of his efforts was the highly successful Loening amphibian.

At first glance, the new Loening aircraft could easily be mistaken for a float-plane. The forward part of the Duralumin hull protruded out beyond the propeller like a float, providing the aircraft with a distinctive profile, and giving rise to its nickname, "The Flying Shoehorn." But it was a true flying boat with the fuselage and hull the same, which construction Loening referred to as a "unitary hull." Wheel wells were built into the hull on each side to reduce drag when the landing gear was retracted, a procedure accomplished by means of a hand crank in the cockpit.

The Loening amphibian was a tractor-type aircraft. This design was made possible by the use of an inverted Liberty 12 engine, which was developed by the U.S. Army and became available in 1923. In this arrangement, the propeller shaft was positioned at the top of the engine, thus allowing the propeller ample clearance over the protruding shoehorn bow below.

Despite the innovative character of this aircraft, one major concession was made to conformity. Grover Loening was a practical man, and he knew from his experience with the Air Yacht that the strut-braced monoplane had not yet found public acceptance. Reluctantly, he abandoned the monoplane design, which would probably have significantly increased performance, and made his amphibian a biplane as conventional wisdom decreed.

Loening's sales target was the U.S. Army. He had sold the biplane amphibian with the guarantee that the aircraft would not only be capable of alighting on land or water, but it would also be superior in performance to the DeHavilland DH-4, which used the same engine.

The prototype first flew on 9 June 1924. It was lightered from the East River plant to Long Island Sound, where there was more room for flight tests. Lieutenant Wendell H. Brookley, U.S. Army, was the test pilot. He executed several takeoffs and landings from the water, and then flew to nearby Mitchell Field, where he repeated the tests on land. Speed trials were next, and these were performed on a measured course in the Sound at very low altitude. During these runs, Brookley apparently allowed the amphibian to get too low. Suddenly it hit the water at high speed, flipped up on its nose, and threw Brookley and Loening into Long Island Sound, unhurt but shaken.

The amphibian was severely damaged in the crash, but the accident had occurred through no fault of the aircraft or its design. Therefore, since the tests up to that point had demonstrated its superior qualities, the Army released a production order for ten of these aircraft. The first of these, designated the COA-1, was delivered on 17 January 1925. The inverted Liberty V-1650-1 engine produced up to 420 horsepower under ideal conditions, to give the airplane a top speed of 121 miles per hour. The gross weight was 5,080 pounds, the wingspan was 45 feet, and the length was 34 feet, 7 inches.

The Army was pleased with the performance of the Loenings, and put them to good use. Lieutenants George C. MacDonald and Victor E. Bertrandias captured two international records for seaplanes on 23 January 1926, flying at speeds of 113 miles per hour for 100 kilometers (approximately 62 miles), and 101 miles per hour for 1,000 kilometers (approximately 621 miles). From 21 December 1926 to 23 April 1927, the Army employed five of these aircraft on a highly publicized Pan American good will flight covering some 22,000 miles. The planes performed well, and were harbingers of the impending development of air transportation throughout the South American continent. The endeavor was marred, however, by a midair collision at Buenos Aires, Argentina, in which two of the participants were killed, and two planes were lost.

The Navy acquired its first Loening amphibian on 9 May 1925, when Lieutenant Thomas P. Jeter delivered the aircraft to the Naval Air Station at Anacostia, Washington, D.C., where it was well received. The OL-1, as it was designated, differed from the Army's COA-1 in that it was powered by an inverted Packard 1A-1500. This engine developed 440 horsepower, resulting in a higher top speed of 125 miles per hour, an increased gross weight of 5,208 pounds, and a shorter takeoff run. Grover Loening, however, always maintained that the Packard engine required more maintenance, and was less reliable than, the Liberty 12, with the result that it detracted from his aircraft's reputation for safety and dependability.

The second OL-1 was delivered to the Navy in mid-December 1925, and was strengthened for launching from a catapult. On 13 January 1926, it was successfully launched from a barge in the Anacostia River, by means of a compressed-air catapult designed by Captain "Dick" Richardson of NC fame.

The Navy also purchased a few Loening amphibians with the inverted Liberty engine instead of the inverted Packards, and designated them OL-2s, to distinguish them from from the Packard-powered OL-1s. The first three OL-2s were acquired during May and June of 1925, and were in fact diverted from the Army's original order, to participate in that summer's Arctic Expedition, sponsored by the National Geographic Society and led by Commander Donald B. MacMillan. The planes were to be used to scout previously unseen Arctic areas, as well as to plant fuel caches at intervals northward, which could then be used like stepping-stones to reach the North Pole. American interest had been spurred by the attempt of the Norwegian Roald Amundsen to reach the North Pole earlier that year using two Dornier Wal flying boats. He had proceeded to within 150 miles of his goal, before being forced to turn back by headwinds which left him insufficient fuel to reach the pole and still return to base thereafter.

A Navy Air Unit was formed for the expedition, under the command of Lieutenant Richard E. Byrd, Junior, and included:

Lieutenant Meinrad A. Schur
Boatswain Earl E. Reber
Aviation Pilot Floyd Bennett
Aviation Machinist's Mate First Class Charles F. Rocheville
Aviation Pilot Andrew C. Nold
Aviation Chief Machinist's Mate Nels P. Sorenson
Chief Aerographer Albert Francis

The dismantled amphibians were loaded aboard the small cargo ship *Peary* in Boston, and the expedition, consisting of *Peary* and the sailing vessel *Bowdoin*, departed from Wiscasset, Maine, on 20 June 1925 and proceeded northward. They arrived at Etah on the northwest corner of Greenland, eleven and a half degrees of latitude from the pole, on 1 August, and quickly set to work assembling the aircraft. By the 4th, all three were flying. The weather

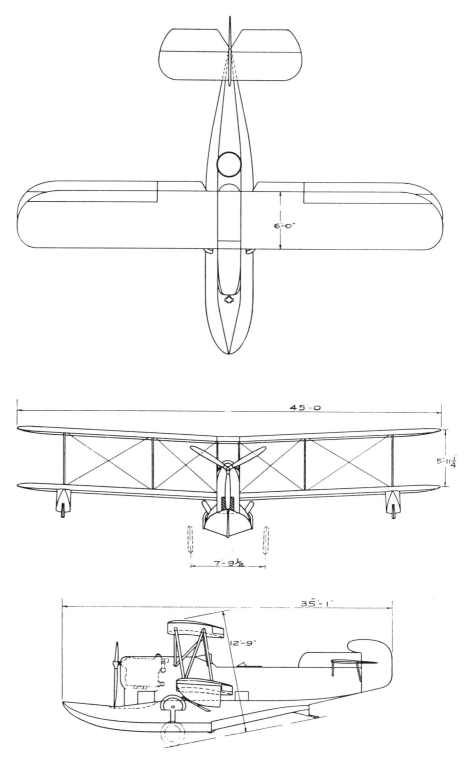

The Loening OL-2.

was poor most of the time, and the flying was often accomplished under hazardous conditions. Only two fueling bases were established, with the farthest being 107 miles from the ship, but considerable photographic survey work was accomplished. The expedition was forced by ice and bad weather to leave Etah on 22 August, by which time the three Loenings had flown over six thousand miles and had surveyed more than thirty thousand square miles of the frozen Arctic. Perhaps equally if not more important, the Navy had added significantly to its store of knowledge on cold weather flight operations.

The Loening OL-5 was the first airplane built for the Coast Guard. (U.S. Coast Guard)

Six OL-3s mounting Packard engines and equipped with tail hooks were purchased by the Navy between June 1926 and August 1927. One of these was used to demonstrate the versatility of the Loening aircraft, when it successfully flew off the carrier *Langley* in June 1926; thereafter, carrier takeoffs and landings by Loening amphibians became commonplace.

Two additional Liberty-powered OL-2s were purchased in February 1926 and assigned to the U.S. Marine Corps at Brown Field, Virginia. One OL-4, also with a Liberty engine, was assigned to make a survey of Venezuela, while three others were purchased especially for use in the Navy's 1926 Alaskan survey, conducted under the command of Lieutenant Ben H. Wyatt.

The first aircraft ever manufactured for the U.S. Coast Guard were three OL-5s, delivered in October 1926. These featured improved Liberty engines, developing 435 horsepower. After being test-flown by Ensign Leonard M. Melka, one was delivered to the Coast Guard station at Cape May, New Jersey, and the other two to the station at Gloucester, Massachusetts. These aircraft, equipped with reinforced hull bottoms and machine guns, were particularly useful in Coast Guard rescue operations, and in the apprehension of offshore rum-runners.

In August 1926, the Navy ordered twenty-seven improved Loening amphibians, designated OL-6s, all of which were delivered between December 1926 and August 1927. Six of these were earmarked for the U.S. Marine Corps, three were assigned to China for use on the Yangtze River Patrol, and three were sent to the Philippines. One OL-7 model, designed especially for carrier operations, was built with folding wings. The wings were hinged to the center sections, and swung aft into a compact package. Unfortunately, this airplane was 200 pounds heavier and 7 miles per hour slower than the OL-6s, and the concept was abandoned.

One OL-6 was refitted with a Pratt and Whitney 400-horsepower Wasp radial air-cooled engine to become the first OL-8, 400 pounds lighter than the OL-6. The Navy ordered forty of these, which were modified further after the delivery of the first twenty to become the OL-8A. This model mounted the 450-horsepower Pratt and Whitney R-1340B engine, which gave the OL-8 an increased service ceiling, but no increase in speed, over that of the OL-6. Lieutenant Commander Arthur W. Radford (later Admiral Radford and Chairman of the Joint Chiefs of Staff) used four of these airplanes on his Alaskan Survey of 1929. His air detachment, operating from the seaplane tender *Gannet* (AVP-8), logged some 700 flight hours and surveyed over 50,000 miles of Alaskan territory in four months.

One other major modification of this successful airplane was made in 1928, when Loening decided to compete for a share of the private and commercial markets. The result was a cabin amphibian called the C-1-W, with three large windows and four plush, leather covered, swivel seats. It had a single cockpit,

The Loening Cabin Amphibian, 1928.

a Pratt and Whitney Wasp engine, and was very much like the OL-8A in performance as well as in other characteristics. A C-2-C six-passenger version, with a wider extended cabin and direct access through a hatch to a two-place cockpit, was also built, and had a 525-horsepower Wright Cyclone engine. A C-2-H variation was essentially the same airplane with a 525-horsepower R-1690 Pratt and Whitney Hornet engine.

Beckwith Havens, a naval aviator in World War I and an experienced flying boat pilot,* accepted a position selling the new cabin amphibians. A number were purchased by small air services and charter companies, and several were acquired by organizations like Pan American Airways and Western Air Express (later Western Airlines). Two C-2-H Loening aircraft were purchased by the Navy and outfitted as aerial ambulances with the designation XHL-1. Five of these aircraft eventually found their way to China in 1929, as equipment for the pioneer China National Aviation Corporation (CNAC).

In 1928, whether as a result of a premonition or just luck, Loening sold his company near the peak of the stock market, which would fall so dramatically the following year. The Loening organization then became part of the Keystone Aircraft Company, a subsidiary of the giant Curtiss-Wright combine. This company subsequently produced OL-9s for the Navy, and marketed a four-place amphibian biplane known as the Keystone-Loening Commuter in the commercial market.

Subsequently, Loening formed a small research and development company to experiment with new ideas. He also participated in the founding of Pan American Airways, and the Grumman Aircraft Engineering Corporation. Grover Loening lived to be 87. His contributions to American aviation have been recognized by many awards over the years, including the Collier Trophy in 1921, the President's Medal of Merit in 1948, the Eggleston Medal of Columbia University in 1949, the Wright Memorial Trophy in 1950, the Air Force medal in 1955, the Guggenheim Medal in 1960, and numerous other personal honors and awards. In addition to his Flying Yacht of 1921 through 1923, and

*See Chapter One, pages 13–15—Havens and VerPlanck fly a Curtiss F-Boat to victory in the Great Lakes Reliability Cruise of 1913.

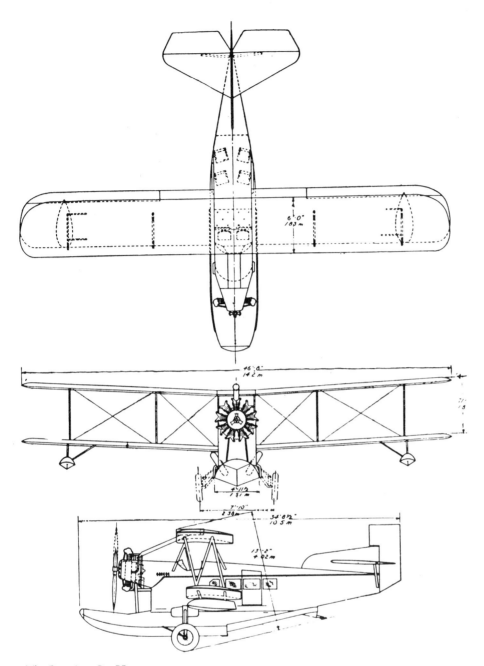

The Loening C-2-H.

the many versions of the Loening Amphibian, he produced the little-known XS2L-1 Scout Plane,* a one of a kind amphibian, and a small two-place monoplane pusher-type flying boat, the XSL-1,† both for the Navy.

Another prominent individual associated with the design and manufacture of amphibious aircraft was Igor Sikorsky. In the late 1920s and the 1930s, he

*The XS2L was a tractor-type amphibian with folding wings. The 400-horsepower Pratt and Whitney R-985 engine and the upper wing sat atop a pylon, which also enclosed the pilot and rear gunner. Wingspan was 34 feet, 6 inches. Overall length was 29 feet, 5 inches, and gross weight was 3,737 pounds. Only one was built.

†The XSL-1 was not an amphibian. It was powered by a Warner Scarab 110-horsepower engine. Wingspan was 31 feet, overall length was 27 feet, 2 inches, and gross weight was 1,500 pounds. This aircraft was modified and became the XSL-2, with a Menasco B-6 engine of 160 horsepower. Dimensions remained the same, but maximum speed was increased from 101 to 116 miles per hour, while gross weight increased to almost 1,700 pounds. Only one was built.

A Western Air Express Loening C-2-H lands at Santa Catalina Island off California. (Western Airlines)

produced a series of amphibians which were extensively used by the U.S. Navy and by various commercial carriers and other private industries and individuals.

The U.S. Navy's first Sikorsky aircraft was one of five S-36 models built in 1927. It was acquired for possible use as a patrol plane, and hence was given the Navy designation XPS-1. Although slightly smaller than the follow-on S-38, with an upper wingspan of 71 feet, and an overall length of 36 feet, 8 inches, the S-36 looked much like its more successful progeny. The Navy quickly discovered that its two 220-horsepower Wright Whirlwind J-5 engines were not powerful enough to make the XPS-1 an effective airplane for service use. It experienced difficulty breaking free of the water on takeoff, and had a maximum speed of only 110 miles per hour, with an unimpressive service ceiling of only 9,000 feet.

These performance deficiencies were overcome by the S-38, introduced in 1928. The Navy purchased two of these aircraft, designated the XPS-2, with machine guns mounted in cockpits fore and aft, later removed. These aircraft had more than twice the horsepower of the S-36, provided by two Pratt and Whitney R-1340B engines of 450 horsepower each. The top speed was increased to 125 miles per hour and the service ceiling was raised to 19,400 feet. The XPS-2 had a wingspan of 71 feet, 8 inches, and an overall length of 40 feet, 3 inches. The gross weight was 9,885 pounds. Both of these aircraft were assigned to Utility Squadron One (VJ-1B), attached to the tender USS *Aroostook*. One of these later went to VJ-1F, attached to the USS *Argonne,* while the other went to the air station at Coco Solo, Panama. One of the two was still serving with the USS *Wright* as late as 1933.

Four Sikorsky S-38Bs were ordered by the U.S. Navy on 3 April 1929, and designated PS-3s as they were delivered. They featured Pratt and Whitney R-1340C engines, and were similar to the XPS-2s in most respects. One noticeable change in appearance was a slanted windshield, designed to improve aerodynamic qualities. By 1930, one of these was serving as ship's aircraft on board the *Aroostook,* while another was employed by the Commander, Scouting Fleet, as his flag aircraft. In the latter part of 1930, all the PS-type (S-38) aircraft were redesignated as transports. By that time, the XPS-1 had been

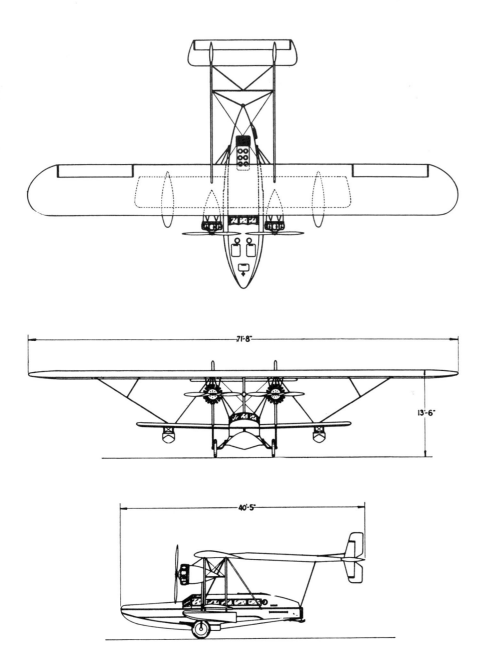

The Sikorsky S-38.

deleted from the Navy inventory, and the two XPS-2s became XRS-2s, the XPS-3s became XRS-3s, and three Sikorsky model S-41s ordered that same year became RS-1s.

Although used by the Navy, the Sikorsky S-38 sesquiplane amphibian was designed primarily to serve as a commercial transport, and it proved to be well adapted to early airline operations. These were times when airfields were scarce, and fueling stops between cities might consist of no more than a quiet stretch of water and a small station-barge. NYRBA and Pan American used a number of these aircraft to open up South America to air commerce in the late 1920s and '30s. They were ideal for feeder operations and for short-haul airlines such as Inter-Island Airways (later Hawaiian Airlines) and Canadian Airways, which operated an S-38 between Vancouver and Victoria. Western Air Express operated their Sikorsky amphibian from Los Angeles via Wilmington, California, to Avalon Harbor at Santa Catalina, where the aircraft was accessed by boat. Vern Carstens flew explorer Martin Johnson's zebra-striped S-38 *Osa's Ark* over some sixty thousand miles of African wilderness.

This S-38 contested the right-of-way with a crocodile in New Guinea's Kikori River during a landing in 1937—and lost. (Sikorsky Aircraft Corp.)

After their appearance in 1928, the S-38s seemed to have spread over the globe, from the southern tip of South America to chilly Alaska, Canada, and Greenland. They flew as airliners in China, and with the French Aeromaritime Company in North Africa, served with a Swedish charter line in Scandinavia, and with oil companies over the jungles of New Guinea.

One S-38 had a particularly colorful career and an unusual end. Originally purchased by Pan American in September 1929, it was flown by Colonel Charles Lindbergh and Captain Basil Rowe on the first air mail run from Miami, Florida, to the Panama Canal Zone in April 1930. It was later sold, and eventually became the property of the Papua Oil Development Company, Limited, of Port Moresby, New Guinea. In December 1937, while landing in the Kikori River, it collided with a crocodile, and was taxied into shallow water where it sank.

Several other S-38s also came to sudden ends. One S-38 operated by China National Aviation disappeared without trace while on a flight between Shanghai and Canton in April 1934, and another, operated by the New Guinea Petroleum Company, was destroyed on the ground on Java in February 1942 by Japanese fighter planes.

The S-38, though referred to by many people as the "Ugly Duckling" or the "Flying Tadpole," was a superior performer, and a record-setter as well. On 21 July 1930 Sikorsky's venerable test pilot Captain Boris Sergievsky set two international records for Class C2 seaplanes with an S-38 powered with two 575-horsepower Wasp engines. The aircraft lifted a total weight of 1,000 kilograms to an altitude of 26,929 feet, thus setting records for both a 500 and 1,000-kilogram payload simultaneously. On 11 August Sergievsky broke yet another world record with the same airplane, carrying aloft a load of 2,000 kilograms to a height of 19,709 feet.

The S-38 was such a success that Sikorsky also produced a smaller version, the S-39, which made its first flight on 24 December 1929. Unlike the S-38, this aircraft was a parasol-wing monoplane like the S-40 Clippers and later S-41s. The prototype mounted two four-cylinder British Cirrus engines developing 115 horsepower each. Sikorsky, a firm advocate of multi-engine aircraft for the sake of safety, felt that single-engine designs introduced an unnecessary element of risk into air travel. He and Loening, who had an opposite point of view, exchanged correspondence on the subject and the issue remained a matter of aeronautical controversy for some time. Unfortunately, the S-39 prototype did little to support Sikorsky's contention, because it experienced engine failure on its third flight and crashed on 30 December 1929. The second engine was insufficient to keep the aircraft airborne.

After this incident, the United Aircraft Corporation, of which the Sikorsky Company had become a part in 1929, insisted that a single, nine-cylinder, 300-horsepower radial engine be installed on the S-39. This power plant was

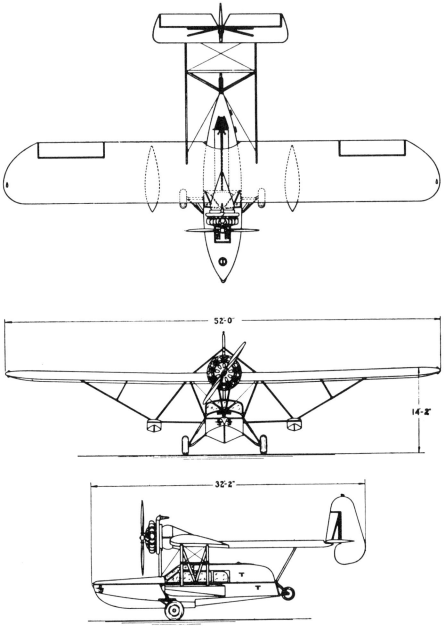

The Sikorsky S-39.

manufactured by Pratt and Whitney, also a subsidiary of United Aircraft. Sikorsky reluctantly gave the approval to mount a single Wasp Junior engine on subsequent models of this aircraft.

The S-39 was envisioned as a private amphibian for wealthy sportsmen. It was built in two versions, the four-place S-39A and the five-place S-39B. Both had improved all-metal hulls, with better takeoff and landing characteristics than either the S-38 or the S-41. The wingspan was an even 52 feet, the length overall was 31 feet, 11 inches, and the gross weight was 3,700 pounds. The S-39 had a top speed of 115 miles per hour, cruised at about 98, and had a range of 375 miles. In general, it performed well. The timing of this airplane's introduction, however, left much to be desired, coming only two months after the October stock market crash that paralyzed the national economy. Only twenty-three S-39s were built, and only one of these, the YIC-28, was purchased for military use. It was retired by the Army in 1934. Another S-39 was acquired by Martin Johnson and named *Spirit of Africa*. This aircraft was painted a

Martin and Osa Johnson's S-39 *Spirit of Africa* had a giraffe-like color scheme. (Sikorsky Aircraft Corp.)

cream color with brown splotches like a giraffe, and was used in Johnson's African explorations along with the zebra-striped S-38 *Osa's Ark*. Later it accompanied Johnson on an expedition to Borneo. It survived until November 1942, when it was lost after an open sea landing in the Gulf of Mexico, made in an attempt to rescue two downed aviators.

The Sikorsky model S-41 was a monoplane with increased wing loading, embodying many improvements lacking in the S-38. It was larger, seating a total of sixteen, and was therefore much more efficient for commercial airline operations. The wingspan was 78 feet, 9 inches, while the overall length was 45 feet, 2 inches. Two 575-horsepower Pratt and Whitney engines propelled the S-41 to a top speed of 131 miles per hour, and a cruising speed of 115. The gross weight was 13,800 pounds, and the service ceiling was 16,000 feet. The S-41 had a normal cruising range of 575 miles, which could be extended to over 800 if some of the payload was sacrificed in favor of fuel, or if it was overloaded, as occasionally happened in early airline operations. The S-41 had a few operating idiosyncrasies, which were never fully eliminated by further development, because only seven were produced. It was too large for most private pilots and small charter-flight operators, and too small for the rapidly expanding major airlines. Furthermore, it was introduced during a time of economic crisis, when many companies were utilizing whatever aircraft they already had, and in many cases struggling to survive. The S-41 model was ultimately abandoned in favor of the S-40, first of the great Clipper flying boats.

The Navy purchased three S-41s, and designated them RS-1s. The first of these was assigned to the U.S. Marine Corps, and later went to Haiti. Another was attached to the air base at Pearl Harbor, and a third was assigned to VJ-2S attached to USS *Wright*. None of the RS aircraft appear on the Navy inventory after 1933.

A particularly popular Sikorsky amphibian was the S-43, a medium size all-metal twin-engine transport used by Pan American, and especially suited to the kind of overwater operations engaged in by Inter-Island Airways in the Hawaiian Islands.*

*Inter-Island Airways Limited began regularly scheduled airline service on 11 November 1929 with Sikorsky S-38s. Sikorsky S-43s were acquired by the airline in the mid-1930s. This company later became Hawaiian Airlines.

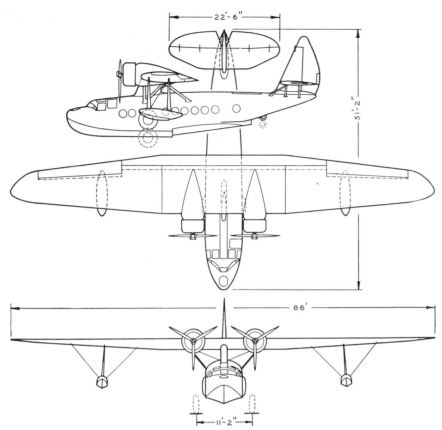

The Sikorsky S-43A.

The S-43 was designed as a nineteen-place aircraft, including a crew of three, but could be configured to seat up to twenty-five. It was powered by two 750-horsepower Pratt and Whitney R1650-52 engines, and at 7,000 feet the A model had a top speed of 194 miles per hour and a cruising speed of 178. The service ceiling was 20,000 feet. The cantilever wing spanning 86 feet was perched atop a short pylon protruding from the top of the hull. The overall length was 51 feet, 2 inches, and the gross weight was 19,500 pounds. The B model was an inch longer, and had a gross weight of 20,000 pounds. Its service ceiling was 19,000 feet, while the maximum range was 800 miles, about 25 miles more than the S-43A. Twin vertical stabilizers and rudders gave the S-43B a slightly different appearance.

The S-43 was a fast airplane with outstanding performance characteristics, and was purchased by companies world-wide. Howard Hughes bought one intending to use it for his record-breaking flight of 1938 around the world, but instead he ultimately flew a faster Lockheed aircraft introduced about that time. The S-43 was later used as a test aircraft to experiment on design concepts for the H-4 Hercules. Following an unfortunate crash and sinking in Lake Mead, Nevada, in the early 1940s, Hughes had the aircraft raised and restored to its original condition at considerable cost. Afterward, for a reason known only to him, it was stored unused in a hangar for many years.

The U.S. Army purchased a few S-43s as OA-8s, and at least one as an OA-11. The U.S. Marine Corps acquired two, and the U.S. Navy purchased fifteen, which were all designated JRS-1s. Eight of these went to San Diego for service with VJ-1.

Sikorsky built an unusual amphibian scout aircraft for the Navy in 1933, known as the XSS-2. This airplane was powered by a single Pratt and Whitney R-1340D-1 engine of 550 horsepower, and had a top speed of almost 160 miles per hour. Its service ceiling was 22,600 feet, and the gross weight was 4,133

Navy JRS-1 amphibians of VJ-1 squadron. The JRS-1 was the Navy version of the Sikorsky S-43A. (U.S. Navy)

pounds. The XSS-2 was very different from other Sikorsky aircraft. It had a single set of wings, 42 feet long, which were gulled close to the hull with the engine strut-mounted overhead. This amphibian was compact, 32 feet in length, with a crew of two, and was intended for use as a carrier or catapult-launched scout and observation aircraft. However, only the prototype was built, and the design was never ordered into production.

One of the more outstanding amphibian flying boats of the 1930s was produced by the Douglas Aircraft Company, Incorporated,* headed by Donald W. Douglas. This airplane was the all-metal twin-engine Dolphin monoplane built for light transport use, and purchased by all four U.S. military services, the Army, Navy, Marine Corps, and Coast Guard. The Dolphin was produced in several different models, but the basic airframe remained virtually unchanged in all. The prototype used two nine-cylinder Wright R975E Whirlwind engines of 400 horsepower each, which produced a maximum speed of 145 miles per hour and a cruising speed of 117. It carried two pilots and six or seven passengers. The wingspan was 60 feet, and the overall length was 44 feet, 4 inches (45 feet, 3 inches on later versions). An unusual feature of this aircraft was its auxiliary wing, 20 feet in length, which served as a brace for the strut-mounted engines and at the same time provided lift. Designated XRD-1 by the Navy, this airplane had a gross weight of 8,000 pounds, and a service ceiling of 18,000 feet.

The Dolphin was first flown on 30 September 1930, and was ready for delivery in June of the following year. The Coast Guard purchased three early models designated RDs, and ten of a later type, designated RD-4s. Because of the stout hull, the Coast Guard Dolphins were used extensively and successfully for open-sea rescue.

In total, the Navy purchased ten Dolphin aircraft in several versions, designated the XRD-1, RD-2, and RD-3, for use as utility transports. The RD-2 and RD-3 were both powered with Pratt and Whitney R-1340-96 engines

*Now McDonnell Douglas.

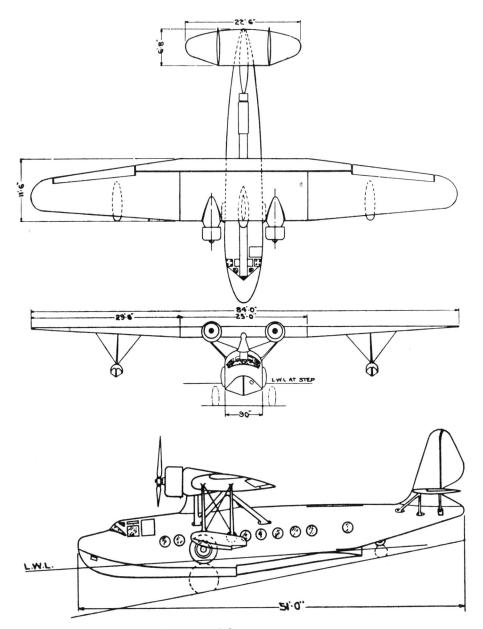

The Sikorsky S-43B. Note the twin tail fins.

developing 450 horsepower, which increased the speed of the RD-2 by as much as 8 miles per hour. The various RD-type aircraft were assigned to Naval Air Stations Anacostia, Norfolk, and San Diego, to Fleet Air Bases at Pearl Harbor and Coco Solo, and to utility squadron detachments aboard tenders. Among other uses, they served as excellent flag and VIP aircraft.

Most of the Douglas Dolphins produced were bought by the military services. A few, however, went to private owners, and five were purchased by the Wilmington-Catalina Airline.

Another fine amphibian which made its appearance in the mid 1930s was the Fairchild 91 Jungle Clipper, built by the Fairchild Aircraft Corporation of Hagerstown, Maryland. Pan American ordered six of these sleek aesthetically pleasing aircraft for use by its subsidiary, Panair Do Brazil, in serving the Amazon River valley. Only two were actually delivered, however, in 1936, and the order for the remaining four was cancelled. These were finally completed and sold, with one being purchased by scientist and explorer Dr. Richard Archbold, and another going to speed boat manufacturer and enthusiast Gar Wood. Two more were exported to Japan.

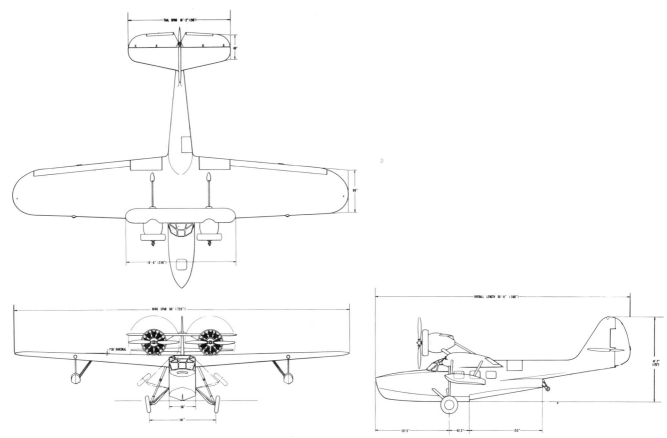

The Douglas RD-2 Dolphin. (McDonnell Douglas Corp.)

The Fairchild 91 was an all-metal high-wing monoplane, with a single 800-horsepower Pratt and Whitney Hornet engine mounted above the cockpit. In 1936 it was probably the fastest single-engine amphibian in existence, with a maximum speed of over 170 miles per hour at 3,000 feet and a cruising speed of 155. The gross weight was 10,500 pounds, and the maximum range was in excess of 700 miles. This airplane had a wingspan of 56 feet, an overall length of 46 feet, 8 inches, and carried ten persons, including two pilots. Since landings and takeoffs on the Amazon River run were made almost exclusively on or from the water, the retractable landing gear was eventually removed to save weight. Thus, the Fairchild 91s operated as flying boats until they were retired in 1945. Because of its demonstrated speed and reliability, a slightly modified version of this aircraft was proposed to the Navy as a scout and observation plane, designated the XSOK-1. A mockup was built, but no operating models were ever produced.

In 1930, the Grumman Aircraft Engineering Corporation had appeared on the scene; although it started as a small operation, it soon became a major supplier of aircraft to the U.S. Navy. This organization was headed by LeRoy Grumman, who was himself naturally oriented toward the Navy. Graduating from Cornell University in 1916 as a mechanical engineer, Grumman was soon caught up in World War I, and enlisted in the Navy as a Machinists Mate 2nd Class. The Navy sent him to MIT for a preflight course in aeronautics, and from there he went to flight training. Designated Naval Aviator number 1216, he spent additional time at MIT, and was subsequently assigned to the Naval Aircraft Factory, Philadelphia. There, while working as a test pilot and project engineer, he met Grover Loening, who persuaded him to leave the Navy and come to work as manager of the Loening plant in New York. It was undoubtedly his work with Loening that made him a devotee of the

The Coast Guard used Dolphins extensively for open-sea rescue. (U.S. Coast Guard)

amphibian flying boat. When Loening sold the operation in 1928, Grumman gathered together a few of the organization's top men, and started his own concern. Loening himself, who had handpicked these men and knew their talents, invested a substantial amount of money in the Grumman venture.

In the beginning this fledgling company repaired damaged Loening amphibians, designed and built seaplane floats for the Navy, and even made truck bodies, while establishing itself in the aircraft industry. During this same period, it also designed and built the prototype of the XFF-1 fighter, and was rewarded with a Navy production contract for twenty-seven of this model.

In 1932, Roy Grumman and William T. "Bill" Schwendler redesigned the Loening Xo2L* to produce the XJF-1 Grumman amphibian biplane, whose familial ties to the Loening line were evident. The Grumman amphibian, however, was more streamlined, and its overall performance was considerably better. The landing gear mechanism, which retracted the wheels in such a way that they were stowed flush with the hull, was strictly a Grumman innovation.

The Grumman XJF-1 was first flown on 4 May 1933 by test pilot Paul Hovgard, and attained maximum speeds of up to 164 miles per hour. The engine was a 700-horsepower Pratt and Whitney R-1535-62, with two rows of seven cylinders each. The wingspan was 39 feet, and the overall length was 32 feet, 7 inches. The gross weight was 4,831 pounds, and the service ceiling was 21,500 feet.

The XJF-1 was delivered to the Navy in May 1933, and after exhaustive evaluation by the test facility at Anacostia, a contract was awarded to Grumman for twenty-seven JF-1s. From that time forward, this family of aircraft was known as Ducks, a name which had sometimes been applied to their Loening progenitors.

Except for using different engines, the succeeding models of the Ducks were essentially the same. The JF-3 employed a nine-cylinder Wright R-1820-08 engine of 750-horsepower. The J2F-1 through J2F-5 also used various versions of this engine. The J2F Ducks differed in external appearance from their JF predecessors in that they had an extended bow, which gave the J2F an overall

*The Xo2L-1 was powered by a Pratt and Whitney R-1340C engine of 450-horsepower, and was a greatly improved version of the OL-9. Wingspan was 37 feet, and overall length was 29 feet, 10 inches. Gross weight was 4,053 pounds, and maximum speed was 132 miles per hour. The Xo2L-2 used a Pratt and Whitney R-1340-D1 of 550 horsepower, and had a maximum speed of 141 miles per hour. Gross weight was 4,829 pounds, and service ceiling was 15,600 feet. It was essentially the same airplane, but was 33 feet, 3 inches in length.

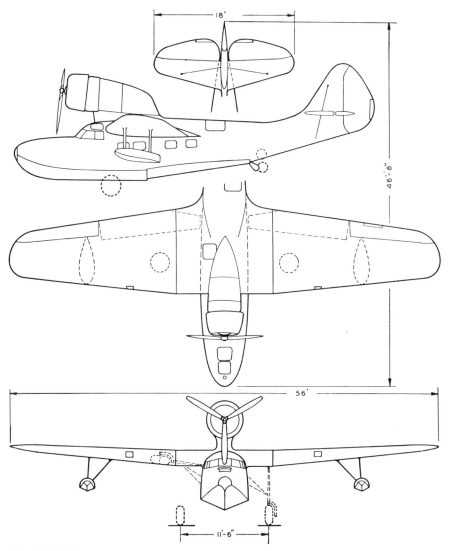

The Fairchild 91.

length of 34 feet. Otherwise, all dimensions remained the same. Most J2Fs carried 30-caliber machine guns in the rear cockpits, and bomb racks under the wings. Beginning with this model, many also carried stationary forward-firing 30 caliber guns. These aircraft were used extensively by the U.S. Navy, Coast Guard, and Marine Corps for scouting, patrol, rescue, antisubmarine warfare, photo-reconnaissance, and general utility missions. The Army Air Corps also obtained one for test and evaluation, and twelve were exported to Argentina.

The Columbia Aircraft Company, which sprang up during the war and disappeared sometime after the end of hostilities, built Ducks under contract from Grumman. Columbia produced 330 J2F-6s with R-1820-54 engines, which developed 1050 horsepower and provided top speeds of up to 190 miles per hour. Altogether, Grumman and Columbia built 645 Ducks between 1933 and 1945. After the war, Columbia built two prototypes of a monoplane version of this aircraft. These XJL-1s featured retractable tricycle landing gear, and they performed well during Navy evaluation. Despite this, no production models were ordered.

The Ducks performed a variety of wartime tasks, but are probably best remembered for their search-and-rescue role. Many a downed aviator owes his life to this sturdy little airplane, which often went out in treacherous weather, took off and landed in heavy seas, and defied hostile fire to rescue

The Grumman XJF-1 was a greatly improved version of the Loening amphibians. (Grumman Aerospace Corp.)

them. One story of a courageous Coast Guard pilot, his crewman, and their J2F-5 Duck, especially deserves mention.

In November 1942, Lieutenant John A. Pritchard, Jr., was assigned as aviation officer aboard the Coast Guard cutter *Northland* operating off the coast of Greenland. The weather in this area is particularly hazardous for flying during the winter months, but it was also a rewarding hunting ground for the deadly German U-boats to ambush Allied shipping. On 23 November Pritchard, in the ship's launch, had led a rescue party ashore on Greenland to pick up three downed Canadian Air Force flyers. A few days later on 28 November, his services were again in demand, and he took off from the icy seas in the *Northland*'s J2F-5 Duck with Radioman 1st Class Benjamin Bottoms, in an attempt to locate the crew of an Army Air Corps B-17 that had crashed on the ice cap. Using the Duck's DF equipment to home on weak signals from the downed plane, Bottoms led Pritchard inland over the cap to the stranded flyers. Ignoring their warnings not to land, Pritchard found what appeared to be a marginally suitable spot some four miles away, and attempted a wheels-down landing. The surface snow was soft and the wheels dug in, but the seaplane hull with its long protruding snout prevented the plane from flipping over on its nose, and it slid to a halt. Leaving Bottoms to maintain radio contact with the ship, Pritchard trudged across the crevasse-ridden ice cap to the downed men. Two of them were injured, but with the help of the third he managed to get them back to the Duck. He loaded the two injured airmen into the plane, and promised to return for the third man the next day. Then after retracting his useless landing gear, he applied full power for takeoff. The three-bladed prop, driven by 850 horsepower, clawed the air, and the plane bumped, bounced, and skidded on its bottom over the snow-covered ice cap until at last it was airborne. The flight back to the ship was without incident.

Pritchard was true to his word, and the following morning the Duck was again lowered over the side. Bottoms was with him as they took off in a light snow, and made their way back to the remaining airman. Again Pritchard

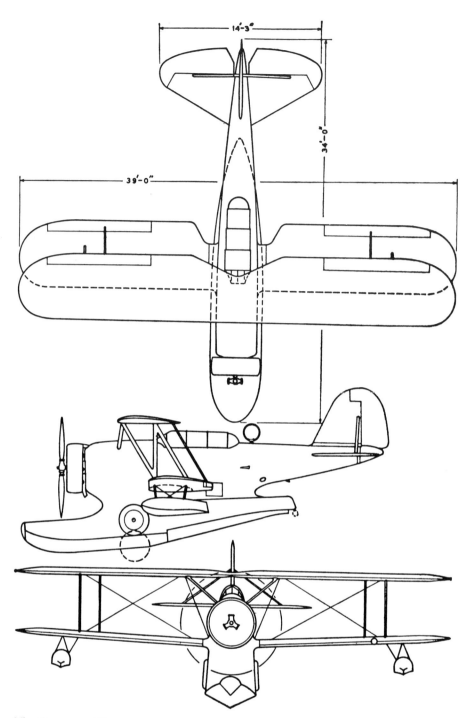

The Grumman JF-1.

man finally aboard, the little Duck slid, careened, and pulled itself into the air. Bottoms reported to the ship that they had made it off the ice cap once more. Then they apparently ran out of luck. A heavy snow storm blanketed the area, and what occurred next is unknown. The three were never heard from again. Pritchard and Bottoms were each posthumously awarded the Distinguished Flying Cross for their rescue efforts.

On 31 May 1937 the Grumman Aircraft and Engineering Corporation flight-tested the largest aircraft it had yet undertaken to produce. This aircraft, the Grumman Goose, was designed for the commercial market, but was also purchased in large numbers by the military services. Grover Loening was responsible for the original specifications, Roy Grumman and Bill Schwendler

executed a successful landing, this time without wheels, and with the last air-

The Grumman Goose was designed for the commercial market, but was also purchased in large numbers by the military services. (Grumman Aerospace Corp.)

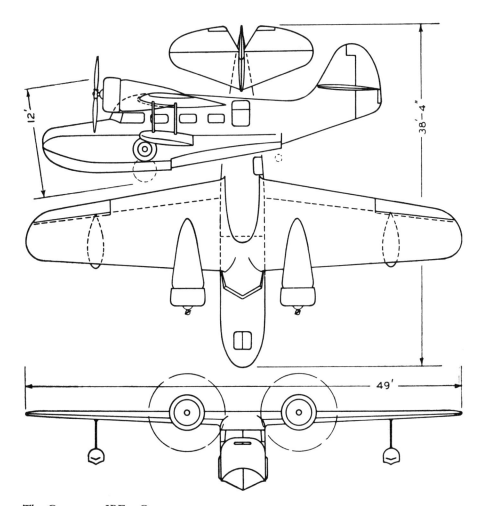

The Grumman JRF-1 Goose.

did the basic design, and Ralston Stalb filled in much of the engineering detail. Designated the G-21 by the manufacturer, the Goose mounted twin Pratt and Whitney R-985 engines, each of which developed 400 horsepower for cruising. It carried ten persons, including pilots, and was a popular private airplane from the beginning.

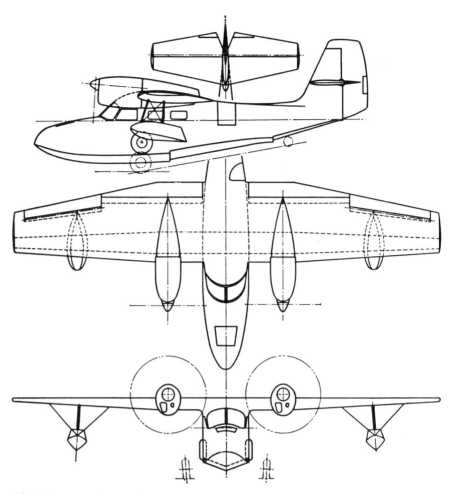

The Grumman J4F Widgeon.

The Navy acquired its first Grumman Goose in 1938 for evaluation as a utility aircraft. Ten more were ordered and delivered in 1939 and 1940 as JRF-1 and JRF-1A's, the latter type being confiigured for aerial photography and target towing. This airplane had a 49-foot wingspan, and a 38-foot, 6-inch length overall. Its maximum speed was 192 miles per hour, with a cruising speed of approximately 150. The JRFs were usually configured to carry two pilots and six passengers. Subsequent versions differed from the early models in small ways. Some, like the JRF-4 and -5, were equipped to carry depth bombs and engage in antisubmarine warfare, while the JRF-6B was outfitted for navigator training. During the period from 1939 to 1945, the Navy acquired more than 250 of these aircraft, in various models. The Coast Guard bought 16 JRFs, while the Army Air Corps purchased more than 30, and some were exported. In total, 345 were produced. In the postwar period, many were acquired by feeder airlines, charter flying services, and private owners, and some are still flying today. Antilles Air Boats, a company founded by Captain Charles Blair, uses about twenty of these Grumman aircraft in both scheduled and unscheduled flights throughout the Caribbean. This company lays claim to being the world's largest existing seaplane airline.

One postwar commercial conversion of the Goose by McKinnon Enterprises of Sandy, Oregon, featured four 340-horsepower Lycoming engines, and had a cruising speed of 225 miles per hour.

Another Gruman design intended for the commercial market was the G-44 Widgeon. This project was nurtured by Roy Grumman, in an attempt to increase commercial sales by offering an airplane very similar to the popular Goose, at half the price. Indeed the Widgeon was, in many respects, a smaller

Leroy Grumman (left) and business manager Jake Swirbul stand beside a G-44 Widgeon built for the civilian market. (Grumman Aerospace Corp.)

version of the G-21. The wingspan was shortened by 9 feet, and the length was reduced by 7 feet 5 inches. Its two 200-horsepower L440C-5 Ranger in-line engines powered the Widgeon to a top speed of 153 miles per hour, and a cruising speed of 138. The gross weight was 4,525 pounds, and the maximum range was 800 miles. The Widgeon carried two persons in the cockpit and three in the cabin in the commercial version. Widgeons configured for military use generally carried only three persons, depending upon the mission.

The G-44, flown by Roy Grumman and company pilot Bud Gillies, was first tested on 28 June 1940. The first production models were sold almost as fast as they could be produced. Immediately after the attack on Pearl Harbor, however, the U.S. Army, Navy, and Coast Guard took the entire output. Eventually, some went to the British, who called them Goslings, and a few were made available to the Brazilians, who used them for coastal patrol.

The U.S. Navy purchased most of the Widgeons produced, and designated them as J4Fs. The Coast Guard, which acquired twenty-five of these aircraft, also used this basic designation, while the Army Air Corps referred to theirs as OA-14s. Like the larger JRF Goose, the Widgeon served primarily in a utility role during World War II, but it was also used as a patrol aircraft, and was even configured for antisubmarine warfare. In this mode, it was capable of carrying a 325-pound depth charge slung under one wing. Inadequate as this may seem, it was with just such a war load that a Coast Guard

The Grumman Mallard was sold to feeder airlines, charter services, and other private corporations and individuals. (Grumman Aerospace Corp.)

Widgeon flown by Ensign Henry C. White sank the German submarine U-166 on 1 August 1942, in the Gulf of Mexico near the mouth of the Mississippi River.

By mid 1944, with the end of the war near, Grumman again began producing Widgeons for the civilian market. After the war, those Widgeons retired from military service were among the more popular surplus aircraft. A French company also produced about thirty of these amphibians, known as SCAN-30s, under a license arrangement with Grumman. A number of them were modified for increased performance, and several of these are operating today. Among them are the McKinnon Super Widgeon with two 275-horsepower Lycoming engines, and a cruising speed of 170 miles per hour, and Pacific Aircraft Engineering Corporation's Gannet with its radial, air-cooled Lycomings of 300 horsepower each, and a cruising speed of 170.

The third aircraft in the Grumman twin-engine amphibian series was the Mallard. This model could carry ten or twelve persons, depending upon its employment. It was sold to feeder airlines, charter services, and other private corporations and individuals. None were purchased by the military services. The Mallard was larger than the Widgeon and Goose, and stressed passenger comfort and convenience. It had a 66-foot 8-inch wingspan, and was 48 feet 4 inches in overall length. Powered by two Pratt and Whitney R-1340-S3A1 engines of 600 horsepower each, it had a top speed of 215 and a cruising speed of 180 miles per hour with a service ceiling of 23,000 feet.

The Mallard first flew on 30 April 1946, and was produced until the middle of 1951. Fifty-nine of these aircraft were built in total, and a number are still in use. Antilles Airboats presently has two Mallards in service, configured to carry fifteen persons.

While Grumman intended the Mallard primarily for the commercial market, the company had by no means abandoned the potential military role of the amphibian. For the latter application, Grumman developed the prototype XJR2F-1, called the Albatross. This airplane, primarily the work of Ralston Stalb, was designed as a utility transport, but was also used extensively for search-and-rescue operations. The XJR2F-1 was first flown in October 1947, and the model was produced from then until 1964. The Air Force purchased a large number of these aircraft, which it designated the SA-16A. The Navy bought well over one hundred Albatross aircraft, which were first labeled JR2Fs, then UF-1s, and finally HU-16s. The Coast Guard found these aircraft particularly suited to rescue work, and their designations generally followed Navy practice.

The original JR2F version had a wingspan of 80 feet, and an overall length of 62 feet 1 inch. Powered by two Wright 1820-76 engines of 1,425 horsepower each, the JR2F had a maximum speed of 255 miles per hour, and a cruising speed of 158. The gross weight was 32,000 pounds, the service ceiling was 22,000 feet, and the range was 2,200 miles. In 1956/57 a major modification to these fine aircraft increased the wingspan to 96 feet, 8 inches, the overall length to 62 feet, 10 inches, the gross weight to 37,500 pounds, and the range to 3,000 miles. Top speed was reduced to about 234 miles per hour. The Air Force designation of this model was SA-16B, while the Navy and Coast Guard designated theirs the HU-16D and E.

The Air Force retired their Albatross aircraft in 1973, turning over some thirty-seven to the Coast Guard. The last Navy Albatross splashed down at Pensacola on 13 August 1976, and was turned over to the U.S. Naval Aviation Museum there. The Coast Guard has retained some of these venerable search and rescue aircraft on active service. The Albatross still holds eleven world records for amphibians.

As World War II came to an end, Grumman began to develop new designs for postwar business. The company experimented briefly with light private aircraft, one of which was an amphibian flying boat named the Tadpole. This all-metal monoplane, designated the G-65, was a two-place high-wing aircraft, with a 125-horsepower Continental C-125 engine mounted pusher style over the wing. It was a compact little light plane, with a wingspan of only 35 feet, an

Table 11-1. Grumman Albatross International Records

Date	Record	Pilot
13 August 1962	Speed—1000 km. without payload—231.96 mph. Speed—1000 km., 1000 kg payload—231.96 mph. Speed—1000 km., 2000 kg payload—231.96 mph.	Cdr. Wallace C. Dahlgren, U.S. Coast Guard
11 September 1962	Altitude—1000 kg. payload—29,475 ft. Altitude—2000 kg. payload—27,404.93 ft.	Lcdr. Fred Franke, U.S. Navy
16 September 1962	Speed—5000 km., 1000 kg payload—151.39 mph.	Lcdr. Richard A. Hoffman, U.S. Navy
25 October 1962	Distance—straight line without payload— 3,571.65 miles	Cdr. W. Fenlon, U.S. Coast Guard
19 March 1963	Speed—1000 km., 5000 kg payload—153.65 mph.	Capt. Glenn A. Higginson, U.S. Air Force
20 March 1963	Altitude—5000 kg. payload—19,747 ft. Greatest Payload—to alt. of 2000 meters— 12,162.9 lbs.	Capt. Henry E. Erwin Jr., U.S. Air Force
4 July 1973	Altitude—without payload—32,883 ft.	Lt. Col. Charles H. Manning, U.S. Air Force

The Coast Guard still retains some Grumman Albatross amphibians as search and rescue aircraft. (U.S. Coast Guard)

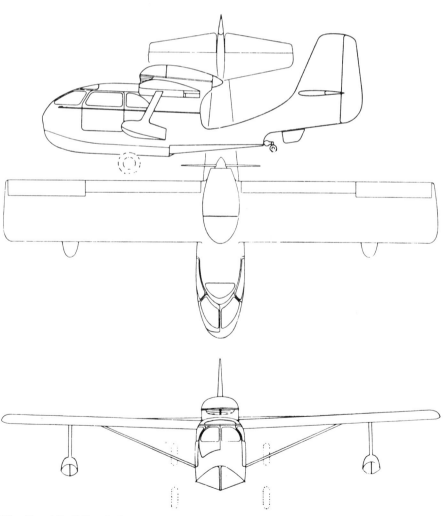

The Republic RC-3 Seabee.

overall length of 23 feet 6 inches, and a gross weight of 2,100 pounds. The first flight was made by Roy Grumman and Hank Kurt on 7 December 1944, and, although the Tadpole performed well, it was never placed into production. The unit cost was a major factor in this decision.

Perhaps the most significant development at that time in a light amphibian flying boat was the Republic RC-3 Seabee. This was a four-place all-metal aircraft which, because of its simplified design, was marketed in quantity for about $6,000 each. It was a pusher-type airplane powered by a single six-cylinder Franklin air-cooled engine of 125 horsepower. The wingspan was 37 feet, 8 inches, while the length overall was 27 feet 10 3/4 inches. The gross weight was 3,000 pounds, and the maximum range was about 560 miles. The top speed was 120 miles per hour, while the cruising speed was 103. For a light plane, the Seabee had a fairly roomy interior, and was suitable for a business trip, a family junket, or a hunting or fishing expedition to a remote lake. First flown in November of 1944, the Seabee was an immediate success, and Republic Aviation was at first unable to keep up with demand for the airplane. One thousand and sixty of these aircraft were produced between 1944 and 1947, and some are still in use today.

A number of other amphibian flying boats produced in the United States are worthy of mention. Among these are the Cox-Klemin amphibians, Grover Loening's Duckling, James H. Eastman's three-place Sea Pirate, G. Sumner Ireland's five-place Neptune and two-place "Privateer," the Spencer-Larsen four-place amphibian, and the Great Lakes XSG-1 observation aircraft built for the Navy. An excellent five-place single-engine plane known as the Seabird was manufactured of stainless steel by Fleetwings Incorporated, of Bristol, Pennsylvania, and a twin-engine aircraft called the Trimmer Amphibian, constructed of molded plywood, was produced by Commonwealth Aircraft Incorporated, of Kansas City, Kansas.

While the amphibian seems to have gone the way of other flying boats, a few hardy light plane enthusiasts persist in its promotion. The Colonial Aircraft Corporation manufactured a light amphibian flying boat in the 1950s called the Skimmer, and an improved version of this aircraft known as the Buccaneer is currently marketed by Lake Aircraft of Houston, Texas; an early version of the Buccaneer, designated the LA-4, set a distance record for light amphibians on 2 September 1964 when, piloted by G. L. Hunt, it flew from Reykjavik, Iceland, to Belfast, Ireland. A few homebuilt designs with names like Osprey and Taylor Coot, and the Volmer Sportsman, the Anderson Kingfisher, and the Spencer Air Car, also help to keep the light amphibian flying boat concept alive.

CHAPTER TWELVE

The Last Buoy

THE BIG COMBAT FLYING BOATS had done well during World War II, and had more than lived up to expectations, but by 1946, the Catalinas, Coronados, and Mariners were old and tired. In spite of the fact that the major airlines were abandoning big seaplanes for faster, more efficient land-based planes, however, the flying boat was to remain for a while longer as an important component of naval aviation.

The P5M Marlin, Martin Model 237, was a worthy successor to the old war boats. The designers of this aircraft borrowed liberally from the PBM, employing the familiar gull wing of similar dimensions. But the extended hull was markedly different, with a length-to-beam ratio of 8:5:1. The long afterbody resulted in smoother operation in rough water, and greatly reduced the tendency to dive into the water like a porpoise, which had often been a problem with earlier designs. It was the first aircraft to use the Martin "Hydroflaps," which were extendable flap-like appendages located below the waterline at the end of the hull. They could be extended one at a time or together, and, used in conjunction with the model's reversible pitch propellers, they made the Marlin highly maneuverable on the water. For an airplane of that size, it was also very easy to control in the air, because of its power-boosted controls and spoiler ailerons.

The contract for the prototype was awarded on 26 June 1946, and the new patrol aircraft, designated the XP5M-1, was first flown at Middle River, Maryland, on 30 May 1948 by company test pilots O. E. "Pat" Tibbs and Wilbur Smith. This airplane was powered by two Wright R-3350 engines of 2,700 horsepower each. Its armament included radar-controlled power turrets in the nose and tail, and a third power turret in the dorsal position, all with twin 20-millimeter guns. The nose and dorsal turrets were later removed on the prototype, and eliminated from the design of the production model. Eventually, the tail turret was also removed.

There followed a period of about a year and a half of test and evaluation, and in July 1950, a somewhat modified version of the prototype was ordered into production.

The first P5M-1 production aircraft flew on 22 June 1951. The forward gun turret had been replaced by a bulbous nose section, which housed a large search radar antenna and gave the aircraft a distinctive profile. Another change was in the design of the cockpit, which was raised to provide increased visibility. As on the prototype, the tail section consisted of a high single vertical fin and rudder, with a low conventional horizontal stabilizer and elevators. This airplane was powered by two improved Wright Cyclone R-3350-30W compound engines* of 3,250 horsepower each. These were mounted on the wings at the angles formed by the gull design. The nacelles were elongated under the wings, and contained large bays, which could be used either for bombs or disposable fuel tanks to extend the range. Permanent fuel tanks were located in the hull and wings.

*Engines which have auxiliary turbines designed to use exhaust gases to provide increased power; also known as turbo-compound engines.

The Martin Marlin P5M-1 was the first aircraft to use hydroflaps. They were used on the water, one at a time for turning, or together as water brakes. The pilot actuated the hydroflaps by depressing the tops of the rudder pedals as he would toe brakes in a plane taxiing on land. (Martin Marietta)

A P5M-1 Marlin nests in a rubber dock alongside a tender for servicing. (U.S. Navy)

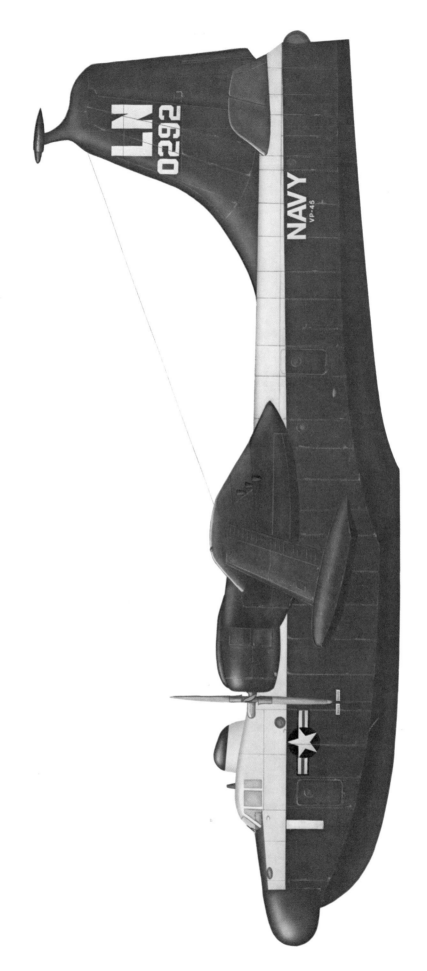

The P5M Marlin was a worthy successor to the old war boats. It could carry and deliver on target torpedoes, bombs, depth charges, mines, and rockets. (John Ficklen)

The Convair XF2Y-1 Sea Dart fighter was a supersonic flying boat with retractable skis. (U.S. Navy)

The Sea Dart's skis had small beaching wheels on the aft end for taxiing up onto land. (U.S. Navy)

The P5M-1 could carry torpedoes, bombs, depth charges, mines, and rockets, and had a gross weight of about 74,000 pounds. The maximum speed was 234 miles per hour at altitude, while cruise speed was about 150, depending upon the load. The maximum range was almost 3,000 miles.

At about the time the first P5M-1 models were coming off the Martin production line, work had begun on the west coast of the United States on one of the most imaginative flying boat projects yet undertaken—the XF2Y Sea Dart. This aircraft was a twin-jet fighter-interceptor, built by the San Diego division of Convair; the first one was launched on 16 December 1952. The Sea Dart was a true flying boat, the fuselage and hull being the same. A delta-wing aircraft, the Sea Dart had no horizontal stabilizer or elevators, but instead relied on "elevons" on the trailing edge of the triangular wing. It rode low and flat in

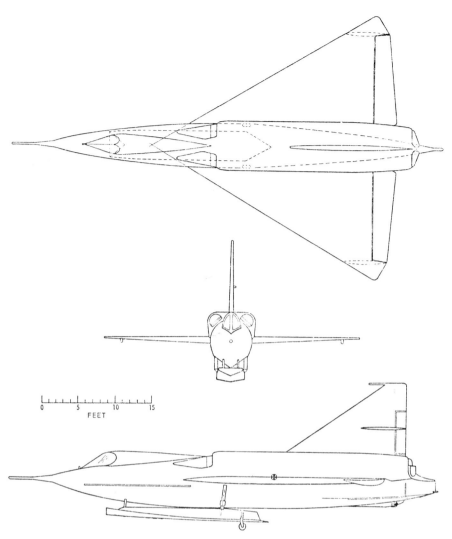

The Sea Dart in single-ski configuration. (U.S. Navy)

the water while taxiing, but rose on a pair of hydroskis on the takeoff run. This procedure was reversed during landing, with the plane first touching down on the skis, and then settling back on the hull in the water as speed decreased. Small beaching wheels on the aft end of the skis and on the underside of the tail could be used to taxi on land for short distances, and the plane could enter and exit the water under its own power. These aircraft could thus be deployed to forward areas where no airstrips existed, to operate from the beaches, where they could respond on a moment's notice to enemy thrusts by taxiing a few feet down the beach and into the water for immediate takeoff. The Sea Dart was also designed to be capable of operating almost entirely from the water, in locations where there were no suitable beaches. A large hull access door permitted minor engine repairs on the water, and an air-transportable maintenance float which could handle three of these fighters simultaneously for heavier maintenance was developed in 1953.

The Sea Dart had a wingspan of 33 feet, 8 inches, and an overall length of 52 feet, 7 inches. The empty weight was 16,000 pounds, and the gross weight for takeoff was 22,300 to 24,000 pounds, depending upon mission configuration. It had a combat radius of over 300 nautical miles at an altitude of 35,000 feet, and a maximum cruising range of over 1,100 miles, which could be extended further by in-flight refueling. For combat armament, it could carry a maximum of forty-eight 2.75-inch folding-fin aircraft rockets, or it could be configured with four 20-millimeter aircraft cannon.

The prototype first flew on 9 April 1953.* This model was originally powered by two Westinghouse J34-WE32 turbojet engines, each capable of producing 3,400 pounds of thrust. The second Sea Dart had two Westinghouse J46-WE-2 engines, each of which provided 4,600 pounds of thrust in normal operation, and 6,000 pounds using afterburners. On 3 August 1954, this aircraft, flown by Convair's C. E. Richbourg, exceeded Mach 1 during a test flight, and thus has the distinction of being the first seaplane to travel faster than the speed of sound.† Unfortunately, on 4 November of that year, it exploded in flight, killing the test pilot. A number of these aircraft were subsequently cancelled, and of the total of nineteen originally ordered, only five were actually built. The prototype aircraft was reconfigured with a single ski, somewhat resembling a surfboard, and was employed in further hydro-ski experiments. By 1956, only one Sea Dart remained in test status, while the other four were placed in storage. The program was discontinued shortly thereafter.

The Sea Dart project was neither the only nor the most extensive U.S. Navy venture into jet-powered flying boats. On 31 October 1952 the Martin Company was awarded a contract for two experimental four-engine Model 275 turbojet flying boats. This airplane, designated the XP6M-1 Seamaster, was to be an all-weather high performance mine-laying aircraft, also capable of long-range reconnaissance operations. Martin's wealth of experience with flying boats, and its work with the T-tail and the rotating weapons door, made that company the logical choice for the development contract. George Trimble headed advanced design at that time, and was responsible for developing the external configuration of the aircraft.‡ He vividly recalls some of the problems encountered:

> The P6M had to fly at 600 knots [almost 700 miles per hour] on the deck to properly deliver mines.§ No airplane of any such size had flown to that high an indicated airspeed. The structural requirements were formidable—particularly the effects of structural flexibility on longitudinal stability.
>
> The bottom of the hull incorporated a mine door which rotated about a fore-and-aft axis, and on top of which the mines were mounted. This door had been perfected on the XB-51, and was also used on the B-57. But for the P6M, the door also had to take landing loads, since the step was in the middle of it.‖ Takeoff and landing speed was 150 knots [approximately 173 miles per hour].

Three different versions of the P6M were actually produced and flown. Basic dimensions were almost exactly the same for all three, with the wingspan 102 feet, 7 inches, the overall length 134 feet, 4 inches, and the maximum height 32 feet, 5 inches, measured from the keel to the top of the tail section.

The new jet engines originally programmed for the XP6M-1 failed during development, and as a result, alternative engines had to be decided upon and retrofitted into the design. The engine selected was the Allison J71-A-4, which provided a maximum of 13,000 pounds of thrust each. The J71-A engines were used on both the XP6M-1 and the YP6M-1 aircraft. These substitute engines, while adequate for test purposes, caused maintenance difficulties, and did not provide sufficient power to allow these two models to reach their optimum performance levels. Nevertheless, flight-test results were heartening.

---

*Initial flight tests were flown by E. D. "Sam" Shannon, Chief of Experimental Flight of the San Diego division of Convair.

†It was fully expected that the Sea Dart would be a Mach 1.5 fighter when full potential had been reached.

‡In the latter stages of development of the P6M, Trimble was Vice President of Engineering for the Martin Company, and is now President of the Bunker-Ramo Corporation.

§Normal cruising altitude was 40,000 feet.

‖The rotating mine door was actually part of the hull bottom. When the door was closed, a pneumatic seal around its periphery made the mine compartment watertight.

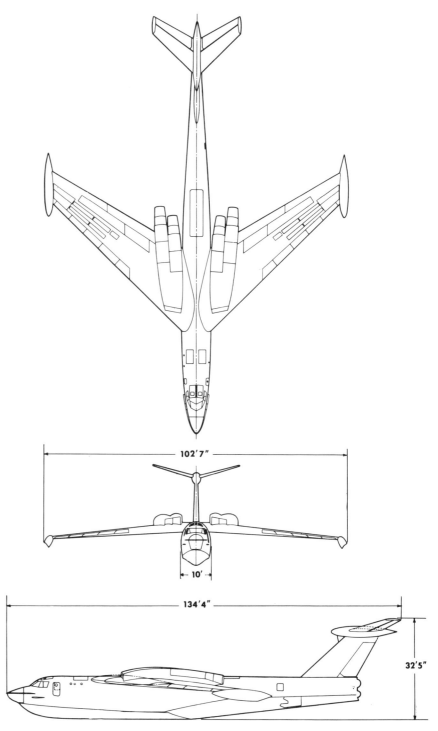

The YP6M-1 Seamaster. (Martin Marietta)

The first XP6M-1 was flown at Middle River, Maryland, by George A. Rodney and M. Berhard, on 14 July 1955. Rodney was manager of all flight-test activities, and Chief Project Pilot throughout the program. He had this to say about the Seamaster:

> The P6M was the first successful application of jet propulsion and high speed aerodynamics to a seaplane. It was truly a Mach 1 aircraft, with all the other performance characteristics of comparable land-based aircraft,

A special beaching cradle with flotation provisions could be engaged or disengaged without assistance from a beaching crew. Once firmly locked to this cradle, the P6M could taxi into or out of the water, as well as over the ground. (Martin Marietta)

that is, there was no performance penalty for it being a seaplane. With its rotary weapons door, it could separate weapons at higher speeds (600 knots) than any aircraft of its day. With its high-ratio hull, it required no special piloting techniques, except in extremely heavy seas. It would handle sea states of three to five feet with ease, and could cope with sea states in the six to nine foot region. It was the first seaplane designed to live in the water and be serviced from either surface ships or submarines. Engines could be changed while [the aircraft was] in the water, [the tops of the engine nacelles were hinged for easy access] and it could be fully rearmed [mines were loaded through an overhead hatch in the mine compartment] and refueled on the water. It utilized a taxi-in beaching gear concept, which enabled the pilot to taxi out of the water without even pausing to install the beaching gear, and once out of the water, he could taxi the aircraft in the same manner as a land-based plane. It was one of the first airplanes to have power-operated controls, and as a result, had handling characteristics almost similar to a fighter. It was also one of the first aircraft, I believe, to incorporate an inertial navigation system, and a computer-controlled weapons delivery system.

Table 12-1. P6M Seamaster flight test program

	P6M-1	YP6M-1	XP6M-1
Engine	Allison J71-A-4	Allison J71-A-6	Pratt & Whitney J-75-P-2
Maximum thrust	13,000 pounds	13,000 pounds	17,500 pounds
Maximum speed at sea level	555 knots 639 mph (approx.)	595 knots 685 mph (approx.)	628 knots 723 mph (approx.)
Normal gross weight at takeoff	160,000 pounds	171,000 pounds	188,000 pounds
Number of aircraft flown	2	6	3
Duration of flight test program	July 1955– November 1956	January 1958– August 1959	February 1959– August 1959

Source: Chief Project Pilot George A. Rooney.

The data gleaned from the flight test program suggests that there was good potential for further development. For example, Rodney indicated that the airplane was flown at a maximum gross weight of about 196,000 pounds, but said, ". . . It would have easily gone higher than that." The performance of the Seamaster, even during the test program, broke several world records, which unfortunately could not be claimed because such information was classified at that time.

The P6M was designed to have a four-man crew, which included a pilot, copilot, navigator-bombardier, and radioman-electronic countermeasures operator. Armor plate protected crew members and essential controls, and there were provisions for quick exit in case of emergency. The XP6M-1 had ejection seats for the pilot and copilot, while the other two crewmen used a quick exit chute on the flight deck. The YP6M-1 and P6M-2 had ejection seats at all four positions. All crew compartments were pressurized and airconditioned.

On 28 January 1955, as the first prototype neared completion, the Navy awarded a second contract to Martin for six somewhat improved follow-on test aircraft, to be designated YP6M-1. The program progressed well for another ten months, and then on 7 December 1955, tragedy struck. Three Martin employees and one Navy pilot were performing a routine test flight aboard the first XP6M-1, which had previously been test-flown in excess of fifty flight hours without incident. No telemetry equipment was on board. The most plausible explanation of what happened is that a malfunction occurred in the control system, which caused a violent pitchdown with an estimated force of negative 9.0 "g's." The resulting stress was so severe that the engines separated from the aircraft, and the wings buckled at the roots before the plane plunged into the Potomac, near the St. Mary's River junction. There were no survivors of this tragic crash.

Almost a year later, on 9 November 1956, the second XP6M-1 came to a disastrous end near New Castle, Delaware. The plane had taken off that day from Middle River, flown by a Martin crew consisting of the pilot R. S. Turner, copilot W. E. Cunningham, flight engineer W. L. Compton, and flight test engineer T. M. Kenney. This time the aircraft was equipped with telemetry instruments, with a ground monitor operating.

At about 3:30 P.M. Turner executed a descent at Mach 0.9 from 25,000 to 21,000 feet, where he eased back on the power to level off. At that time he discovered that the aircraft had developed a nose-down tendency, and that he had to exert an unusual amount of back pressure on the controls. Moments later, the situation reversed itself, and the plane began a slow climb. Turner pushed forward on the yoke, only to find that the pitch-up became even more pronounced. Later, in describing what happened, he said,

The stick was placed forward at full arm's length and required about eighty pounds of force. The airplane did not respond at all to the extreme control deflection. The 'g' forces became so heavy that my chin was forced down on my chest, and my view was greatly restricted. At this time I heard over the VHF radio, "She's breaking up."*

All four crewmembers ejected from the aircraft, and parachuted safely to the ground. The stricken plane went into a descending spiral, until it reached 3 or 4,000 feet, where it exploded and burned, scattering wreckage for many miles.

This second XP6M-1 had been flown a number of times prior to the accident, and had logged more than forty flight hours at varying speeds, altitudes, and attitudes. The pilots who had flown it were pleased with the plane's performance and handling characteristics. What then had happened on this particular day to cause things to go awry?

It was later established that the horizontal tail configuration had been modified for this particular flight, as part of a tail-shake test. Unfortunately, the modification was based upon wind tunnel data later found to be faulty, and the change was determined to have been responsible for the plane's erratic behavior and subsequent loss. The official accident investigation reported no evidence of pilot error or structural failure, and found

> . . . no basic functional, design or flying deficiencies . . . which might have contributed to the accident or which would impair the future service utility of the aircraft.†

In spite of these two unfortunate incidents, both the Navy and the Martin Company were sure that the Seamaster would be a success. Work on the six follow-on YP6M-1 test aircraft continued, and on 29 August 1956 twenty-four additional planes, designated P6M-2s, were ordered into production by the Navy. These aircraft mounted more powerful Pratt and Whitney J-75-P-2 jet engines, which produced 17,500 pounds of thrust each, and provided a significant increase in performance. The program seemed well on its way to fruition, with the P6M clearly having the potential to usher in a new era for the flying boat.

Although the Seamaster was built ostensibly as a mine warfare aircraft, it had capabilities far beyond that limited mission. As a long-range bomber, it had potential to equal and perhaps even surpass the performance of the B-47 and the B-52. In addition to possessing some exceptional operational characteristics, it would also have been considerably less vulnerable than its land-based counterparts, because it was not dependent for support upon stationary air bases of known location. Instead, the Seamaster could rendezvous with a tender or a submarine at prearranged forward positions for refueling, rearming, and maintenance. Test data indicates that it would have been a formidable weapons delivery platform, whether at an altitude of 40,000 feet, or close to the surface, eluding enemy radar while boring in to the target. But in the 1950s, long-range strategic bombing had already been established as the preserve of the U.S. Air Force, and ranking naval officers may have been reluctant to reopen any controversy on that subject. Perhaps even more significant is the fact that the Seamaster could conceivably have developed into a competitor of the aircraft carrier as a means of projecting U.S. naval air power. In any event, it appears that there were few influential supporters of the increasingly costly P6M program, especially if it meant a reduction of funds available for carrier aviation. It was also about this time that the advent of the missile-launching Polaris submarine with its enormous strategic potential made the need for a long-range sea-based strike aircraft highly questionable.

*The Glenn L. Martin Company, *Accident Investigation*, Vol. 1, XP6M-1 Seamaster Ship No. 2 ER 9066, Baltimore, Md. January 1957, p. 1.
†*Ibid.*, p. 27.

The P6M had the potential to revolutionize naval aviation, and create limitless possibilities for new generations of flying boats. (Martin Marietta)

On 21 June 1957 the Seamaster program was cut back from twenty-four to eighteen P6M-2s. Meanwhile, work continued on the six YP6M-1s, the first of which was test flown on 20 January 1958. Production delays, added expense, and the strategic concerns already mentioned, led to a further reduction in November of that year, leaving the six YP6M-1s and ten P6M-2s remaining. Then on 24 August 1959 the Navy terminated the program altogether. By that time, all YP6M-1s had been completed and flown for a composite total of almost 500 flight hours, while three P6M-2s had reached the flight line and had collectively logged over 100 hours in the air. The remaining P6M-2s were in varying stages of completion. All the P6Ms, including those already flying, were stripped of useable equipment, and the airframes were scrapped. Not one example of this extraordinary aircraft remains in existence today.

The sound of the sleek hulls being torn apart by the scrappers' torches and hammers signaled much more than the demise of a great aircraft. It was in fact the death knell of the American flying boat. Only the P5M Marlin remained in production, and its days too were clearly numbered.

Following the major modification in 1953, the P5M-2 had become operational the following summer. This improved version mounted R-3350-32 WA engines of 3,450 horsepower each. The bow chine was lowered slightly to minimize the amount of spray passing through the propellers while water-borne, and it sported a new T-tail with the horizontal stabilizer and elevators set atop the high vertical fin. The MAD* sensing head was contained in a tapered cylindrical casting protruding aft from the point where the two tail planes joined.

The P5M-2, like the earlier version, was primarily designed as an antisubmarine warfare aircraft, and boasted the latest in ASW electronics equipment. In the bulbous nose was mounted an AN/APS-44 radar antenna, which under good conditions was capable of detecting as small a target as a submarine's snorkel, at a respectable distance. Beneath the starboard wing tip, it carried a carbon arc searchlight, the beam of which could be directed from the cockpit by the copilot to illuminate a suspected snorkel or a surfaced submarine at night. It carried sonobuoys which could be dropped into the water in prescribed patterns, to gather and transmit active or passive sonar information back to the aircraft. On the raised flight deck just behind and slightly below the cockpit sat the technicians, who operated the sophisticated electronics gear. Each collected information from his specialized equipment, and fed it to an officer known as the "TACCO," or Tactical Coordinator. It was this officer's job to evaluate all the information and derive the position, course, and speed of the known or suspected submarine. After this was accomplished, the pilot could be directed in for an attack. For this function, the Martin Marlin could be armed with a lethal variety of weapons, from depth charges or homing torpedoes carried in the bomb bays, to high-velocity rockets mounted under the wings.

The P5M crews practiced antisubmarine tactics interminably, because the submarine had a definite advantage. Only timely action by a skilled crew of professionals acting together could result in the sinking of a submarine. Many practice exercises were conducted against friendly submarines, which surfaced at the ends of the exercises to critique the performances of the plane crews.

In addition to exercises of this kind, the flying boats spent much of their time on long tedious patrols far off both coasts of the United States, in efforts to detect and track Soviet submarines. With their increasing missile capabilities, these submarines could be expected to play an important role in any surprise attack on the United States. The patrols continued day after day, and involved endless hours of search with pitifully few contacts. Nevertheless, it was a job that had to be done, and the flying boats did it well. Crew members were usually proficient at several positions, and switched around frequently during patrols to keep themselves alert. On these long flights, the duties of cook customarily fell to the ordnanceman, and some were very adept at preparing meals in the small galley beneath the flight deck.

Sometimes the aircraft itself provided excitement to enliven an otherwise routine patrol. On one such flight in 1959, *Fine-Art Three*,† a Bermuda-based

---

*AN/ASQ-8 Magnetic Anomaly Detection device.
†Plain language radio call-sign used to identify flying boat Number 3 of Patrol Squadron 45.

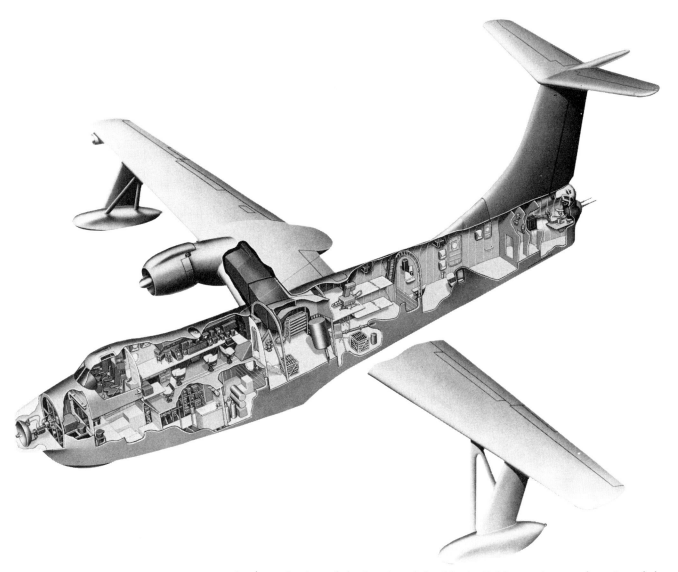

A schematic view of the interior of the Martin P5M-2, an improved version of the P5M-1 design with more powerful engines and a T-tail. (U.S. Navy)

P5M-2 from VP-45, took off from the Naval Air Station, Jacksonville, Florida. The patrol plane commander was Lieutenant Commander James S. "Steve" Christensen, an experienced flying boat pilot who had flown PBM rescue planes during World War II.

On this particular day, the clouds hung low over the ocean, and Christensen leveled off just beneath them at an altitude of 1,000 feet, as they passed over the Florida coastline and headed out to sea. The mixture controls were eased back into the lean position, the ordnanceman passed two cups of black coffee up into the cockpit, and the long day began. About 200 miles out, the port engine suddenly and without warning lost power and stopped running. The plane commander quickly moved the mixture controls to rich, hoping he could coax the recalcitrant engine back to life, but to no avail. He reached up and pushed the button to feather the propeller and reduce drag. At 1,000 feet, there was little altitude to spare, and, having consumed little fuel at this point, the aircraft was too heavy to fly for very long on one engine. The fuel jettison system was actuated, but it was a slow process, and it quickly became apparent that the airplane would go into the water before it lost enough fuel weight to keep flying. Christensen told the crew to brace for an open sea landing, while the copilot, Lieutenant j.g. Kennedy B. Snow broadcast an emergency "MAYDAY"

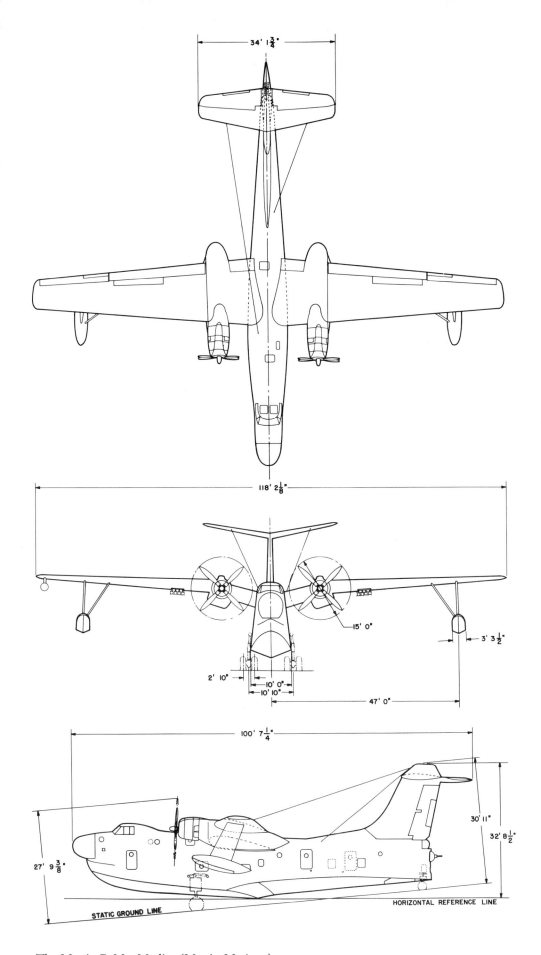

The Martin P5M-2 Marlin. (Martin Marietta)

message with their position over the radio, hoping that someone would receive it. Seconds later, the plane settled onto a big swell with a loud smack, bounced back into the air, came down on the next crest, bounced once more, and stuck fast on the third contact with the water. Miraculously, the aircraft survived the hard landing unscathed. Not a rivet had popped, nor had a single seam opened, but they were down in the open sea some 200 miles from Jacksonville, with little chance of getting airborne again. They would simply have to taxi the boat home.

Lashing the pedals so that the rudder was deflected just enough to keep the aircraft on course, they began their long, slow journey. Corrections in heading were made by small power adjustments on the one good engine.

About two hours after the landing, a Lockheed P2V Neptune appeared overhead, and ascertaining that the problem was not critical, soon departed. A Coast Guard P5M arrived shortly thereafter and diverted a nearby liner, the *Ocean Monarch*, to the scene. The aircraft taxied in her wake for about four hours, and then the *Monarch* turned to head back toward her destination, already well behind schedule. During this time, a Lockheed WV Constellation remained in company 2,000 feet overhead. Shortly after sunrise, they were greeted by a Navy blimp from NAS Glenco, Georgia; the Navy tug *Umpqua* arrived on the scene a short time later, followed by a Coast Guard cutter. But despite all the offered assistance, the aircraft pushed on under its own power, and at about 4:00 P.M. that afternoon, some twenty-six hours after takeoff, it taxied into the turning basin at Mayport, Florida, and dropped anchor. Another patrol had ended.

The last of the P5M-2 aircraft came off the Martin production line toward the end of 1960. One hundred and forty-five of this version were built, of which ten were sold to the French.

The Navy began phasing out the P5s in the early 1960s, with some squadrons initially trading their flying boats for P2V Neptunes, and later, for the new Lockheed P3A Orions as they became available. In 1964, experiments were conducted using a jet engine mounted in the tail of a P5M-2, to provide the aircraft with an increased performance capability and a longer operational life. Although the installation appears to have been successful, no other P5Ms were similarly modified.

The Marlins performed one last mission of historical significance before their retirement. The Vietnam War was moving into high gear in the mid 1960s,[*] and the North Vietnamese were making every effort to keep the Viet Cong forces in the south supplied, despite counter-efforts to stop them. A favorite tactic was to run supplies in by sea, using small junks posing as fishing vessels or coastal cargo carriers, both of which blended with legitimate seaborne traffic to confound their American and South Vietnamese antagonists. Larger amounts of military equipment and ammunition were sent in by bigger steel-hulled trawlers. The U.S. Navy responded with a patrol system of ships and aircraft, which coordinated their surveillance activities along the entire coast of South Vietnam in operation "Market Time."

As in previous hostilities, the flying boats were able to gain an advantage by operating from a tender positioned in the forward area. In this case, they located at Cam Ranh Bay on the coast of South Vietnam, and consequently wasted no time transiting to patrol stations. Heavy maintenance and support was available at the Sangley Point Naval Station in the Philippines, some 800 miles across the South China Sea. The P-5s were armed with high-velocity rockets and machine guns mounted on the hatch combings, so that they would be equipped to deal with intruders and to prevent the delivery of war materials over the beaches.

*By this time these aircraft had been redesignated. P5M-1s became SP-5As and P5M2s became SP-5Bs.

Fine-Art Eight of VP-45, previously *Fine-Art Three*, was taxied almost 200 miles to safety after an emergency landing in the open sea off the coast of Florida. (U.S. Navy)

The last "Market Time" patrol flown by a P-5 in the combat zone was flown on 11 April 1967, with Commander Seventh Fleet, Vice Admiral John Hyland, aboard. The last tactical patrol in the western Pacific was flown from Sangley Point by Commander H. E. Longino and Commander Philippine Patrol Air Group, Captain H. S. Ainsworth, on 10 May 1967. From the Philippines, the P-5s made their final flights to Japan, where they were dismantled and cut apart for scrap.

The flying boat, which had been an American contribution to the progress of manned flight, had become an American legend. They had been the first airliners, the first U.S. warplanes to engage in combat and the first commercial means of crossing both the Atlantic and Pacific by air. They had explored the steaming jungles of Africa, New Guinea, and the Amazon River Valley, and had spanned the Arctic wastes where man had never ventured before. They rescued hundreds of aviators and seamen as they bobbed about helplessly in the treacherous sea, and they roamed the world's oceans at will like great sea birds, at home in their element.

A crew gathers on the wing of a P5M-2 to catch a breeze and swap stories. (Capt. S. P. Halle Collection)

The flying boats were distinctive in the world of naval aviation, not only in the historical context, but also because they added a special sense of esprit de corps and a colorful splash of character. It is an understatement to say that those who flew the old boats will not easily forget them. Somewhere in the recesses of almost every flying boat pilot's mind, there is a black stormy night over the ocean, an uncertain position, a single-engine emergency, or perhaps an open sea landing, that still brings a furrow to the brow. But he may also remember a night flight to Trinidad under a blanket of stars, the soft red lights of the instrument panel, and quiet hours swinging on a buoy in the Caribbean or the South Pacific. He may conjure up from the past a cool dip after a grueling patrol, or a warm tropic night when the crew gathered on the wing to catch a breeze and swap stories.

Few would deny that the boats represented a special way of life. Each one had its own personality derived partly from its particular mechanical idiosyncrasies, and partly from the human characteristics of its crew. Each crew in turn was a close-knit entity unto itself, and the flying boat was the focal point—its reason for being. It was at once a home away from home, a faithful steed, a weapon of war, and a fickle machine which above all must be respected and maintained. Each crew member knew the significance of his job, and his responsibility to the crew. They spent long hours together as a proficient team, and there was pride in the crew and the boat, and a feeling of being part of something unique.

On 6 November 1967 the last SP-5B flying boat of the only remaining seaplane squadron in the Navy made its final landing in San Diego Bay, where some fifty-five years before, Glenn Curtiss had momentarily coaxed his first flat-bottomed flying boat into the air. Now, as the pilot eased the big seaplane alongside the familiar black and yellow ring, that golden age had come to an end. Miniature waterspouts formed under the propellers, as the throttles were thrown into reverse and back again. "Buoy made, Sir," reported the bowman. The mixture controls were moved smartly into the idle cutoff position, and the great boat shuddered and was still. Then there was only the sound of the waves lapping against the hull, and the cry of a solitary gull.

Bibliography

BOOKS

Aircraft Year Book for the years 1919-1962.

The Aleutians Campaign, June 1942-August 1943—Combat Narratives. Washington, D.C.: Office of Naval Intelligence, U.S. Navy, 1945.

Allen, Richard Sanders. *Revolution In The Sky*. Brattleboro: The Stephen Greene Press, 1964.

Arthur, Reginald Wright. *Contact; Careers of U.S. Naval Aviators*. Washington, D.C.: Naval Aviation Register, 1967.

Bowers, Peter M. *Boeing Aircraft Since 1916*. London: Putnam and Co., 1968.

Buchanan, A. R. (ed.). *The Navy's Air War*. New York: Harper & Brothers Publishers, 1946.

Curtiss, Glenn H. *Flying Boats, Aeronautical Motors, Aeroplanes, Hydroaeroplanes*. New York: The Curtiss Aeroplane and Motor Corp., 1919.

Davies, R. E. G. *Airlines of the United States Since 1914*. London: Putnam, 1972.

Dickey, Philip S. *The Liberty Engine 1918–1942*. The Smithsonian Annals of Flight, Vol. 1, No. 3, Washington, D.C.: National Air and Space Museum, 1968.

Duval, G. R. *American Flying Boats; A Pictorial Survey*. Truro: D. Bradford Barton, 1974.

Duval, G. R. *British Flying Boats and Amphibians 1909-1952*. London: Putnam & Company, 1966.

Fahey, James C. *The Ships and Aircraft of The U.S. Fleet*. New York: Ships and Aircraft, 1941.

Fahey, James C. (ed.). *U.S. Army Aircraft 1908-1946*. New York: Ships and Aircraft, 1946.

The Flight Across the Atlantic. New York: Curtiss Aeroplane and Motor Corp., 1919.

Flying Officers of the U.S.N. Washington, D.C.: Naval Aviation Warbook Committee, 1919.

Garfield, Brian. *The Thousand Mile War*. New York: Ballantine Books, 1975.

Green, William. *Flying Boats*. Vol. 5 of the series "War Planes of the Second World War." New York: Doubleday and Co., 1962.

Grenfell, Russell. *The Bismarck Episode*. London: Faber and Faber, 1948.

Harris, Sherwood. *The First to Fly*. New York: Simon and Schuster, 1970.

Hatfield, David D. *Howard Hughes H-4 Hercules*. Los Angeles: Historical Airplanes, 1972.

Horvat, Joseph J. *Above the Pacific*. Fallbrook: Aero Publishers, 1966.

Jablonski, Edward. *Seawings*. New York: Doubleday & Co., 1972.

Johnson, Edward C. *Marine Corps Aviation: The Early Years*. Washington, D.C.: U.S. Government Printing Office, 1977.

Josephson, Matthew. *Empire of the Air; Juan Trippe and the Struggle for World Airways*. New York: Harcourt, Brace and Co., 1944.

Karig, Walter, and Purdon, Eric. *Battle Report*. Pacific War: Middle Phase. New York: Rinehart and Co., 1947.

Keats, John. *Howard Hughes*. New York: Random House, 1966.

Killen, John. *A History of Marine Aviation 1911-68*. London: Frederick Muller, 1969.

King, Ernest J. and Whitehall, Walter M. *Fleet Admiral King: A Naval Record*. New York: W. W. Norton & Co., 1952.

King, H. F. *Aeromarine Origins*. Fallbrook: Aero Publishers, 1966.

Larkins, William T. *United States Marine Corps Aircraft 1914-1959*. Concord: Aviation History Publications, 1959.

Larkins, William T. *U.S. Navy Aircraft 1921-1941*. Concord: Aviation History Publications, 1961.

Loening, Grover. *Amphibian*. Greenwich: New York Graphic Society, 1973.

Lord, Walter. *Day of Infamy*. New York: Henry Holt and Co., 1957.

Lord, Walter. *Incredible Victory*. New York: Harper & Row, 1967.

Matt, Paul R. *Historical Aviation Album*. Collectors Series. Temple City.

Morison, Samuel Eliot. *History of United States Naval Operations in World War II*. Boston: Little, Brown, 1947-1962.
I *The Battle of the Atlantic, September 1939-May 1943*.
III *The Rising Sun in the Pacific, 1931-April 1942*.
V *The Struggle for Guadalcanal, August 1942-February 1943*.

Munson, Kenneth. *Flying Boats and Seaplanes Since 1910*. New York: Macmillan, 1971.

Nowara, Heinz J. et al. *Marine Aircraft of the 1914-1918 War*. Letchworth, Herts: Harleyford Publications, 1966.

O'Neill, Ralph A. and Flood, Joseph. *A Dream of Eagles*. Boston: Houghton Mifflin Co., 1973.

Palmer, Henry R. Jr. *The Seaplanes*. (Famous Aircraft Series). New York: Arco Publishing Co., 1965.

Price, Alfred. *Aircraft versus Submarine*. Annapolis: Naval Institute Press, 1974.

Richardson, Holden C., Beall, Wellwood E. and Manley, Charles W. *Flying Boats*. New York: National Aeronautics Council, 1942.

Roscoe, Theodore. *On The Seas And In The Skies*. New York: Hawthorne Books, 1970.

Roseberry, C. R. *Glenn Curtiss Pioneer of Flight*. New York: Doubleday & Co., 1972.

Rubenstein, Murray and Goldman, Richard. *To Join With The Eagles: Curtiss-Wright Aircraft 1903-1965*. New York: Doubleday & Co., 1974.

Scharff, Robert and Taylor, Walter S. *Over Land and Sea: A Biography of Glenn Hammond Curtiss*. New York: David McKay Co., 1968.

Seaplanes & Motors. Early Military Aircraft of the First World War. Vol. 3. Dallas: Flying Enterprises, 1971.

Sikorsky, Igor I. *The Story of the Winged-S: An Autobiography*. New York: Dodd, Mead & Co., 1967.

Smith, Richard K. *First Across*. Annapolis: Naval Institute Press, 1973.

Studer, Clara. *Sky Storming Yankee: The Life of Glenn Curtiss*. New York: Stackpole Sons, 1937.

Sudsbury, Elretta. *Jackrabbits to Jets: A History of North Island*. San Diego, California. San Diego: Hall & Ojena Publications, 1967.

Swanborough, Gordon and Bowers, Peter M. *United States Navy Aircraft Since 1911*. Annapolis: Naval Institute Press, 1976.

Thetford, Owen. *British Naval Aircraft 1912-58*. London: Putnam, 1958.

Thruelsen, Richard. The *Grumman Story*. New York: Praeger Publishers, 1976.

Turnbull, Archibald D. and Lord, Clifford L. *History of United States Naval Aviation*. New Haven: Yale University Press, 1949.

United States Naval Aviation 1910-1970. Washington, D.C.: U.S. Government Printing Office, 1970.

Van Deurs, George. *Wings For The Fleet*. Annapolis: Naval Institute Press, 1966.

Van Wyen, Adrian O. *Naval Aviation In World War I*. Washington, D.C.: U.S. Government Printing Office, 1969.

Wagner, Ray. *American Combat Planes*. New York: Doubleday & Co., 1968.

Wagner, Ray. *The Story of the PBY Catalina*. San Diego: Flight Classics, 1972.

Wagner, William. *Reuben Fleet: and the Story of Consolidated Aircraft*. Fallbrook: Aero Publishers, 1976.

Westervelt, George C., Richardson, Holden C. and Read, Albert C. *The Triumph of the NCs*. New York: Doubleday, Page & Co., 1920.

Wilbur, Ted. *The First Flight Across The Atlantic May 1919*. Washington, D.C.: Smithsonian Institution, 1969.

Zahm, Albert F. *Aeronautical Papers: 1885-1945*. Vol. 1. Notre Dame: The University of Notre Dame, 1950.

ARTICLES

Aero and Hydro

"Benoist 1914 Flying Boat Described." October 11, 1913.
"Burgess Flying Boat Shows Marked Progress." May 31, 1913.
"Burgess Produces High Powered Boat." August 30, 1913.
"Christofferson Craft Is 100 H.P. Three-Seater." April 5, 1913.
"Flying Boat Cruise To Detroit Started." July 12, 1913.
"The Latest Curtiss Flying Boat." August 9, 1913.
"The New Cooke Tractor Airboat." August 2, 1913.
"New Wright Aeroboat Has Motor In Front." June 13, 1914.
"Patterson-Francis Is Attractive Flying Boat." June 21, 1913.
"Vilas Is First Pilot To Cross Lake Michigan." July 5, 1913.

Aerospace Historian

Bowers, Ray L. "The Energetic Sperrys." Summer 1967.
Hallett, George E. A. "Glenn H. Curtiss' First Off-Water Flight." Winter 1966.
Reynolds, George A. "Flying, Floating, And Fighting Angels." Winter 1971.

Air News

"Grover Loening: Pioneer And Prognosticator." April 1942.
Washburn, Stanley Jr. "Is Kaiser Crazy?" Oct. 1942.

American Aviation Historical Society Journal

Anderson, Carroll R. "Mission to Kavieng." Summer 1965.
Bently, Roger. "American Overseas Airlines." Spring 1966.
Berry, Peter. "The Excalibur." Winter 1975.
Casey, Louis S. "Curtiss Flying Lifeboat." Summer 1965.
Dickey, Fred C. Jr. "Patrol Planes and Patrol Squadrons." Fall 1961.
Gould, Bartlett. "The Burgess Story." Part 3—1913-1914. Winter 1966.
Hardie, George Jr. "ATO and the Big Fish." Fall 1967.
Keller, Charles L. "The Aerial Torpedo." Winter 1975.
Klas, M. D. "Last of the Flying Clipper Ships." Summer 1968.
Klas, M. D. "Plight of the Anzac Clipper." Fall 1972.
Mayborn, Mitch. "The Sikorsky S-39." Spring 1962.
Mayborn, Mitch. "The Ugly Duckling: Sikorsky's S-38." Fall 1959.
Morehouse, Harold E. "Flight from the Water." Fall 1964.
Nalty, Bernard C. and Strobridge, Truman R. "The OL-5 and the Beginnings of Coast Guard Aviation." Fall 1974.
Oliver, Edward B. "The Itinerant Sea Bird." Fall 1971.
Ray, Thomas W. "First Year of Naval Aviation." Fall 1967.
Robinson, Douglas H. "The Commercial Flying Boat Thirty Years Later." Summer 1973.
Rodina, Matthew Edward Jr. "The Grumman Mallard Story." Fall 1975.
Scarborough, William E. "The Consolidated PBY—Catalina to CANSO." Spring 1971.
Scarborough, William E. "The Consolidated PBY, Part II." Summer 1971.
Scheppler, Robert H. and Anderson, Charles E. "The Martin Clippers." Fall 1965.
Tillman, Barrett. "F-5 Flying Boat Dispositions." Summer 1973.

Barton, Charles. "Spruce Goose: Pterodactyl of World War II." *Popular Mechanics*, November 1977.
Butz, J. S. Jr. "Navy Aims At Low Power Atom Seaplane." *Aviation Week*, April 15, 1957.

Cross & Cockade Journal

Layman, R. D. et al. "Allied Aircraft vrs. German Submarines, 1916-1918." Winter 1970.
"Naval Aviation Overseas, 1917-1918." Spring 1963.
Schieffelin, John H. "Boat Pilot." Recorded and Transcribed by David R. Winans. Spring 1970.

"Curtiss Granted Flying Boat Patent." *Aerial Age Weekly*, April 8, 1918.

The Engineers Digest

Rubin, Norman N. "Historical Resume of Coast Guard Aircraft." Part I. March-April 1955.
Rubin, Norman N. "Historical Resume of Coast Guard Aircraft." Part II. May-June 1955.

Rubin, Norman N. "Historical Resume of Coast Guard Aircraft."
  Part III. March-April 1956.
Rubin, Norman N. "Historical Resume of Coast Guard Aircraft."
  Part IV. September-October 1957.
Farrant, Don. "Jack Vilas' Record Flight." *Air Classics*, October 1975.
Goldmerstein, Leon. "How To Find The Way Across The Ocean." *Aeronautics*,
  July 15, 1914.
Grupp, George W. "Coast Guard Aviation Has Come A Long Way." *U.S. Coast
  Guard Magazine*, August 1956.
Gunston, Bill. "The Mighty Mars." *Aeroplane Monthly*, April 1976.
"The Hall Aluminum Story." *Flying Review International*, January 1969.
Mayborn, Mitch. "Sikorsky S-40 Amphibian." *Air Trails*, Winter 1976.
McDougall, Harry. "Rain by Plane." *Aircraft Annual*, 1967.
Mikesh, Robert C. "Dinner Key." *Aviation Quarterly*, vol. 1, no. 1, 1974.
Morris, Frank D. "Four Fliers From Midway." *Colliers*, July 25, 1942.
National Geographic
  Byrd, Richard E. "Flying Over The Arctic." November 1925.
  MacMillan, Donald B. "The MacMillan Expedition Returns." November 1925.
  Miller, William Burke. "Flying the Pacific." December 1936.
Naval Aviation News
  Armstrong, William J. "Dick Richardson—His Life in Aeronautics." April 1977.
  "Patrol Planes—WW II On." August 1961.
  Van Vleet, Clarke. "Beer Bottles, Bombs, and Battles." June 1972.
  Van Vleet, Clarke. "South Pacific Saga." February 1977.
  "VP—Flying Boat Years." July 1961.
Poling, George E. "On The Trail Of The Tradewind." *Airpower*, May 1978.
Reynolds, Bruce. "Pioneer Mechanic." *Flying,* April 1958.
Sims, Don. "U.S.C.G. Aviation . . . A History." *Air Classics Quarterly Review*, Sum-
  mer 1976.
Society of Automotive Engineers *Transactions*. vol. 14, part 1, 1919.
  Coburn, F. G. "Problems Of The Naval Aircraft Factory During the War."
  Richardson, H. C. "Airplane And Seaplane Engineering."
  Towers, J. H. "Operations Of Naval Aircraft."
  Vincent, J. G. "The Liberty Engine."
"The Transatlantic Flight." *Flight,* June 26, 1914.
U.S. Naval Institute *Proceedings*
  Murphy, William B. "They Sailed to the Flying Boat's Future." November
    1965.
  Rankin, R. H. and Rubin, N. N. "The Story of Coast Guard Aviation." June
    1959.
  Serrell, Andrew. "Mars, No Bettah Da Kine." August 1957.
  Westervelt, G. C. "Design and Construction of the NC Flying Boats." Septem-
    ber 1919.
Van Deurs, George. "Captain Mustin and the First Panama Flight." *Shipmate*, De-
  cember 1977.
Webster, W. W. "The Navy PN-12 Seaplane." *Aviation*, May 14, 1928.

UNITED STATES NAVY DOCUMENTS

Aviation History Unit DCNO (Air), *Rodgers Flight to Hawaii 1925*. Washington,
  D.C.: 1945.
Bureau of Aeronautics, *Characteristics, Weights and Performance of U.S. Navy Air-
  planes*. Washington, D.C.: 1 September 1935.
Bureau of Aeronautics, *Report of Advanced Base Operations—Pearl Harbor Based
  Squadrons*. Washington, D.C.: 15 June 1936.
Bureau of Construction and Repair, *Characteristics of Flying Boats, Seaplanes and
  Airplanes*. Washington, D.C.: 1 May 1920.
Bureau of Construction and Repair, *Preliminary Specifications for Fleet Seaplanes*.
  (GB-1) Washington, D.C.: 1920.
Bureau of Construction and Repair, *Types of Aircraft Used in Naval Aviation, 1917-
  1919*. Bul. no. 101. Washington, D.C.: 1 December 1919.

Naval Air Systems Command, History Office, *Notes on Giant Boat* and accompanying documents (LMP) 3 March 1960.

Office of the Chief of Naval Operations. *Characteristics of VP Planes*. Washington, D.C.: 1 April 1935.

Office of the Chief of Naval Operations—Naval Aviation History, *Martin PBM—Operational Notes*. Washington, D.C.: undated.

Patrol Squadron Eleven, *December 7, 1941 Air Raid; Report of*. Kaneohe Bay: 13 December 1941.

Patrol Squadron Forty-Four, *Night Torpedo Attack, 3-4 June; Report of*. LT W. L. Richards' narrative report. 18 June 1942.

Patrol Squadron Twelve, *Report of Raid of December 7, 1941*. Kaneohe Bay: 14 December 1941.

Patrol Squadron Twenty-Two, *Summary of action and damage during Air Raid on December 7, 1941*. Pearl Harbor: 13 December 1941.

Patrol Wing One, *Report of Japanese Air Attack on Kaneohe Bay, T.H., December 7, 1941*. Report of Cdr. Knefler McGinnis. Kaneohe Bay: 1 January 1942.

Patrol Wing Two, *Operations on December 7, 1941*. Report of Rear Adm. P. N. L. Bellinger. Pearl Harbor: 20 December 1941.

Index